Yale French Studies

NUMBER 129

Writing and Life, Literature and History: On Jorge Semprun

SPECIAL EDITOR: LIRAN RAZINSKY

Yale French Studies

Liran Razinsky, *Special editor for this issue*

Alyson Waters, *Managing editor*

Editorial board: Alice Kaplan (Chair), R. Howard
 Bloch, Morgane Cadieu, Ian Curtis, Caroline
 Delaitre, Edwin Duval, Thomas Kavanagh,
 Christopher L. Miller, Maurice Samuels,
 Christopher Semk

Editorial assistant: Robyn G. Pront

Editorial office: 82-90 Wall Street, Room 308

Mailing address: P.O. Box 208251, New Haven,
 Connecticut 06520-8251

Sales and subscription office:

Yale University Press, P.O. Box 209040

New Haven, Connecticut 06520-0940

Designed by James J. Johnson and set in Trump
 Medieval Roman by Newgen North America.
 Printed in the United States of America by Sheridan
 Books, Ann Arbor, Michigan.

ISSN 044-0078

ISBN for this issue 978-0-300-21722-3

LIRAN RAZINSKY

Editor's Preface: Writing and Life, Literature and History: On Jorge Semprun

> We sometimes find ourselves holding the book that the author had to
> write in order to pull himself out of "purgatory," the book in which he
> shows us his burns and secret wounds.
>
> —Claude-Edmonde Magny, *Lettre sur le pouvoir d'écrire*.[1]

LIFE

Jorge Semprun's life spans the twentieth century; he had the strange
and difficult opportunity of living through several of its key moments,
mostly dark ones. His youth was marked by the Spanish Civil War.
Then, exiled in France, Semprun joined the Resistance, experienced
torture by the Gestapo, and survived a period in Buchenwald, becoming one of the most prominent witnesses of the camps. During the
following two decades, as a devoted member of the Communist Party,
he organized Spanish resistance to Franco. But Semprun's rupture and
disillusionment with Communism was dramatic and he became an
important critic of the party. Semprun's itinerary resonates in his
oeuvre, for all these experiences became material for his writing. His
work reflects, accordingly, much of the twentieth century. To take
a broad view of his work, as this volume of *Yale French Studies* attempts to do, is, consequently, to look back at many of that century's
significant junctures.[2]

1. Claude-Edmonde Magny, *Lettre sur le pouvoir d'écrire* (Paris: Climats, 1993
[1947]), 41 (my translation).
2. I want to warmly thank Ursula Tidd, Sara Kippur, and Tsivia Frank Wygoda for
their comments and help with this introduction. Thanks also to Alyson Waters for her
support and help during the preparation of this volume and to Mark Joseph and Guy
Segev for their assistance in producing it.

YFS 129, *Writing and Life, Literature and History: On Jorge Semprun*, ed. Razinsky,
© 2016 by Yale University.

Semprun's status as one of the most interesting literary voices in France and a landmark of *témoignage* has been only partially supported by substantial academic commentary, a shortfall particularly evident in France. Even his death in June 2011 has only now begun to trigger more academic endeavors around his work.[3] The current volume, in presenting an integrative approach to his work, is an attempt to fill this gap. Its publication seems especially timely, and not only because of Semprun's recent death. It corresponds to the huge revival of interest, in contemporary French literature and among scholars and critics, in World War II and the Holocaust, and in literature's concern with history.

Jorge Semprun was born in Madrid in 1923 to a prestigious family of politicians and jurists with republican tendencies.[4] Thanks to his German nanny, he became fluent in German while still a child. He lost his mother at the age of nine and lived with his father, who was appointed civil governor of Toledo in 1936. Following the outbreak of civil war, the family was forced to leave Spain near the end of that year. After two years in The Hague, Semprun went to Paris in early 1939, where he enrolled in the prestigious Lycée Henri IV. He later began studying philosophy at the Sorbonne. In early 1943, the twenty-year-old Semprun, who had become a Communist, joined the Resistance network Jean-Marie Action under the pseudonym Gérard. He was arrested by the Gestapo in October 1943 and tortured before being sent to Buchenwald in January 1944, where he survived until the Liberation. In Buchenwald he worked in the *Arbeitsstatistik*, the internal administration office, thanks to his activity in the Spanish

---

3. Recent volumes dedicated to his work include Ursula Tidd, *Jorge Semprún Writing the European Other* (Oxford: Legenda, 2014); *A Critical Companion to Jorge Semprún: Buchenwald, Before and After*, ed. Ofelia Ferrán and Gina Herrmann (Basingstoke, Hampshire: Palgrave Macmillan, 2014); Daniela Omlor, *Jorge Semprún: Memory's Long Voyage* (Bern: Peter Lang, 2014). Sections on his work may be found in Thomas Trezise, *Witnessing Witnessing: On the Reception of Holocaust Survivor Testimony* (New York: Fordham University Press, 2013) and Sara Kippur, *Writing It Twice: Self-translation and the Making of a World Literature in French* (Illinois: Northwestern University Press, 2015). For a very thorough presentation of Semprun's work, with discussion of individual works and an overview of the research on him, see Ferrán and Herrmann's introduction to their *A Critical Companion to Jorge Semprún*, 1–36.

4. In accordance with his double origin (Spain, France) and bilingualism, Semprun's name is spelled either with or without the accent (Semprún/Semprun). This volume keeps the spelling favored by each author, and the original spelling used for published titles.

Communist Party (PCE) (Communists were dominant in the internal organization of the camp) and his fluent German. This job was probably largely responsible for his survival.[5] Upon Liberation in April 1945 Semprun went back to Paris, where he worked as a translator for UNESCO until 1952 and began an adventurous period of activity in the Spanish Communist Party, a period that ended only in 1964. Starting in 1953, he made regular clandestine trips in and out of Spain as coordinator of underground Communist anti-Franco activity in Spain.

Forced to lie low for a few weeks in a safe house in Madrid in 1962, he wrote his first book, Le grand voyage (The Long Voyage), the first in a series of Buchenwald memoirs.[6] This text came after years of deliberate silence when he had attempted to put the past behind and go on living. Once the well of memory opened, it never closed again until his death. After the success of Le grand voyage (published in 1963), Semprun embarked on a literary career that reaches what is perhaps its high point with L'écriture ou la vie (Literature or Life) (1994).[7]

Most of Semprun's books deal with his experiences during the war and internment, while others deal with his activity as an organizer for the Communist Party, and his experiences in Spain before and after that. Although some of his works—novels and film scripts—are fictions, they are often closely linked to his experiences.

In 1964, around the time he wrote his first book, and after a gradual prise de conscience or evolving critical consciousness fostered by a

5. At various points Semprun has been accused of some degree of collaboration due to his work in the Arbeitsstatistik, even to the point of being accused of having been a Kapo. While these claims seem false (Kapo) or exaggerated (collaboration), it can probably be said that Semprun enjoyed a privileged position, and that like many Communists in Buchenwald, the fact of being a Communist largely helped his survival, and his position in the Arbeitsstatistik allowed him to help other Communist inmates sometimes at the expense of others. His autobiographical Quel beau dimanche! (What a Beautiful Sunday!) contains some apologetic rejections of the accusations against him and attempts to offer his version of the events (Jorge Semprun, What a Beautiful Sunday!, trans. Alan Sheridan [San Diego, New York and London: Harcourt Brace Jovanovich, 1982], 28–29, 88, 119, 152; Quel beau dimanche! [Paris: Grasset, 1980], 32–33, 83, 110, 140). For a quick survey of the accusations and Semprun's defense, see Jaime Céspedes, "Jorge Semprún's Speeches: Self-Fashioning and The Idea of Europe" in Ferrán and Herrmann, 219–32.

6. Jorge Semprun, The Long Voyage, trans. Richard Seaver (NY: The Overlook Press, 2005); Le grand voyage, in Le fer rouge de la mémoire, (Paris: Gallimard [Quarto], 2012), 91–232.

7. Semprun, Literature or Life, trans. Linda Coverdale (New York: Viking, 1997); L'écriture ou la vie (Paris: Gallimard [Folio], 1994).

reading of Solzhenitsyn's *One Day in the Life of Ivan Denisovich*, Semprun clashed with the Party and was excluded from the PCE executive committee, becoming a vociferous opponent of the Party and of the direction Communism had taken. *La guerre est finie* (1966), Alain Resnais's film based on a script by Semprun, retraces some of these events. Notably, as late as 1969, Semprun still defined himself as a Communist[8] and restricted his denunciations to the Party, before a final rupture with Communism as a whole, sharply expressed in *Quel beau dimanche!* (*What a Beautiful Sunday!*), his autobiographical text of 1980. Thus Semprun, originally deported for his activity in the Communist Resistance, and then an important clandestine agent and member of the Spanish Communist Party, was to become a denouncer of Communist practices and Stalinist crimes. "The liberators of Auschwitz came from a country where the Gulag exists!" he reminds us.[9]

Semprun's belated career as a writer did not mean a break with politics. In 1988 he returned to Spain to serve as Minister of Culture under Prime Minister Felipe González (until 1991) and in the 2000s he was, as a public intellectual, increasingly involved with issues of remembering Europe's troubling past in the twentieth century, as well as with its future.[10]

Semprun's biography is rich in literary as well as historical junctures, however. His writing reflects much more than the mental intricacies of a single author in a cocoon. It has become, rather, a meeting point of several of the preoccupations of the French literary world: preoccupations ranging from testimonial writing, through complex work around the tension between truth and fiction, to autobiographical/autofictional concerns, and plays with identity. As Colin Davis writes, from the

---

8. Semprun, interview in *L'express*, cited in *Le fer rouge de la mémoire*, 62.

9. Semprun and Alain Finkielkraut. "Comment transmettre l'inimaginable?" Discussion (Interviewers: Eric Conan, Jean-Marc Gonin), *L'express*, January 19, 1995. Accessed April 6, 2015. http://www.lexpress.fr/actualite/societe/jorge-semprun-et -alain-finkielkraut-debattent-comment-transmettre-l-inimaginable_487336.html (my translation).

In *What a Beautiful Sunday!* the narrator speaks of "the guilt I felt at having lived in the blessed innocence of the memory of Buchenwald, the innocent memory of having belonged to the camp of the just, without the slightest doubt, whereas the ideas for which I thought I was fighting, were serving at the same time to justify the most radical injustice, the most absolute evil: the camp of the just had created and was running the Kolyma camps." (Semprun, *What a beautiful Sunday!*, 150–1; *Quel beau dimanche!*, 139).

10. For a detailed chronology of Semprun's life, see "Jorge Semprun. Vie et oeuvre 1923–2011" in *Le fer rouge de la mémoire*, 13–83.

beginning, Semprun's work was unique in bringing together two op-
posing literary trends in postwar France: Sartre's *littérature engagée*,
which stressed the political responsibility of literary texts, and the experimental techniques of the *nouveau roman*, which stressed art and
language as formal intellectual exploration.[11]

Although Semprun is probably best known for his testimonial
writing on Buchenwald, his oeuvre is diverse and polymorphous.[12]
One of the aims of the current volume is to broaden the research on
Semprun, and to take all the genres of his writing together, some of
them—the screen plays, the novels, and the essays—only rarely stud-
ied, thus allowing the fuller scope of his work to emerge. Alongside
his testimonial writing on Buchenwald (the focus of texts here by
Frank-Wygoda, Chaouat, Dorfman, Razinsky, and Tidd), Semprun has
written novels (discussed here by Davis, Golsan, and Frank-Wygoda),
memoirs of his time in Spain, screen plays, notably for Alain Resnais
and Costa-Gavras (the focus of Coelen's paper here), and essays (Golsan's contribution discusses one of them). Together, the papers collected here constitute an overall assessment of Semprun's work.
They carefully represent the various traditions of writing to which
Semprun belongs—French literature, Holocaust testimony, Spanish
literature, autobiography, the interface of political engagement and
writing, bilingual writing.[13]

Semprun indeed belongs to both French and Spanish literature. As
Kippur shows, research on Semprun tends to bifurcate along national
and linguistic lines; scholars of Spanish literature tend to focus on
his Spanish memoirs whereas in France and the rest of the world he
is much more known for his texts on Buchenwald.[14] (As Bouju shows

11. Colin Davis, "Jorge Semprun," in *Holocaust Literature: An Encyclopedia
of Writers and Their Work*, ed. S. Lillian Kremer (New York and London: Routledge,
2003), 1147. See also Davis' paper in the current volume.

12. Semprun's manuscripts are not deposited, to date, at an institution. Most of
them are held by his daughter Dominique Landman.

13. Contributions to the current volume also deal with texts ranging from Semprun's earliest work—*Le grand voyage* (1963)—to his posthumous writings (Tidd's paper studies the posthumous *Exercices de survie*, 2012). The reception of Semprun's
work is also approached, in Bouju, focusing on the status of his work in Spain, and
Kippur, who studies Semprun's internationalization, specifically the translations of
his work into English.

14. Kippur, "Resisting Self-Translation: Jorge Semprun, Language Authenticity,
and the Challenge to World Literature," in *Writing It Twice*. Kippur thoroughly discusses Semprun's choice of language for his texts, as does Françoise Nicoladzé in *La
deuxième vie de Jorge Semprun* (Castelnau-le-lez: Climats, 1997), 131–42.

here, Semprun's status in Spain hardly compares with the recognition he enjoys in France). The question of whether Semprun is a Spanish author writing in exile or a French author with Spanish origins seems pointless in itself. At any rate, although his writing is in French, with the exception of three books dealing specifically with Spain— *Autobiografía de Federico Sánchez* (*Autobiographie de Federico Sanchez*), *Veinte años y un día* (*Vingt ans et un jour*) and *Federico Sánchez se despide de ustedes* (*Federico Sanchez vous salue bien*)[15] (the latter a self-translation from French)—Spain has always remained a focus of concern and activity for Semprun, and part of his identity. Although Semprun's bilingualism can be looked at on an existential level,[16] it certainly also marks his writing. The bi- or rather multilingualism of his writing actually forms part of his style, as he frequently uses foreign words that he then translates himself, often passing comment on the linguistic transition (as Kippur's paper in this volume brings out), thus raising the question of language, and through it, that of truth and fiction.[17]

WRITING

Although Semprun was prolific, there is a profound unity in his writing, partly due to recurring themes but, more importantly, to an easily recognizable style and tone, and to the insistent use of specific literary techniques and narrative modes. This mixture of modes and techniques creates the unique color of his texts and his inimitable voice as an author. In what follows, I reflect on and make more explicit these basic components of his work.

Chronological Labyrinths

Perhaps the most striking aspect of Semprun's writing is his creative play with chronology. The reader enters a rollercoaster of anticipation and retrospective descriptions where temporal location is often

15. Semprún, *Autobiografía de Federico Sánchez* (Barcelona: Planeta, 2002); *Autobiographie de Federico Sanchez*, trans. Claude Durand and Carmen Durand (Paris: Seuil, 1978); *Veinte años y un día* (Barcelona: Tusquets, 2003); *Vingt ans et un jour*, trans. Serge Mestre (Paris: Gallimard, 2004); *Federico Sánchez se despide de ustedes* (Barcelona: Tusquets, 1992); *Federico Sánchez vous salue bien* (Paris: Grasset, 1993).

16. Thomas Klinkert, "Quand la 'neige d'antan' efface la 'langue originaire.' À propos du bilinguisme de Jorge Semprun," in *Écrire aux confins des langues*, ed. Jeanne Bem and Albert Hudlett, *Creliana*, hors série I (2001): 134.

17. See Kippur, "Resisting Self-Translation."

unclear. As early as *Le grand voyage*, the narrative constantly shifts between times in what Lawrence L. Langer has called "a nonchronological method."[18] Both narrated events and the narrating I are subject to free play with chronology. The events are rarely presented in linear sequence, from early to late (although at times in *Le grand voyage* and *Le mort qu'il faut* (The Dead Man We Needed), for example, some overall chronology is kept but interspersed with numerous digressions[19]). Semprun "creates a Proustian narrative structure that kaleidoscopically conflates time zones."[20]

The narrating I, for its part, is fragmented. As Tidd points out, Semprun's writing clearly conforms to the second phase in Langer's classic two-phase distinction in testimonial writing on the Holocaust, that is, it is focused on the memory of the event rather than on the event itself.[21] The times and whereabouts of his recollections, that is to say, the circumstances in which he was reminded of events, and the times and whereabouts of periods of writing and composition, figure centrally. Semprun moves his readers among these different moments and locations, creating a drama of memory, writing, and recollection that is different from and independent of the narrated events.

An important result of these constant shifts in the time of narration, noted in the pioneering research of Sidra Ezrahi, is the "simultaneity of past, present, and future in Semprun's narrative which [. . .] fixes the Holocaust in the eternal present."[22]

The labyrinthine time structure governing all of Semprun's writing naturally brings to mind memory's tangled structure. "[I]n the fractured chronology [. . .] Semprún highlights the failings and constructedness of memory and narrative," writes Tidd.[23] For Langer, Semprun's use of narrative time "suggest[s] that the voyage to Buchenwald and the experience in the camp have severed past from

18. Lawrence L. Langer, *The Holocaust and the Literary Imagination* (New Haven and London: Yale University Press, 1975), 252.

19. Semprun, *Le mort qu'il faut* (*The Dead Man We Needed*) in *Le fer rouge de la mémoire*, 973–1089 (Paris: Gallimard [Quarto], 2012).

20. Brett Ashley Kaplan "'The Bitter Residue of Death': Jorge Semprun and the Aesthetics of Holocaust Memory," *Comparative Literature* 55/4 (2003): 324.

21. Ursula Tidd, "The infinity of testimony and dying," *Forum for Modern Language Studies* 41/4 (2005): 409.

22. Sidra DeKoven Ezrahi, *By Words Alone: The Holocaust in Literature* (Chicago and London: The University of Chicago Press, 1980), 168.

23. Tidd, "The infinity," 413.

future, that from Buchenwald as center [. . .] the mind radiates and returns without discovering any coherent form to connect these disparate realms of time."[24]

Part of Semprun's artistry with time stems from his heavy use of digressions. These digressions, while disorienting, do not produce the experience of reading a confused narrative, but rather of being in the hands of a self-assured, skilled narrator teasing the reader as he carefully guides her down his chosen routes and suspends the plot at will. Thomas Trezise claims that through the use of "discursive indirection" in narration (Trezise analyzes the opening scene, "The Gaze" of *Literature or Life* but his conclusion can be taken more generally), Semprun "establish[es] an appropriate distance between his experience" and that of readers,[25] creating "a tension between proximity and distance or identification and estrangement."[26]

Repetition

Beyond digressions, frequent changes in the time of narration, and the artful maneuvering of past, present, and future, the play with time in Semprun's work is accompanied by different sorts of repetition. Repetition is evident on three levels: in the actual style of sentences and paragraphs, in the time structure of his texts, and in the recurrence of the same episodes in different texts.

The first level, stylistic repetitiveness, is part of the very texture of Semprun's prose, a kind of verbal excessiveness that often creates a sense of awkwardness: "'Guys, what a beautiful Sunday!' the guy said. / He looked up at the sky and said to the other guys that it was a beautiful Sunday."[27]

The second kind of repetitiveness is in the narration, where events are recounted or alluded to more than once in the same text. The effect on the reader can range from a feeling of unease, as if there is something unpolished in the writing, the author having failed to notice that something has already been said, to a sense of an assertive narrator carefully withholding or disclosing information (in precise quantities), so as to fit his needs and capture our attention.

24. Langer, *The Holocaust and The Literary Imagination*, 285.
25. Trezise, *Witnessing Witnessing*, 205.
26. Ibid., 206.
27. Semprun, *What a Beautiful Sunday!*, 19; *Quel beau dimanche!*, 25. I have modified the published English translation to render the repetitiveness.

This repetition works in tandem with the changes in the time of narration. Events are often first alluded to as yet to come, or as already having been told, in addition to being directly reported. About his own style, Semprun speaks of "this manner of writing in a temporal to-and-fro, between anticipation and turning back."[28]

A third form of repetition found throughout Semprun's oeuvre is one in which similar scenes repeat, often with considerable variation. It is not that, in studying Semprun's lifetime production as a whole, one simply comes across variations, but rather that Semprun's narrators alert us to these revisions, repetitions, and differences in different books (mostly in *Literature or Life* but also elsewhere). Davis shows how such revisions reflect Semprun's ideological changes and an evolving political perspective.[29] Frank-Wygoda, in the current volume, explores one of these scenes, the killing of a German soldier by Semprun and another Resistance fighter.

As with the fragmented time structure, repetitive memories of the camps can result from the very nature of traumatic memory. In this case, the nature of the repetition—static or dynamic—may reveal very different psychic ways of dealing with the traumatic memory (in Freudian terms, "acting out" or "working through"). Semprun's repetition is open and creative and allows for constant renegotiation of the past.[30] Susan Suleiman makes a detailed study of one case of repetition and revision, an episode that Semprun recounts as many as four times—his entry to Buchenwald where he was advised that presenting himself as a student would give him little opportunity to survive the camp. She concludes that "continuous revision is the literary performance of the working through of trauma" in his writings.[31]

Like his distinctive style, revision of the same scenes across books also serves to unify Semprun's various works into an oeuvre, an integrated corpus. One has a sense, says Joë Friedemann, that each new work only came to complete the ones before.[32]

---

28. Semprun, *Adieu, vive clarté* (Paris: Gallimard, 1998), 217. Translation taken from Susan Rubin Suleiman, *Crises of Memory and the Second World War* (Cambridge, Massachusetts and London: Harvard University Press, 2006), 140–41.

29. Davis, "Jorge Semprun," 1147–48.

30. Suleiman, "Revision: Historical Trauma and Literary Testimony. The Buchenwald Memoirs of Jorge Semprún," in *Crises of Memory* (132–58), 139–40.

31. Ibid., 158.

32. Joë Friedemann, *Langages du désastre* (Saint-Genouph: Nizet, 2007), 20.

Semprun himself gradually turns this tendency to repeat and revise into a recognizable feature of his voice as a writer and a necessity of memory work. In explicit remarks, many of which figure in *Literature or Life*, Semprun draws attention to the repetitive attempt at self-representation that is in a way never over because it never yields satisfaction. His memories have to be written and rewritten and the effort is interminable: "one will never be able to tell everything. [. . .] All the possible accounts will never be anything but scattered fragments of an endless, literally interminable, account."[33] (See Razinsky in this volume for an exploration of the theme of the infinity of writing in Semprun.)

Games with Identity

Semprun's work includes autobiographical texts that employ fiction, and novels that contain much that is autobiographical. This playing with genre brings to the fore the question of identity. While we can make a general distinction between Semprun's autobiographical and fictional texts (with a work such as *L'évanouissement* perhaps falling in between),[34] the fictionalization of identity is common to both.

In his autobiographical writing Semprun generally uses the first person but often has recourse to the third person as well. *The Long Voyage* for example moves from the first person "I" to, in a crucial moment toward the end, on arrival at the camp, the third person Gérard. In *What a Beautiful Sunday!*, the first person narrator turns at times to talking of himself in the third person, referring to himself as Gérard,[35] *L'espagnol* (the Spaniard),[36] and *L'enfant* (the child).[37] The second person is also used,[38] and sometimes Semprun moves between a first and third person perspective on himself within two sentences. In one scene the narrator recounts how a friend from the camp fails to recognize him years later when Semprun travels with him on a political mission under a false identity. In a flashback to their time in the camp and using the friend as focalizer, the narrator describes

---

33. Semprun, *What a Beautiful Sunday!*, 105; *Quel beau dimanche!*, 98.
34. Semprun, *L'évanouissement* (Paris: Gallimard, 1967).
35. Semprun, *What a Beautiful Sunday!* 102; *Quel Beau Dimanche!*, 95.
36. Ibid., 84–88 ; 80–83 .
37. Ibid., 115 ; 106.
38. Ibid., 107, 287, 408–17; 99, 259, 368–76.

the figure of Semprun (Gérard as he was called in the camp and as the friend knows him) as "the Spaniard."[39] This episode demonstrates, in the change of perspective from first person to the gaze of another, Semprun's frequent alternation between perceiving from inside, and looking at his experience from the outside

In a crucial moment in *Literature or Life* he describes how, having begun a new book in which he writes from the perspective of a French officer approaching the camp after liberation, he suddenly became aware of what had startled the officer. He became aware of whom this officer's gaze had settled on: it was Semprun himself, the survivor just leaving Buchenwald.[40] In a sense, the use of various names for his narrators, as well as the use of alter egos in his fiction, at bottom means playing with distance from and proximity to one's experience. "I observed myself as my own double—not as the actor, but as the witness of my own life. [. . .] I [. . .] found instinctively that it was easier to speak of oneself from the outside,"[41] says Semprun of his use of literary doubles and alter egos. "In the other books, the first person is the narrator; in *Literature or Life* it is me."[42]

If for Philippe Lejeune, identity between author, narrator, and protagonist is the criterion for autobiography,[43] and if testimony is centered around claims to truth and the personal experience of the survivor, Semprun's playfulness with identities disrupts the texts' claims to authority.

In *The Autobiography of Federico Sanchez (Autobiografía de Federico Sánchez)*, Semprun creates the autobiography of another: his clandestine alter ego, Federico Sánchez. Using that pseudonym, he switches between addressing himself in the second person and passages written in the first person. This book may very well be the epitome of Semprun's play on identities, in which we find dazzling passages such as this one:

39. Ibid., 84–88; 80–83.

40. Semprun, *Literature or Life*, 227–31; *L'écriture ou la vie*, 294–99.

41. Semprun, "Interview with Lila Azam Zanganeh," *The Paris Review, The Art of Fiction* 192 (2007). Accessed April 4, 2015 http://www.theparisreview.org/interviews/5740/the-art-of-fiction-no-192-jorge-semprun.

42. Semprun in R. Vigny. "Lettres ouvertes," *France Culture*, November 9, 1994. Cited in Nicoladzé, 57 (my translation).

43. Philippe Lejeune. "The Autobiographical Pact," in *On Autobiography*, trans. Katherine Leary (Minneapolis: University of Minnesota Press, 1989 [1975]), 5.

"And then there was you (no, not you, Federico: me: you, Sánchez, didn't exist yet [. . .]) [. . .]

If you were in a novel, I repeat, you would remember this first meeting [. . .] [here follows an insipid poem of admiration to "*La Pasionaria*"]

You wrote that. Well, no, it wasn't you: I was the one. My very own self.

I wrote that, many years before I was Federico Sánchez [. . .]"[44]

Semprun's fictional works also display a whole cast of doubles, alter egos, and surrogates. Fictional characters like Juan Larrea in *La montagne blanche* in many ways share Semprun's history.[45] It is as if, despite the fact that Semprun frequently hides behind a smoke screen of narrators and doubles, he can still be seen behind it.

This literary play with identity echoes the fact that Semprun indeed lived a large part of his life under false identities in the Resistance, and in clandestine travels to Spain for the Spanish Communist Party. He is especially fond of giving his narrators and protagonists names that he used in his clandestine activities (Federico Sánchez, Juan Larrea, Rafael Artigas, Gérard). Add to this the fact that some of his clandestine names are themselves borrowed from literary figures, and the whirlpool is complete.

There seems, however, to be a deeper meaning to the fluidity of identity in his writings. As is made clear in *Le mort qu'il faut*, the text in which the issue of switching identities is most evident, taking on another's identity is a direct result of having experienced death. If your own self has in some sense died, you are, in a way, as much another as you are yourself. *Le mort qu'il faut* tells the story of how one day in Buchenwald Semprun took the identity of a dying inmate, a "Muselmann," after being warned that the Gestapo were looking for him. Semprun remained with him in the *Revier* the night he died. The other ritualistically and symbolically died in his stead. The real Semprun had died. If he lived on, it was because he was now merely the ghost of himself, having assumed another man's identity. As Semprun relates in *L'écriture ou la vie*, Juan Larrea, the protagonist of his novel, *La montagne blanche*, and a name Semprun had used in his clandestine activity, commits the suicide that Semprun had managed

44. Semprun. *The Autobiography of Federico Sanchez and the Communist Underground in Spain*, trans. Helen R. Lane (New York: Karz, 1979), 11–12;
45. Semprún, *La montagne blanche* (Paris: Gallimard, 1986).

to avoid, dying Semprun's death and allowing Semprun to live.[46] "It is as if Semprun is killing off his alter egos," Davis summarizes, "in order to make his own survival possible"[47] (see also his paper in this volume). In this vein, Tidd suggests that "the use of aliases and death surrogates is a means to bear witness to the trauma of the inexperienced experience of death."[48] Thus, in a way, the fluidity of identity is enabled by the telling of a life that has become the telling of a death, of an absence rather than of a presence.

Intertextuality

On the second page of *The Long Voyage*, there is a curious, incongruent irruption of intertextuality. The narrator-protagonist has barely begun relating the nightmarish deportation in the overcrowded cattle car when (while bursting into laughter) he tells his fellow deportee, "the guy from Semur": "this is really going to be the Night of the Bulgarians" ("la Nuit des Bulgares").[49] The allusion to Henri Michaux's troubling prose poem is not only explicit in the text, it is part of the life world of the protagonists. Semprun's narrators evoke literature as a constant measure of reality, perhaps as a means to make sense of and deal with it ("I spent the first night of this voyage reconstructing *Swann's Way* in my mind and recalling my childhood").[50] However, since Michaux's is a surrealistic poem of improbable, nightmarish events, it is not clear in what sense literature here helps explain life. Here it seems, rather, only to bring out the profound unreality of being squeezed into a cattle car on the way to Buchenwald. Whether during deportation and in the camp, or writing and remembering decades later, Semprun leans on intellectual tradition for both survival and for memory work. However, the vital significance of literature and intellect do not go entirely unquestioned. When later the (fictitious) "guy from Semur" hears more about the poem from the narrator and says, "if we delved a little deeper, we'd find there's nothing to your Night of the Bulgarians,"[51] he is perhaps expressing a position against the significance and usefulness of literature and intellectual life. Although such a position is rare in Semprun, he occasionally

46. Semprun, *Literature or Life*, 242–46, 293; *L'écriture ou la vie*, 312–17, 375.
47. Davis, "Jorge Semprun," 1146.
48. Tidd, "The infinity of testimony and dying," 412.
49. Semprun, *The Long Voyage*, 9; *Le grand voyage*, 91.
50. Ibid., 72; 130–31.
51. Ibid, 34; 107.

exposes philosophy's insufficiency or errors (an approach observable for example in his quarrels with Wittgenstein and Heidegger; see below).

There is a pronounced and *explicit* intertextual dimension to Semprun's writing. In *Literature or Life* alone, we find a whole library of references to writers, poets, and philosophers. A partial list includes Kafka, Goethe, Malraux, Wittgenstein, Kant, Heidegger, Giraudoux, Thomas Mann, Baudelaire, Valéry, Aragon, César Vallejo, Carlos Fuentes, Celan, Primo Levi, Faulkner, Brecht, Heine, Paul Nizan, Sartre, René Char, and Hermann Broch.[52] Some of the authors Semprun alludes to are not merely evoked, but form haunting obsessions that his writing at times tries to break free of, at times embraces. To an extent, Semprun's intertextuality extends his multilingualism and is testament to his participation in several writing traditions, particularly those of France, Spain, and Germany, his three "homelands." It is also part of his attempt to make himself an emblem of the whole of Europe (as bearer of European memory in the twentieth century), as can be seen, for example, in the essay *L'homme européen*, written with Dominique de Villepin, in which he states that for him Europe is "the privileged homeland of literature, of reading, with its multiple languages").[53]

The labyrinth of explicit intertextual references also serves Semprun's ongoing investigation into the role and essence of writing itself. Again if we take *Literature or Life* as an example, it seems as if the text simultaneously tries to liberate itself from this overbearing tradition, this sea of other writing enfolding Semprun's text, all the while sinking deeper into it as it continues to cite directly and allude to a series of texts and authors. This struggle, then, to liberate writing from tradition brings to the fore Semprun's effort to emphasize authorial presence, and the self-referential aspect of his writing to which we now turn.

---

52. Miguet-Ollagnier discusses the specific significance of many of these names for Semprun, claiming essentially that all these texts help Semprun live and die. Marie Miguet-Ollagnier,"De Serge Doubrovsky à Jorge Semprun: pas de langue maternelle, deux langues maternelles?," in Bem and Hudlett, *Écrire aux confins des langues*, 120–27.

53. Semprún and Dominique de Villepin, *L'homme européen* (Paris: Plon, 2005), 215. My translation.

Playfulness, Reflexivity, and Self-Referentiality

Hide and seek with identity, narrative experimentation with time, repetition, and digressions are perhaps related to the nature of trauma and issues of memory, but they also exemplify a different aspect of Semprun's writing. The feel of Semprun's texts and the particular challenges they pose for the reader stem in great part from their playfulness, despite their dark subject matter. Part of this playfulness can be seen in the narrator's constant drawing of attention to himself, as in the following passage from *What a Beautiful Sunday!*: "'Do you remember the Russians?' says Barizon [. . .] He has just emerged from [a]long meditative silence [. . .]. He had been sipping his brandy in silence for several minutes and the Narrator had taken advantage of that to continue his account of events one Sunday long ago."[54]

This pronounced personalization of the text, not only through narrative that is naturally focused on the writer's experiences, but also and primarily through constant direction of the spotlight to the narrating I and the process of writing—in other words the profound self-referentiality and reflexivity of Semprun's works—is to some extent in contradiction with his desire to comment on a broader range of issues: Europe and its future, Nazi Germany and Stalinism, absolute evil, human fraternity, death as a lived experience. The result is a mixture of the personal and the general, a philosophy through autobiography.

Self-awareness and reflexivity dominate Semprun's prose.[55] The experience of the camps itself is marginalized, as it were, in favor of the act of narration, its choices and dilemmas: how to write about the camps? How to navigate the story in the present? The narrator in Semprun's text is a maestro orchestrating its elements.

Of course, there is always the possibility of a return of the repressed: the narrator, the master voice, is controlled by his own story and by the past that demands to be told and retold. Thus, while experiences of fragmentation, of being the slave of memory, and of

---

54. Semprun,*What a Beautiful Sunday!*, 100; *Quel beau dimanche!*, 93
55. While Semprun's endless reflections on the process of writing do put him in line with French traditions of writing throughout the twentieth century and more recently, he stands out for the referential aspect of his writing, grounded in history and experience.

personal crisis dominate Semprun's text,[56] and while memories of Buchenwald, of torture, and of having to hide one's identity are the center of his narrative, these elements stand in contrast to a very self-assured prose—at times overly self-assured—of an author calmly navigating his ship, easily maneuvering chronology and identity, information disclosure and concealment, and suspense.

The strong metafictional aspect of Semprun's work is also evident when he speaks directly about writing and testimony. Semprun's texts pursue the question of the role and possibility of writing in general and, more specifically, of writing about the camps. He is in dialogue with clichés and conventions in the fields of testimony and philosophy, using not only interviews but also his texts themselves to convey his positions. He remarks cynically, for example, on the famous paradox expressed by Primo Levi (and continued by Giorgio Agamben) that the true witnesses are dead, and so every witness is vicarious:

> Sure, the better witness, the only true witness, in reality, if you ask the specialists, is the one who did not survive, the one who went all the way with the experience, the one who ended up dead. But neither the historians nor the sociologists have yet discovered the solution to the contradiction: how to invite the true witnesses, the dead ones, to their conferences?[57]

He resists the notion of a supposed ineffability of the concentrationary universe: "You can tell all about this experience."[58] He opposes the philosophical belief, which he locates in Wittgenstein, that death is not an event in one's life, making it unknowable.[59] Like Levi and unlike Jean Améry, he believes (not without some doubts—this is also true of Levi) in literature's part in the achievement of some degree of spiritual freedom in the camps:[60]

56. In a detailed study of questions of identity in Semprun, Nicoladzé lays stress on the fractured, divided, and uncertain identity displayed in his texts (*La deuxième vie de Jorge Semprun*, for example, 54, 63), later reunified through writing.

57. Semprun, *Le mort qu'il faut*, 981. My translation.

58. Semprun, *Literature or Life*, 13–14; *L'écriture ou la vie*, 26.

59. "'Death is not an event in life. Death cannot be lived,' this idiot Wittgenstein had written"; Ibid. 193;252 (see also 171;225–26 and Semprun, *L'évanouissement*, 66–70).

60. Jean Améry, "At the Mind's Limits," in *At the Mind's Limits*, trans. Sidney Rosenfeld and Stella Rosenfeld (Bloomington and Indianapolis: Indian UP, 1980), 1–20;

In a concentration camp [. . .] [w]hispering poetry to yourself [...] lends you a sort of solitude, allows you to imagine for an instant that you belong to yourself again. [. . .] [Y]ou are reciting Paul Valéry and suddenly you are alone, autonomous, private. [. . .] [F]or that one second you've managed to escape.[61]

His most famous assertion, however, concerns the need to integrate fiction, "artifice," into historical testimonies of what happened.

FICTION AND REALITY

In a few scenes in his most elaborate text, *Literature or Life*, Semprun dramatizes his positions about testimony, its possibilities and conditions, and its proper execution (such scenes can also be found in other texts by Semprun). The opening chapter of *Literature or Life*, "The Gaze" (given a fresh reading by Dorfman in this volume), presents Semprun leaving the camp the day after Liberation and encountering three British officers.[62] Their response to him and his strategies of speech are "a mise-en-abyme of the relationship that certain kinds of readers have with survivor testimonies."[63]

Other scenes in *Literature or Life* figure a group of survivors about to be sent back to France discussing the right way to talk about their experiences;[64] Semprun watching and commenting on raw newsreel footage taken in the camps upon Liberation;[65] or Semprun after Liberation showing a group of French women the camp's crematorium, only to discover that they have fled in the middle of his account.[66] A scene Semprun has made into a part of his personal myth is of hiding in an apartment in Spain, where his host Manuel, a survivor from Mauthausen, gives a disorganized and chaotic rendering of his

---

Primo Levi "The Canto of Ulysses" in *If This Is a Man*, trans. Stuart Woolf (NY: Orion Press, 1959), 127–34; "The Intellectual in Auschwitz," in *The Drowned and the Saved*, trans. Raymond Rosenthal, (London: Abacus, 1989), 102–20.

61. Semprun, "Interview" in *The Paris Review*. Many examples of the power of poetry and literature are found in *Le mort qu'il faut*. See, for example, 995–99, 1024.

62. Semprun, *Literature or Life*, 3–24; *L'écriture ou la vie*, 3–39.

63. Sharon Marquart, "Authoritative Witnessing and the Control of Memory: On Jorge Semprun's *L'écriture ou la vie*," *French Forum* 36/ 2–3 (2011): 148.

64. Semprun, *Literature or Life*, 122–27; *L'écriture ou la vie*, 64–70.

65. Ibid., 198–201; 258–62.

66. Ibid., 118–22; 159–64. The scene is also discussed in *The Long Voyage*, 69–76; *Le grand voyage*, 129–33.

experiences; Semprun's response is to tell his own story the way he sees fit by writing *Le grand voyage*.[67]

In these scenes Semprun puts forth most clearly, through the protagonists and narrator, his view that in order for testimony to be able to convey the experience of the camps, there has to be fiction. The historical truth in itself is simply not enough (for an exploration of Semprun's position, see Carroll[68]). The truth the survivors have to tell, Semprun believes, is "unimaginable." It can only become credible through the use of "a bit of artifice"[69]:

> The only ones who will manage to reach this substance [a story conveying the reality of the camps], this transparent density, will be those able to shape their evidence into an artistic object, a space of creation [. . .] Only the artifice of a masterly narrative will prove capable of conveying some of the truth of such testimony.[70]

Semprun is very insistent about this need for artifice, repeating it not only in these model scenes of testimony and elsewhere in his text, but also in interviews. Upon examination, it seems that the justification for it differs from one reiteration to another. On one level, fiction is necessary because the truth to be told is unimaginable, the facts are insufficient in themselves: "The truth we experienced is not credible, and this is a fact the Nazis relied upon in terms of their own legacy, for future generations," Semprun says in an interview. "If we tell the raw, naked truth, no one will believe us. [. . .] [L]iterature alone is capable of reinventing and regenerating truth."[71] In this sense, it is the fundamental otherness of the Nazi camps, the way they surpass what we think is believable, that requires imagination to describe them.

In another statement regarding the need for fiction, although credibility is still at stake, an additional factor is involved—the listeners: "'Telling a story well, that means: so as to be understood [*de façon à*

67. Semprun, *Literature or Life*, 239–40; *L'écriture ou la vie*, 309–310. The anecdote is also related, for example, in *What a Beautiful Sunday!*, 58–61; *Quel beau dimanche!*, 60–61. Marquart offers a criticism of scenes like these and the beliefs they embody for potentially restricting forms of response to trauma and witnessing narratives that are not in alignment with them (158).

68. David Carrol, "The Limits of Representation and the Right to Fiction: Shame, Literature, and the Memory of the Shoah," *L'esprit créateur* 39/4 (1999): 68–79.

69. Semprun, *Literature or Life*, 124; *L'écriture ou la vie*, 166.

70. Ibid., 13; 25–26.

71. Semprun, "Interview" in *The Paris Review*.

être entendus]. You can't manage it without a bit of artifice. Enough artifice to make it art!'"[72] Listeners' willingness to listen is not a given. They have limits and possibilities and one must accommodate one's story to them to be heard; the events have to be told in specific ways. So fiction, in this sense, is a compromise one has to make if one is to have listeners at all. Already in his first encounter with people from the outside, in the scene in the chapter "The Gaze," Semprun brings up the question: "But can people hear everything, imagine everything? Will they be able to understand? Will they have the necessary patience, passion, compassion, and fortitude? I begin to doubt it, in that first moment, that first meeting with men from *before*."[73]

The need to engage listeners is not only related to the nature of the events to be told, but also hinges on more ordinary matters. Fiction is not a choice; it is inevitable. Putting facts and events into a narrative means employing fictional strategies. This creates unease because of the nature of the particular facts and events to be told, but it seems almost impossible to avoid. The events are insufficient in themselves, they do not tell a story, and to relate them coherently would mean precisely to tell a story. One makes representational choices to create a narrative. Thus, the problem with Manuel's Mauthausen account is that "[i]t was disorganized, confused, too wordy, mired in the details: there wasn't any overall vision, everything was seen in the same light [...] a firsthand account that was rough [...] an avalanche of facts."[74] The images in the raw footage from the camps in the newsreel are "silent" (*muettes*) without a "commentary" that would "situate" and "decipher" them.[75] Showing is not enough; one needs to comment on facts; commentary means elaboration, and this means invention.

And on yet another level, fiction is required because the events, the historical facts, are simply not what one has to tell: "'What's at stake here,'" Semprun reports himself telling a group of survivors arguing about how to communicate the experience of Buchenwald, "'is the exploration of the human soul in the horror of Evil... We'll need a Dostoyevsky!'"[76] What has to be told is "radical Evil,"[77] the facts of the camps being merely a reflection of it. The radical evil goes beyond

72. Semprun, *Literature or Life*, 123; *L'écriture ou la vie*, 165.
73. Ibid., 14; 26–27. Italics in the original.
74. Ibid., 240; 310.
75. Ibid., 200; 261–62.
76. Ibid., 127; 170.
77. Ibid., 87–88; 119–20.

any one event, or any one account. Only fiction, only a Dostoyevsky can expose it.

This praise of fiction clashes, however, with the fundamental requirement of testimony: to tell the truth, to relate what happened. As Suleiman puts it: "Here, then, is the crux of literary testimony: Semprun as survivor-witness claims incontrovertible veracity for his testimony as a whole; but Semprun as writer claims the right to take certain liberties when they are 'more effective than simple reality.'"[78] So whereas witnessing entails the claim to an authoritative position and a commitment to truthfulness, Semprun undercuts these claims with his autobiographical playfulness and his masks and camouflage, doubles and surrogates, and the fictional liberties he takes.

SEMPRUN'S LITERARY LEGACY

Semprun's belief in the need for fictional or poetic elaboration of Holocaust testimonies could seem ethically troubling, but, be that as it may, the very first witnesses refer to such a need (Robert Antelme in his forward to *The Human Race*,[79] and to some extent Charlotte Delbo in the epigraph to *None of Us Will Return*[80]). In Semprun's work, this need is more explicit and the play between fiction and reality more deliberate. It is not just, for example, that in the entirety of his work, fictional texts include autobiographical elements, but also that, and more importantly, on several occasions in *Literature or Life* he admits that he invented elements of earlier texts (notably, the "guy from Semur" in *Le grand voyage*).[81]

Today, when firsthand testimony about the camps has become less and less possible, the question of how fiction can represent the concentrationary universe is more acute than ever. We are witnessing a literary period, especially in France, where the interface between history and literature is increasingly investigated, where new authors

---

78. Suleiman, *Crises of Memory*, 137. Suleiman does not consider this mode of testimony of Semprun impermissible. For an extended discussion of the literary liberties Semprun takes, see Suleiman's chapter on him in *Crises of Memory*, 132–58.

79. Robert Antelme, *The Human Race*, trans. Jeffrey Haight and Annie Mahler (Evanston, Il: The Marlboro Press/Northwestern, 1998), 4.

80. Charlotte Delbo, *Auschwitz and After*, trans. Rosette C. Lamont (New Haven and London: Yale University Press, 1995).

81. Semprun, *Literature or Life*, 262; *L'écriture ou la vie*, 336–37. Another case of invention is that of Hans, the Jewish friend of the narrator in *Le grand voyage*. See *Literature or Life*, 35–37; *L'écriture ou la vie*, 53–55.

and public taste increasingly converge in an attempt to understand history, specifically World War II and the extermination process, through fiction. Suffice it to cite the heated debates around Littell's *Les Bienveillantes* (*The Kindly Ones*), Yannick Haenel's *Jan Karski*,[82] and Laurent Binet's *HHhH*. Semprun's insistence on the need to introduce fiction into stories of deportation and the camps, to fictionalize the past and to clothe memory in literary garments, gains special interest as a premonition of current trends of Holocaust remembrance in an age without witnesses. Indeed, in an interview with *Paris Review*, Semprun speaks of "younger generations, who have not witnessed but will be able to imagine,"[83] and apropos of the Haenel-Karsky affair, he remarks that "if young novelists can no longer take hold of memory, memory will become arbitrary and solemn."[84]

In 2006 when Jonathan Littell's controversial novel, the narrator of which is an SS officer, *Les Bienveillantes* came out, Semprun's enthusiastic support of the book, in the media and as a member of the jury that accorded Littell the Goncourt Prize, played an important role in legitimizing it. Semprun's ethical authority as a witness and the credibility accrued through lifelong commitment to writing about the camps allowed a book that mixes writing about extermination with outrageous sexual descriptions, to leap over any possible initial hurdles to its reception. The aesthetic and moral commitments that may have inclined Semprun to support *The Kindly Ones* are those central to his project of testimony. Above all, Semprun's strong belief that writing about the camps needs to employ artifice seems to have led him to be much less defensive than others about Littell's fictionalizing the perpetrator's experience. As we have seen, Semprun's position not only allows for fiction to be written about the

---

82. See Richard J. Golsan, "L'Affaire Karski: Fiction, History, Memory Unreconciled," *L'esprit créateur*, 50/4 (2010): 81–96, for a thorough exposition of the Karski debate.

83. Semprun, "Interview" in *The Paris Review*.

84. Semprun, "Je n'aime pas trop le mot Shoah." Interview with Agathe Fourgnaud, *Le point*, February 25, 2010. Accessed April 10, 2015, http://www.lepoint.fr/culture/2010-02-25/semprun-je-n-aime-pas-trop-le-mot shoah/249/0/427647. Fabrice Humbert, author of *L'origine de la violence*, another representative of the new literature on World War II and the Shoah, states things clearly: "We are all indebted to him [Semprun], it is he who has authorized us to write fiction on this subject" (my translation). Interview with Grégoire Leménager, "Génération Littell," in *Le nouvel observateur*, July 5, 2010. Accessed April 10, 2015, http://bibliobs.nouvelobs.com/romans/20100705.BIB5425/generation-littell.html.

camps, it also stresses that since what matters is not the exactitude of a particular detail, but the effort to convey the truth at the heart of the camps, fiction is crucial. "In fifty years, collective memory will refer to Littell and not to Hilberg," he tells the *Frankfurter Allgemeine Zeitung*: "Only writers can transmit and renew memory."[85] Secondly, Littel explores in his novel the radical evil that, as we have seen, for Semprun constitutes this truth at the heart of the camps. Thirdly, Semprun, who was in the end a harsh critic of Communism, pointed to the resemblance of the Gulags to the Nazi camps in some of his work, and would certainly have appreciated this dimension of Littell's novel.

*   *   *

Semprun's writing has its weaknesses. In less successful moments, the self-referential remarks and pronounced extradiagetic interventions, as well as repetition on the level of actual sentences, lead to a certain surplus in his writing, a wordy style that sometimes slides toward the verbose or even the narcissistic. In better moments he deploys small miracles of memory and writing. One also senses in Semprun's work, particularly in the last decades of his life, a pronounced effort at self-fashioning or self-construction, the creation of a specific persona, an effort that sometimes seems excessive.[86] Such control and self-assuredness are always, however, at least in his writing, prone to the resurfacing of the shadows of the past.

Semprun leaves behind not only some wonderful texts and a fifty-year-long corpus of testimonial writing but also a strong commitment to resistance to totalitarianism in all its forms, and a profound example of the way literature can engage with the political world without renouncing its independence from it.

85. Semprun, "*Ohne die Literatur stirbt die Erinnerung*," Interview in the *Frankfurter Allgemeine Zeitung*, February 8, 2008: 35. Translation by Wolfgang Assholt, who also notes the lack of influence this position had in Germany. Assholt, "A German Reading of the German Reception of *The Kindly Ones*," in *Writing the Holocaust Today: Critical Perspectives on The Kindly Ones*, ed. Aurélie Barjoet and Liran Razinsky (Amsterdam and New York: Rodopi, 2012), 234.

86. See Céspedes "Jorge Semprún's speeches," for an analysis of this effort to fashion a specific public persona in his speeches.

BRUNO CHAOUAT

Jorge Semprún's Remembrance of Jewish Fate[1]

BEYOND "COMPETITION AMONG VICTIMS"

This essay maps out critical encounters between Jorge Semprún and
the Jews, specifically exploring Semprún's understanding of the difference between the fate of Jews and that of other victims—of fascism, Nazism, and totalitarianism.

Avoiding the trap of what historian Jean-Michel Chaumont has
polemically labeled "competition among victims,"[2] Semprún's approach to history and memory is closer to Michael Rothberg's paradigm of "multidirectional memory," a notion that strives to overcome
competitive memories, highlighting the specificity of each historical
experience without precluding mutual learning from traumatic memories (inasmuch as one can learn from such negativity, inasmuch as
suffering can ever be found useful or productive in shaping new forms
of solidarity and establishing justice).[3]

In a sober dialogue published in 1995, Semprún echoed Elie Wiesel's insistence on the distinctness of Jewish fate and the separation of
Jewish experience from other tragic collective experiences, a distinctness that does not trivialize others' trials:

1. Special thanks to Alan Astro for his thoughtful comments. And many thanks to
Carol de Rosset for editing.

2. See Jean-Michel Chaumont, *La concurrence des victimes* (Paris: La Découverte,
1997).

3. Michael Rothberg, *Multidirectional Memory: Remembering the Holocaust
in the Age of Decolonization* (Stanford: Stanford University Press, 2009), 19. On
ethics and the crisis of theodicy in the aftermath of genocide, see Emmanuel Levinas, "La souffrance inutile," in *Entre nous: Essais sur le penser-à-l'autre* (Paris:
Grasset, 1991).

YFS 129, *Writing and Life, Literature and History: On Jorge Semprun,* ed. Razinsky,
© 2016 by Yale University.

Historical chance is solely responsible for the fact that the final solution was not final, but it came progressively closer to finality. Thus, the establishment of the industrial system of extermination constituted by the gas chambers and all that it implies—that is what constitutes the total difference as well as the difference in the lived experience.[4]

Semprún's awareness of the specificity of Jewish experience is unambiguous, especially in terms of distinguishing it from deprivation and torture resulting from political commitment, and, in Semprún's case, as an effect of engagement in Communist resistance, which led to his internment in Buchenwald in 1944.[5]

Torture is a major theme in Semprún's works, starting with *L'évanouissement* (The Fainting Fit) (1967), his most esoteric meditation on the impossible experience of death, a meditation nurtured by the philosophy of Martin Heidegger and Ludwig Wittgenstein.[6] *L'évanouissement* is suffused with screen memories and lost memories, personal experiences superimposed on collective ones. The *récit* recapitulates the themes of existentialism and the experience of mortality, or rather, the missed encounter with death for which fainting is a synecdoche. *L'évanouissement* shows that Semprún never took lightly the fate of any victims of recent history—those of fascism, Nazism, Stalinism, Communism. Without drifting into anti-modern or anti-American rhetoric,[7] Semprún never trivialized the atrocities

4. Jorge Semprún and Elie Wiesel, *Se taire est impossible* (Paris: Editions mille et une nuits, 1995), 13. All translations from the works of Semprún that have not been translated into English are my own.

5. On the controversial suggestion of an ontological continuity between Nazi dehumanization, ethnic cleansing, and the Serbian war, see Semprún's drama *Le retour de Carola Neher* (Paris: Gallimard, 1998).

6. Semprún, *L'évanouissement* (Paris: Gallimard, 1967), 66-69. Semprún's reflections on torture culminate in his posthumous *Exercices de survie* (Paris: Gallimard, 2012).

7. See *Mal et modernité* (Paris: Climats, 1995). The poignant relation between father and son, Jorge and Jaime Semprún, remains unexplored to this day. Jorge outlived his son Jaime by one year (the latter died in 2010). Jaime, to whom Jorge's first book is dedicated, was an elegant essayist in his own right and the founder of the new Internationale Situationniste, a movement inspired by Guy Debord's critique of modernity, capitalism, and the entertainment industry. Unlike his father, who once denounced in anti-modern and anti-American rhetoric a failure of critical thought, Jaime Semprún's ideology was radically anti-modern and anti-American. By contrast, Jorge Semprún wrote, as though targeting his son's ideology: "The critique of Americanism, of machines and progress—of that which Heidegger calls *Machenschaft* in his posthumous

of modern evil, as evidenced in *Mal et modernité*, nor the bombing of Hiroshima in particular, evoked in *L'évanouissement* with a lyricism that recalls Marguerite Duras's and Alain Resnais' 1959 *Hiroshima mon amour*:

> Ball of fire [. . .] ball of flame kilometers high. Sky of fire [. . .] sky of flame, fire up to the highest sky. Flower of smoke in the summer sky. Sky of ashes, sky of soot in the summer sky. (*L'évanouissement*, 106).

The reader aware of Semprún's intimate acquaintance with Paul Celan's poetry, especially "Todesfuge" (1948),[8] could easily be (mis) led into believing that Semprún is speaking of Auschwitz and the Holocaust. While the tropes (smoke, ashes) hint at Holocaust literature and testimony, Semprún is actually evoking the bombing of Hiroshima, yet without minimizing the Holocaust.

ETHICS AND POLITICS

A few years before *L'évanouissement*, in 1963, Semprún published *Le grand voyage*,[9] his literary début and possibly his most felicitous piece of autobiographical writing. This memoir, although sui generis in terms of its literary voice, draws inspiration from Robert Antelme's account (*L'espèce humaine*, 1947), especially in its Marxist, straightforward conception of Resistance, antifascist struggle, and deportation; as his narrator states, "it's simply a question of instituting a classless society" (*The Long Voyage*, 47). Even closer to Antelme are Semprún's considerations regarding man's indestructibility:

> But in the camps man also becomes that invincible being capable of sharing his last cigarette butt, his last piece of bread, his last breath, to sustain his fellow man. . . . [M]an doesn't become that invincible animal in the camps. He already is. It's always been a part of his nature, an inherent possibility. (60)

---

book—whether that critique presents itself within a right-wing or a left-wing ideological or semantic context, is always the symptom of weak thought. Or vulgar thought. Or both. Of a pre-critical thought in any case; that is to say, postmodern thought" (*Mal et modernité*, 57-58). Jaime proved his father wrong by elaborating one of the most refined critiques of modernity in the late twentieth century.

8. See "Une tombe au creux des nuages," in Jorge Semprún, *Le fer rouge de la mémoire* (Paris: Gallimard, 2012), 726.

9. Semprún, *Le grand voyage* (Paris: Gallimard, 1963). English translations are from Semprún, *The Long Voyage*, trans. Richard Seaver (New York: Grove Press, 1964).

For Semprún, suffering, alienation, exile, deprivation serve a purpose: the advent of a classless, just society. Yet Semprún's Marxist pragmatism is always tempered by an ethics of human encounter. In a conversation with a German soldier, the narrator distinguishes between politics and ethics in a moment reminiscent of Camus or Levinas:

> "You hope I'll die. . ."
> "I hope the German army will be annihilated. And I hope that you will come out of it." (*The Long Voyage*, 54)

This recognition of the tension between politics and ethics accounts for Semprún's early condemnation of Communism's crimes and his ensuing exclusion from the Communist Party in 1964, one year after the publication of his first book. One could object that there is something outrageous in Semprún's attention to the German soldier's face, to the human singularity of the enemy, when the enemy is Nazi Germany. Yet this is precisely what allows us to understand Camus's paradoxical claim that violence is inevitable, even as it is unjustifiable. Speaking of Kaliyaev and the other "meurtriers délicats" of his play *The Just*, Camus wrote in 1951:

> It is possible that they too, while recognizing the inevitability of violence, nevertheless admitted to themselves that it is unjustifiable. Necessary and inexcusable—that is how murder appeared to them.[10]

The ability to maintain this paradox may distinguish those who, like Semprún and Camus, were able to condemn the gulag, from those who justified the atrocities of Communism in the name of historical reason. This ability also sheds light on Levinas's declaration that even an S.S. man has a face,[11] and perhaps also illuminates Antelme's ethical axiom that there is only one human species (the affirmation of the unity of victim and perpetrator, a unity that ultimately brought about the collapse of S.S. logic).[12] Semprún was too much of a humanist to be a flawless Marxist.

10. Albert Camus, *The Rebel* (New York: Vintage Books, 1991), 169.
11. Emmanuel Levinas, *Entre nous*, 244.
12. No need to mention all the literature on Robert Antelme's *L'espèce humaine*, from Maurice Blanchot's *L'entretien infini* (Paris: Gallimard, 1969), to Martin Crowley's *Robert Antelme: Humanity, Community, Testimony* (Oxford: Legenda, 2003), especially the numerous commentaries on Antelme's famous sentence: "The S.S. can kill a man but cannot turn him into something else."

TO A PASSERBY

The first occurrence of the question of the Jewish fate in Semprún's literary work occurs in *Le grand voyage*. It takes place on the rue de Vaugirard, in occupied Paris in 1941 or 1942, when the narrator crosses paths with a woman with a Slavic accent, in need of immediate assistance. The narrator feels compelled to respond to her after witnessing the indifference, apathy, or fear of others on the street, no doubt a typical scene in Paris under German occupation. The foreigner, a Baudelairean of sorts,[13] melancholic and restless enough to be in mourning like Baudelaire's memorable "passante," stares at the passers-by:

> One would have thought—that is, I thought—that she was looking for an urgent answer to some vital question in the eyes of the passers-by. She looked the passers-by up and down, as though assessing them: were they worthy of hearing her secret? (*The Long Voyage*, 87-88)

The scene is one of staring into the face, "dévisager," to ascertain whether one can trust a stranger, or, in this case, place one's fate in a stranger's hands merely by addressing him or her. The essential questions are ethical and metaphysical: To what extent can one trust a face? Which face can be trusted in times of war against civilians? Who will respond and why would they respond to the fate of the Jews? Why not merely choose to pass by?

After the woman addressed the narrator, he wonders why she assumed that it was safe to address him and not others. She says: "You looked as though you were hoping that I would speak to you" (90). Expecting to be spoken to, to be called upon to respond—such is Semprún's ethical disposition. Expecting to be addressed—this sums up his ethical *Stimmung* as non-indifference or, as Levinas would have it, *désintéressement*, and thus his ability to hear and heed the fate of the Jews as well as the fate of the victims of Soviet Russia.

One year later, on the journey that takes him to Buchenwald and that forms the core narrative of *Le grand voyage*, the narrator remembers the woman:

> I wonder whether, finally, she took this voyage that we're taking [. . . .]. I still don't know that, if indeed she has taken this voyage, she

---

13. For a direct engagement with Baudelaire in general and the poem "A une passante" in particular, see Semprún's *Adieu, vive clarté* (Paris: Gallimard, 1998).

hasn't taken it the same way we are. Because there's still another way of traveling, for the Jews, I was to see that later. I have only a vague picture of this voyage that she has perhaps taken, because I still don't have a clear picture of the kind of voyage they make the Jews take. Later on I'll have a clear picture. (93)

After the war, the narrator of *Le grand voyage* meets the woman again in a park, and notices the Auschwitz tattoo on her arm. She does not recognize him. This juncture of the conversation is a dialogue of the deaf: she does not know he was the man who stopped, does not recall their encounter in occupied Paris, and only then does he realize the hiatus that separates the experience of the Jews from that of political survivors:

"No one has *ever* helped me. . . ."
"I was helped all the time. . . . ."
"You're not a Jew, that's all." (96)

One of the distinctive traits of Jewish fate is what Andre Neher called the "silence of Auschwitz," the solitude of the Jews, their dereliction.[14] Semprún's experience of the war and of political struggle in general is one of solidarity. This scene of misrecognition encapsulates the *différend* between Jews and Résistants.

RESTORING THE VOICE

Throughout Semprún's literary work, there are other encounters with Jewish fate, Jewish experience in the Soviet Union, and the Holocaust. In *Le grand voyage*, another memory crops up—the arrival of "the slow, staggering column of Polish Jews" (162). At that moment, Semprún recalls the death of Jewish children. As he writes in this book composed sixteen years after the war:

[T]hat death is already adolescent, it's reaching that serious age of the postwar children, these post-voyage children. They are sixteen years old, the age of that ancient, adolescent death. And maybe I shall be able to tell about the death of the Jewish children, describe that death in all its details, solely in the hope—perhaps exaggerated, perhaps unrealizable—that these children may hear it, or that even one of them may hear it, were it only one of those children who is reaching the

14. André Neher, *L'exil de la parole: du silence biblique au silence d'Auschwitz* (Paris: Editions du Seuil, 1970).

solemnity of his sixteen years, the silence of his sixteen years, their exigency. (162)

To the extent that *Le grand voyage* is dedicated to his son Jaime, "because he is sixteen," the account of the Jewish children's death can thus be seen as also addressed to his son. It is meant to be a transmission of a Holocaust memory by a non-Jewish father to his son, a way to incorporate into a non-Jewish family who took part in Communist and antifascist Resistance, the history of the Holocaust as part of that legacy without harnessing the Holocaust, its history and its memory, to the antifascist struggle; i.e., without cannibalizing that history, and consequently, preserving a respectful distance between the author's personal experience and that of the Jews:

> I can tell the story of the Jewish children from Poland, not as a story that has happened to me especially, but above all one that happened to the Jewish children from Poland. That is, now, after these long years of willful oblivion, not only am I able to tell this story, I feel compelled to tell it. I have to speak out in the name of things that have happened, not in my own name. The story of the Jewish children in the name of the Jewish children. The story of their death on the broad avenue which led up to the camp entrance, beneath the stony gaze of the Nazi eagles, surrounded by the laughter of the S.S., in the name of death itself. (163)

No need to resort to Giorgio Agamben's byzantine analysis of Primo Levi's alleged "paradox of the witness" who cannot bear witness and to the aporia of witnessing, a cause célèbre in postmodern theory.[15] The reader is merely exposed here to Semprún's humble recognition of the finitude of human experience, as well as to the moral obligation to bear witness to the unwritten history of the death of the Jewish children of Buchenwald. The experience of a child is not the experience of an adult, and that of a Jewish child is incommensurable with that of a non-Jewish adult. To tell the story of the Jewish children hunted down in Buchenwald, in the name of those children, in the name of their death, is not to usurp their place or to speak in their stead. It is an attempt to de-personalize the narrative, objectivize the memoir, and let history speak through the voice of a privileged witness. The scene that follows is that of a child-hunt: fifteen Jewish

---

15. See Giorgio Agamben, *Remnants of Auschwitz: The Witness and the Archive*, trans. Daniel Heller-Roazen (New York: Zone Books, 2000).

children, between 8 and 12 years old, the last survivors of one train-load of Polish Jews, hunted down and murdered by S.S. men and their dogs (*The Long Voyage*, 163-66).

The idea of speaking in the name of the dead returns in Semprún's work, at times explicitly as a response to Levi's seemingly paradoxical declaration regarding the powerlessness of the witness.[16] In *L'écriture ou la vie*,[17] published more than thirty years later, Semprún writes: "Clearly, we must sometimes speak in the name of the missing. Speak in their name, in their silence, to give them back their power of speech" (137). But while Semprún's explicit reference to Levi is deferential if critical, his hidden allusion to Agamben and his theory of the impossibility of bearing witness is ironic. In *Le mort qu'il faut* (The Dead Man We Needed), published in 2001, a few years after the French translation of Agamben's *Remnants of Auschwitz*, and not by chance a book centered on the theme of the "*Muselmann*," Semprún wrote:

> [T]he best witness, the only authentic witness, in fact, according to experts, is the one who has not survived, the one who went through the entire experience and ultimately died of it. But neither the historians, nor the sociologists, have so far been able to resolve this contradiction: How can one invite the authentic witnesses, i.e., the dead, to their colloquia? How does one make them speak?[18]

Semprún here excoriates, with corrosive irony, the deconstructive trend in testimony theory since the 1990s, especially the paradox of witnessing that one can find in Agamben's work. It is also interesting to read *Le mort qu'il faut* against the backdrop of Agamben's *Remnants of Auschwitz*. Semprún's "*Muselmann*" is the opposite of Agamben's: he has a face, a past; he listens and interacts. In short,

---

16. Levi articulates that powerlessness in *The Drowned and the Saved* (New York: Summit Books, 1988):

> We survivors are not only an exiguous but also an anomalous minority: we are those who by their prevarications or abilities or good luck did not touch bottom. Those who did so, those who saw the Gorgon, have not returned to tell about it or have returned mute, but they are the 'Muslims,' the submerged, the complete witnesses, the ones whose deposition would have a general significance. (83-84)

To be sure, such an expression of powerlessness is as much an effect of survivor's guilt as of some ontological aporia of witnessing.

17. Semprún, *L'écriture ou la vie* (Paris: Gallimard, 1996). English translations are from Semprún, *Literature or Life*, trans. Linda Coverdale (New York : Viking, 1997).

18. Semprún, *Le mort qu'il faut* (Paris: Gallimard, 2002), 17.

he is human, whereas Agamben needs, for the sake of theory, to depersonalize, de-historicize, deface, and ultimately, dehumanize his *Muselmann*, who is a purely abstract, theoretical creature.

In this way, Semprún reasserts his own position as a legitimate witness of history, and also as a privileged witness to the fate of the Jews. One mission of literary representation for Semprún is to restore the voice of the dead rather than complacently rehash the inadequacy of the language of fiction to communicate extreme experience in general and the Holocaust in particular. On this, Semprún certainly agrees with Robert Antelme,[19] that powerful testimonies need the supplement of fiction.[20]

FIGURING THE JEWS

In *Quel beau dimanche!*,[21] published in 1980, Semprún formulates philosophical and political reflections on terror and totalitarianism and establishes a controversial parallel between Communism and Nazism, between the Nazi Lager and the Gulag. At the heart of the book, the author reminisces about fifteen Jewish survivors of Częstochowa who were transported from Polish camps to Buchenwald shortly before the liberation of the camp. In poignant, lucid pages, Semprún dwells on the specific fate of the Jews, on centuries of persecutions that resulted in the myth of Jewish passivity, and on the double bind with which Zionism is confronted. A necessity for breaking with the anti-Semitic myth of Jewish passivity, Zionism is also a normalization of Judaism and its possible betrayal. Few European writers have understood the Jewish fate with such empathy and clear-sightedness as Semprún. Simultaneously, Semprún was at times uneasy dealing with Judaism, especially with its unfamiliar, perhaps less secularized, or less Westernized incarnations.

What strikes one first in Semprún's account is his own momentary subscription to the topos of Jewish passivity, and even his apparent reliance on the cliché of Jews who were "being taken like sheep

19. On Antelme, artifice and testimony, see my "Ce que chier veut dire: les ultima excreta de Robert Antelme," in *Revue des sciences humaines* 261 (Lille: Presses Universitaires de Lille, 2001), 148-62.

20. *L'écriture ou la vie/Literature or Life*, 123.

21. Semprún, *Quel beau dimanche!* (Paris: Grasset, 1980). English translations are from Semprún, *What a Beautiful Sunday!*, trans. Alan Sheridan (San Diego: Harcourt, Brace, Jovanovich, 1982). Although I have modified most translations, page references are to that edition.

to the slaughter"—in sharp contrast with the epic and even heroic experience of Resistance and antifascist struggle that dominates his oeuvre (an oeuvre that may have more in common with that of Malraux, Sartre, and even Antelme, than with that of Blanchot, Duras, or Bataille):

> Seeing them huddled against each other in that lingering drizzle, one could imagine their infinite patience, their resigned anticipation of the disasters to come, a resignation that life had cruelly taught them. They were nothing but that infinite patience, that unshakable resignation. Their vital force was but the mortal weakness of a herd made to stand in place. (*What a Beautiful Sunday!*, 279-80; translation modified)

Semprún here approximates the postmodern, philo-Semitic and somewhat ambiguous characterization of Jewishness à la Maurice Blanchot, later taken over by Jean-François Lyotard—passivity, resignation, and infinite patience.[22] Yet here one will find neither philo-Semitic celebration of that passivity, nor anti-Semitic contempt for Jewish fatalism. Semprún merely observes: those Jews who arrive from Polish camps have exhausted all their abilities to resist, and perhaps—this is the moment of metaphysical extrapolation and of the anti-/philo-Semitic cliché—that sense of resignation and acceptance has been transmitted to them by centuries of persecution.

In contrast with those fifteen Jewish survivors, Semprún stages the character of Daniel, who is both a political prisoner and a Jew. Daniel, who will reappear in *Le mort qu'il faut*, is himself an avatar of the fictional character of Hans who appears in Semprún's first *récits*, *Le grand voyage* and *L'évanouissement* (unless it is the other way around: Hans may be a recollection of Daniel). Hans is a Jewish character who joined the Resistance in order not to die as a Jew, to refuse the fate of the Jews. But Hans is also a Jewish ego-ideal, a sort of narcissistic projection of the Resistant as a Jew and of the Jew as the "pure" figure of resistance to socio-economic oppression. The following quote reminds us that Semprún was no stranger to Marguerite

---

22. See especially Maurice Blanchot's essay "Etre Juif," in *L'entretien infini*, and Jean-François Lyotard's *Heidegger et "les juifs"* (Paris: Galilée, 1988). On the "figural Jew" and the French philo-Semitic tradition from the nineteenth century up to postmodernism and deconstruction, see Sarah Hammerschlag's *The Figural Jew: Politics and Identity in Postwar French Thought* (Chicago: University of Chicago Press, 2010).

Duras's apartment on the rue Saint-Benoît. The reader will recognize Duras's unique voice in the use of *conditionnel pré-ludique*[23] that is her signature:

> We would have invented Hans, as an image of ourselves, the purest image, the closest to our dreams. He would have been German, because we were internationalist: in each German soldier shot down in an ambush, we did not target the foreigner, but the most murderous essence, and the most blaring one of our own bourgeoisie, i.e., of the social relations that we wanted to change in ourselves. He would have been Jewish because we wanted to liquidate all oppression and because the Jew, even passive or resigned, was the intolerable image of the oppressed. (*L'évanouissement*, 169-70)

Twelve years later, in *Quel beau dimanche!*, Semprún suggests that Daniel, like Hans, is the Jew who opted for Resistance and took his own fate in his hands, and thus rejected alleged Jewish acceptance, passivity, and resignation. However, Semprún's view of Jewish identity has developed and matured. He has become suspicious of the philo-Semitic, self-serving narrative that construed the Jew as eternal victim—a narrative that up until 1967 (year of *L'évanouissement* and perhaps not coincidentally of the Six-Day War) tended to reduce anti-Semitism to social oppression and class struggle.

Let us return to the fifteen Jews from Poland. Resignation and acceptance border on cowardice and even betrayal when the fifteen Jews do the Nazi salute, thus provoking shame both in Daniel, the combative, political Jew, and the narrator (*What a Beautiful Sunday!*, 286). The initial reaction to the "ghetto Jewish" mentality, i.e., acceptance and passivity that border on "Stockholm syndrome" (siding with one's tormentor), is shame. Those seemingly passive, suffering Jews appear shameful to Daniel, the political Jew, and to the narrator whose core ethical value is uncompromised resistance to fascism— whether in the form of Franco's Spain or Nazism. But those Jews are memorable because they emblematize for Semprún the tragic history of European Jewry. They are not emblematically Jewish for Semprún; rather, they are the very negation of the Jew, the Jew imagined or

---

23. Linguists use this mode to refer to children's playful talk. In English, children would say before a game of impersonation: "You be the doctor. . ." In French: "Toi tu serais le docteur. . ." Duras scholars have borrowed it to account for the writer's imaginary scenarios.

shaped by anti-Semite and philo-Semite alike. Pace Sartre, it is not so much that the Jew is a creation of the gaze of the anti-Semite; instead, the passive, accepting, suffering Jew is nothing but an effect of a European history of combined anti-Semitism and philo-Semitism:

> You will have remembered up until your last minute the Jews of Częstochowa, standing petrified, making a superhuman effort to stretch out their arm in a Nazi salute. Having become truly Jewish, i.e., quite the opposite, having become the very negation of the actual Jew, having become consistent with the image that a certain history has given of the Jews. An openly anti-Semitic history that can tolerate Jews only as wretched and submissive, in order to despise them all the while exterminating them. Or another history, more insidious, that sometimes is not aware of its own anti-Semitism, that even denies it, but that can tolerate the Jews only when they are oppressed, are victims; only when it is possible to have compassion for them, and on occasion to lament their extermination. (287; translation modified)

Semprún wrote those lines in 1979-80. He had grasped with a remarkable acuity the dialectic between anti-Semitism and philo-Semitism throughout the European representation of the Jews as passive victims. The core pages of Semprún's book are thus an attempt at breaking the vicious circle of Jewish suffering. No less than Albert Memmi or Sartre in his time, Semprún calls forth a liberation of the Jew from the gaze of the other.[24]

Semprún then asks one of the fifteen Jews why they performed the Nazi salute. The Jew shrugs, as though struck by the futility of the question, as though it were a perfectly normal thing to do. The narrator of *What a Beautiful Sunday!* then learns that those fifteen Jews surrendered to the Germans to avoid being taken by the Russians: "The Russians, he shouts, don't you know that the Russians hate the Jews?" (287). This is a moment of awakening for Semprún (at least in retrospect, since those pages are written in 1979), a moment when he is first exposed to Russian, and Soviet, anti-Semitism, even though the anecdote seems apocryphal since the Jews at the time massively preferred the Russians to the Germans. Yet at that moment, on the occasion of remembering the Jews of Poland, their resignation, the tragic choice between the Russians and the Nazis, and their imagined preference for the latter, Semprún recounts his support, in Janu-

24. See Albert Memmi's diptych *Portrait d'un Juif* (Paris: Gallimard, 1962), and *La libération du Juif* (Paris: Gallimard, 1966).

ary 1979, for the Russian dissident Edward Kuznetsov detained in
Brezhnev's gulag, who deliberately accepted his own Jewishness:

> But through his sheer will to be Jewish Edward Kuznetsov stood in
> total opposition to the Jews of Częstochowa. He did not endure any-
> thing, he did not accept anything, he did not subject himself to any-
> thing: he was Jewish, freely, irrevocably. He was Jewish despite all
> opposition: despite himself, despite an important part of himself at
> least. (*What a Beautiful Sunday!*, 290; translation modified)

Semprún's words about the Polish Jews and about Edward Kuznetsov
are ambiguous and even opaque. First, they imply that the Jews of
Częstochowa were somehow subjected to some Sartrean bad faith.
Why? That Semprún suggests that the Polish Jews who arrived to
Buchenwald were not *authentic* Jews in the Sartrean sense of the
word is baffling, besides the fact that the Germans terrorized them
into performing the Nazi salute, or that Russian anti-Semitism had
so terrorized them that they would comply with their new guards
and tormentors. Yet Semprún appears to portray them in a manner
that resonates with Jan Karski's portrayal of the ghetto Jew in Claude
Lanzmann's *Shoah*. Karski at first identifies and finds social and cultural affinities with one of the Polish Jews he meets, who will inform
him of the fate of European Jewry, and will ask him to communicate
that fate to the free world. Yet Karski's portrayal of the Jews is not im-
mune to anti-Semitic stereotypes, and one recalls his malaise when
the Jew suddenly morphs from a "Polish nobleman" like him into
a ghetto Jew, as soon as they have entered the ghetto. This is a moment of breakdown in Karski's testimony, when identification with
the "civilized," European Jew is no longer possible, and when even
the initial dynamic of empathy seems to collapse. Karski says:

> What struck me was that now he was a completely different man—
> the Bund leader, the Polish nobleman. [. . .] He is broken down, like a
> Jew from the ghetto, as if he had lived there all the time. Apparently,
> this was his nature. This was his world.[25]

Semprún's reader experiences something similar to the listener of
Karski's testimony, if less spectacular and dramatic. On the one
hand, there is Daniel, the political, assimilated, European, Jew, with
whom identification is unambiguous; on the other hand, the "ghetto

---

25. Claude Lanzmann, *Shoah: An Oral History of the Holocaust* (New York: Pan-
theon Books, 1985), 158-59.

Jews"— passive, resigned, corresponding to the anti-Semitic carica-
ture, who trigger shame.

Another difficulty arises as well. Why does Semprún consider that
Kuznetsov is Jewish against at least part of himself, while at the same
time showcasing his Jewishness as an example of *authentic* Jewish
identity—a chosen, willed, Jewish identity? These are hermeneutic
hurdles that I cannot resolve but that need to be highlighted.

On the same pages, Semprún recalls historian Jean-Pierre Vernant's speech at the support event for Kuznetsov. In his speech, Vernant justified Zionism on the grounds of the alienated situation of
Jews in the Soviet Union, an alienation that plunged the Jews into
existential and political nothingness. For Vernant, the only way of
becoming "something" was by "creating a fatherland," by "being a
Zionist": "And this is so true that for masses of people, being Jewish
and being a Zionist amount to the same thing" (*What a Beautiful
Sunday!*, 292; translation modified). However, Zionism was not as
simple a solution for Semprún as it was for Vernant:

> Zionism has played and continues to play this grand role, even though
> it carries within itself its own contradiction, the seed of its ideal de-
> struction, since it leads the Jews to become a people like all other
> peoples, a State like all other states. (293; translation modified)

Semprún here appears as a dialectical, Hegelian thinker. Zionism for
him is a necessary moment in the history of the Jewish people that
carries within itself the seed of its own overcoming, or *Aufhebung*.
What is called today "post-Zionism," and which ought not be understood as anti-Zionism or as anti-Israelism but instead in a historic-
dialectical sense, is merely the teleological accomplishment of Zionism. "Post-Zionism" is inscribed within the Zionist project of the
so-called normalization of the Jewish people. And thus Zionism is but
a legitimate step, or rather is endowed with a provisional legitimacy.
Jews are faced with a double bind; while the idea of national sovereignty was necessary for their emancipation, it also carried the risk of
the destruction not merely of Zionism (the overcoming, the suppres-
sion of Zionism through normalization), but of the very metaphysical
core of Jewish identity. This is by no means an original idea; it has
nurtured intense debate within the Jewish world since the inception
of political Zionism. But let us examine how Semprún remaps it, how
he reformulates the dialectic of Jewish identity—between land and
Book, physical territory and exile, Israel and the diaspora, and how

what is historically necessary may be metaphysically deleterious, how a tension can occur between history and metaphysics and how this tension has been at the core of the debate about Zionism:

> But this, which is true at the level of history, this need for the Jews to own a normal State, is simultaneously a mortal risk for them at the metaphysical level. Indeed, the Jewish people are, if not the chosen people (an inconceivable proposition), the people of the Book. A contradiction expressed in their inalienable right to be a people like all other peoples, with a land and a State—even though that right [. . .] once a concrete reality, has gravely wronged latent Arab rights [. . .]— and whose flipside is the metaphysical impossibility of being merely a people like other peoples, the metaphysical need to be Pierre Goldman's people and not just Menachem Begin's people. (*What a Beautiful Sunday!*, 293-94; translation modified).

Beyond the allusion to the wrong that the creation of Israel has done to the Palestinians, the problem lies in the tendency to split history and metaphysics, temporal and spiritual, a tendency in which one recognizes Christianity's DNA. However, Semprún seems less inclined to embrace such a split than to prefer a more dialectical view of Jewish identity. For him, the latter spreads on two levels or layers—the layer of history and that of metaphysics, the layer of politics and sovereignty (nation and territory) and that of study (the Book). Both layers are complementary rather than mutually exclusive. Jewish identity is a synthesis of Begin and Goldman, rootedness in a land and in statelessness, normalization and exception. Such dialectical identity is:

> . . . expressed in the impossibility, both material and spiritual, for the State of Israel, of absorbing all of the Jewish people, to subsume the Diaspora, to the extent that the latter bears witness as much to the Jewish national identity as does the Jewish state itself. (294)

WHITE-OUT

In all of Semprún's works, the past is often conjured by the uncanny memory of a snowstorm. Its first occurrence can be traced to *L'évanouissement*; when the narrator undergoes anesthesia, the memory of the snow suddenly arises (146). The spring snowstorm was a real one that the author experienced in Paris on May 1, 1945—a seemingly exultant memory of the Allies' victory and of the liberation of the camps. The snow, however, is not merely emblematic of a joyful, springtime memory at the end of the war. It also triggers traumatic memories and screen memories. Through the logic of free associations, dizzying digressions, embedded narratives, and unhinged chronology that characterizes Semprún's autobiographical writing, the snow also triggers the memory of Buchenwald and the Holocaust.

By a coincidence that turns writing into an "anti-fate," as Malraux would have it, or rather, that turns the accidents of life into a literary choice, it is on another May 1— in 1964, in Salzburg — that Semprún receives the Formentor prize, in a ceremony wherein the poet Carlos Barral offers his fellow writer the first Spanish edition of *Le grand voyage* (*Literature or Life*, 272). The copy of that first edition, however, is quite peculiar. Due to Franco's censorship, the book could not be printed in Spain and was in process of being printed in Mexico. However, the edition would not be ready for several weeks. All that Barral could give Semprún was a hard cover with numbered, blank pages. The whiteness of those pages triggered in Semprún's imagination the memory of the May 1945 blizzard, and as is always the case with the image of snow for Semprún, the memory of deaths and of the camps ensues. On this specific occasion, the whiteness evokes a *memento mori* through the discrete echo of fifteenth-century poet François Villon's famous phrase "*les neiges d'antan* [the snows of yesteryear],"[26] itself an evocation of the ancient topos of the *Ubi sunt*:

> On May 1, 1945, a snow squall had fallen upon the red flags of the May Day parade at the precise moment when a group of deportees in striped uniforms had swung out into the Place de la Nation. At that instant, on that first day of renewed life, the swirling snow had seemed to remind me that it would always bring with it the presence of death.
>
> Nineteen years later, the span of a generation, on May 1, 1964, in Salzburg, the snow of yesteryear had once again fallen on my life. It had erased the printed traces of the book I'd written in one headlong stretch, in a safe house on the Calle Concepción-Bahamonde in Madrid. The snow of yesteryear blanketed the pages of my book, burying them beneath a powdery shroud. The snow had erased my book, at least in its Spanish version. (*Literature or Life*, 273)

26. I am referring to Villon's poem "Ballade des dames du temps jadis" and to the anaphoric line "*Mais où sont les neiges d'antan?* [But where are the snows of yesteryear?]"

Semprún reads Franco's censorship as erasure, death, and amnesia (a common trope for censorship that one can trace back to Milton's writings).[27] Here, however, erasure and amnesia compel the writer to rewrite the same book interminably, thus explaining why Semprún's reader experiences a sense of *Durcharbeitung* and interminable self-analysis:

> The sign was easy to interpret, the lesson easy to draw: I had not yet accomplished anything. This book it had taken me almost twenty years to be able to write was vanishing once more, practically as soon as it had been finished. I would have to begin it again: an endless task, most likely, transcribing the experience of death. (273)

The first book, *Le grand voyage*, written almost twenty years after the experience of his "death," faints or vanishes ("*s'évanouissait*"). Hence the second book that bears the name of that fainting, *L'évanouissement*—as though it were the whitening, the blanking out of the first, and as though the structure of Semprún's work were that of a rewriting on an erased or vanished manuscript—is a palimpsest. The reader then has an experience of reading that is that of rereading the same, rewritten book.

Ultimately, the fate of the Jews is somehow tied to that experience of memory and erasure, to that interminable task of rewriting. Semprún's grandchildren Thomas, Mathieu and Cécilia (children of his daughter, Dominique), appear in *L'écriture ou la vie*, a book dedicated to Cécilia. After having made, throughout his previous works, an effort to distinguish between his own experience as a political prisoner and survivor and the fate of the Jews in the Holocaust, *L'écriture ou la vie* ties the two experiences together and makes this linkage into a pivotal element on the literary plane. For Cécilia, granddaughter and dedicatee of *L'écriture ou la vie*, Semprún will fill the white pages of the first Spanish edition of *Le grand voyage* with the story of a Jewish child and Buchenwald survivor:

> I will write on those blank pages, for Cécilia Landman, the story of Jerzy Zweig, a little Jewish child in Buchenwald. [. . .] I will write

27. See John Milton, *Areopagitica, A Speech for the Liberty of Unlicenc'd Printing to the Parliament of England* (1644). See also my discussion of the tropes of censorship from Milton to Chateaubriand, Bruno Chaouat, *Je meurs par morceaux. Chateaubriand* (Lille: Presses Universitaires du Septentrion, 1999).

down for her, in the blank pages of [*Le grand voyage*], the story of
Jerzy Zweig, the Jewish child we saved, whom I met years later in
Vienna, in another life: life. (*Literature or Life*, 276-77)

The story of Jerzy Zweig is yet to come; or rather, it will never come
to us from Semprún himself. Was it ever written on the white pages of
the Spanish edition of *Le grand voyage*? Has it remained unpublished,
forever archived?[28] What matters here is less to provide empirical answers to those questions than to note that for Semprún, remembering
Jerzy Zweig in particular and the fate of the Jews in general remained
an open-ended task inextricably tied to that of self-writing—a task
finally that Semprún also deemed from the very beginning as one
of transmission, of passing something on to others—and, perhaps, of
one's self-writing, self-erasure, and one's own passing away.

28. I have not found the story of Jerzy Zweig in the books published between
L'écriture ou la vie and *Exercices de survie*.

COLIN DAVIS

What Fiction Doesn't Say: Reticence in Semprun's Novels

"[W]ho says what to whom in fact?"[1]

When reading Semprun's prodigious literary output, it is hard to forget his remarkable life, from exile and imprisonment in Buchenwald to the clandestine struggle against Franco's regime, expulsion from the Communist Party, success as an author and a period as Minister of Culture in post-Fascist Spain. His work is almost invariably, irresistibly treated as a form of testimonial life writing, tied to his experience, especially (though not exclusively) to his experience of Buchenwald, and also more broadly to his standing as a preeminent witness to European history and politics in the twentieth century. To dissociate the man from his work might seem, Régis Debray suggests, simply absurd.[2] Semprun was an extraordinary person whose traumatized and resilient engagement with the dense fabric of reality is reflected in his writing.

Semprun's best-known and most-studied works are the ones that can most easily be read as autobiographical in some sense: his first book, *Le grand voyage* (1963), and then what Suleiman calls his "Buchenwald memoirs,"[3] *Quel beau dimanche!* (1980), *L'écriture ou la vie* (1994) and *Le mort qu'il faut* (2001).[4] These books estab-

---

1. Jacques Derrida, *Donner la mort* (Paris: Galilée, 1999), 175; *The Gift of Death and Literature in Secret*, trans. David Wills (Chicago and London: University of Chicago Press, 2008; 2nd edition), 131. In the main text, where published translations have been used, the first reference is to the French edition and the second to the English-language version; otherwise, translations are my own.

2. Régis Debray, "Semprun en spirale," in Jorge Semprun, *Exercices de survie* (Paris: Gallimard, 2012), 9–13 (9).

3. Susan Rubin Suleiman, *Crises of Memory and the Second World War* (Cambridge [Mass.] and London: Harvard University Press, 2006), 137.

4. Jorge Semprun, *Le grand voyage* (Paris: Gallimard, 1963); *Quel beau dimanche!* (Paris: Grasset, 1980); *L'écriture ou la vie* (Paris: Gallimard, 1994); *Le mort qu'il faut* (Paris: Gallimard, 2001).

YFS 129, *Writing and Life, Literature and History: On Jorge Semprun*, ed. Razinsky, © 2016 by Yale University.

lish the standing of their author as a Buchenwald survivor struggling to represent and to understand his personal experience and
its broader historical, philosophical, and political significance. They
may incorporate fictional elements. In *Le grand voyage* for example,
the narrator is called Gérard rather than Jorge, and the "guy from
Semur" is not based on a single real person. Even so, encouraged
by the knowledge that Semprun was known as Gérard in the Resistance, critics have generally treated the book as principally testimonial. Semprun's most self-consciously *fictional* works have by
and large been neglected by scholars. If they are discussed at all,
it has most commonly been to the extent that they reflect and re-
fract Semprun's more overtly testimonial works and, like them, deal
with the difficulty of representing and understanding the experience
of the concentration camps.

So what is the place of fiction in Semprun's literary output? A
much-quoted passage from near the beginning of *L'écriture ou la vie*
provides a ready answer. Here, Semprun expresses his distinctive position on the possibility of narrating the experience of Buchenwald.
He rejects the view that it is unnarratable. Everything can be said, so
long as testimony can become "an artistic object, a space of creation.
Or of re-recreation. Only the artifice of a masterly narrative will
prove capable of conveying some of the truth of such testimony."[5]
So narration is possible, but it will also be interminable, requiring
art and artifice. And it will also inevitably entail falling into what
Semprun calls "repetition and working over (*la répétition et le ressassement*)" (24/14; translation modified). This conception of the attenuated speakability of experience explains and justifies the most
characteristic formal features of Semprun's written style in both his
novels and his testimonial works: it is digressive and repetitive, constantly returning to key incidents and episodes, reviewing and renar-
rating them, teasing at language in order to draw out new strands of
meaning, and flitting restlessly between different periods in time in
order to convey the multi-layered density of experience and memory. Artifice, and therefore fiction, further the overall purpose of approaching ever more closely, if never definitively fixing, "the truth of
testimony."

5. Semprun, *L'écriture ou la vie*, 23; *Literature or Life*, trans. Linda Coverdale
(New York: Penguin, 1997), 13.

In this account, then, "repetition and working over" are textual devices that serve an identifiable end. What is repeated and endlessly reviewed is the truth of testimony, which can be stated *only* through that process of repetition and review. Fiction is justified, perhaps even necessary, because there is no simple, direct, natural, artifice-free means of communicating the complexity of the real. The key point here is that there is something preceding repetition, something that is repeated: a reality that can be narrated even if it is never fully contained in any one version. In this article I suggest that this only partly explains the significance of fiction as it is explored and instantiated in Semprun's novels. The view of repetition as the repetition *of something that precedes it, locatable in history and memory*, co-exists—a little uneasily—with a quite different practice, in which what repetition repeats is dispersed, cut off from any ultimate source in history or experience.

REPETITION AND REFERENTIALITY IN TRAUMA STUDIES

The question here is: *what does repetition repeat?* This also raises the issue of reference: is there something behind the text which precedes it and toward which it gestures, even if it cannot be fully communicated? Semprun's work as an author of fiction began in the 1960s, when the French literary scene was dominated by the so-called *nouveau roman*, which opposed the tenets of Sartrean committed literature by insisting on the autonomy of literature. In this context, what mattered most was the experimental "adventure of writing" rather than the sociopolitical responsibilities of the artist. Semprun's fiction is heavily marked by his sympathy for the aims and practices of the *nouveaux romanciers*; but unlike much of their work, it constantly foregrounds the historical and political contexts in which it is set. His characters are typically survivors or children of the survivors of the Nazi concentration camps, or victims of Stalinist repression, or exiles from Fascist Spain, or some combination of all of these. In terms of literary history, Semprun's achievement as an author is that he occupies an intermediary position, negotiating the line—and showing that there is no necessary conflict—between formal innovation and political relevance.

Semprun's literary writing appears to be almost ideally suited to contemporary Trauma Studies. If hard-line poststructuralism in the

1960s and 1970s can be depicted (more by its opponents than its best supporters) as resolutely textualist and unhistorical, one of the gains of Trauma Studies has been to reinstate the referential function of art. Thomas Elsaesser describes trauma theory as "[a theory] of recovered referentiality."[6] It insists on a relation between the world of the text and something that precedes and lies outside it, even if that "something" is not immediately available to consciousness and representation. Freud developed his theory of trauma in response to the experience of shell-shocked combatants in the First World War. In what has become one of the key references of modern Trauma Studies, he describes the survivor of a train accident who initially walks away unscathed and apparently unaffected, but who, after a period of latency, develops symptoms that can be traced back to an earlier traumatic experience.[7] Trauma entails a delayed response; it becomes apparent after—sometimes a long time after—the event(s) that inaugurated it. In such cases the trauma may be difficult or even impossible to reconstruct and to communicate, but it remains indubitably, incontrovertibly *real*. This point is echoed in what have become the canonical texts of Trauma Studies. In *Unclaimed Experience* Cathy Caruth refers to Freud's account of the railway accident as showing "not only *the reality* of the violent event but also *the reality* of the way that its violence has not yet been fully known."[8] Discussing Camus's *La peste*, Shoshana Felman suggests that, in the novel, "the allegory seems to name the *vanishing of the event* as part of its *actual historical occurrence*."[9] The founding traumatic event, whatever it might be, is *real*; its absolute, extra-textual reality is vigorously affirmed even if it cannot be known or narrated by the traumatized subject. Trauma Studies, in these key works, entails a kind of *mitigated realism*: *mitigated*, because the "reality" that lies behind it is never fully available; but *realism* because the actual historical truth of the underlying traumatic event is not doubted. Michael Rothberg's term "traumatic realism" captures this conception. The works he

6. Thomas Elsaesser, "Postmodernism as Mourning Work," in *Screen* 42/2 (2001): 193–201 (201).

7. Sigmund Freud, *Moses and Monotheism*, in *The Origins of Religion*, Pelican Freud Library, vol. 13 (Harmondsworth: Penguin, 1985), 309.

8. Cathy Caruth, *Unclaimed Experience: Trauma, Narrative, and History* (Baltimore and London: Johns Hopkins University Press, 1996), 6; my emphasis.

9. Shoshana Felman, in Shoshana Felman and Dori Laub, *Testimony: Crises of Witnessing in Literature, Psychoanalysis, and History* (New York and London: Routledge, 1992), 103.

discusses, for example by Charlotte Delbo and Ruth Klüger, are *traumatic* insofar as their subject resists direct representation and may therefore require nonrepresentational, nonreferential practices of writing; but they are also *realist* insofar as they refer to a reality that precedes and informs them. Traumatic realism, according to Rothberg, shares the modernist distrust of representation, but "it nevertheless cannot free itself from the claims of mimesis, and it remains committed to a project of historical cognition through the mediation of culture. The abyss at the heart of trauma entails not only the exile of the real but also its insistence."[10] The Holocaust is no less real for being unspeakable.

REPETITION AS REVISION

In her important reading of Semprun's Buchenwald memoirs, Suleiman refers to Freud's famous account of the *fort-da* game in *Beyond the Pleasure Principle*, and she distinguishes between repetition as a desire for mastery and repetition as a sign of the death instinct. This is in turn related to the distinction between narrative memory and traumatic memory: the latter (using another set of Freudian terms) "acts out" trauma (remaining obsessively trapped within its confines) whereas the former entails "working through," moving toward (even if never fully achieving) understanding and reconciliation. Semprun's version of repetition is, she argues, more akin to working through. In fact she prefers to call it "revision": "a process whereby the memory of a traumatic past event is not merely repeated but continually reinterpreted in light of the subject's evolving preoccupations and self-understandings" (140). Revision is, she says, "Semprun's characteristic signature as a writer" (141). This form of repetition permits—indeed it positively thrives on—variation and artifice. Examining different accounts of an incident that occurred shortly after his arrival at Buchenwald, Suleiman accepts variations between them because "The witness can be mistaken, even though his account is given in good faith [. . .]. A testimony is always, necessarily, one incomplete version of an event" (152). The use of artifice may seem to threaten the status of the relevant works as literal testimony, but Suleiman is nevertheless content to accept that "whatever liberties he may take

---

10. Michael Rothberg, *Traumatic Realism: The Demands of Holocaust Representation* (Minneapolis and London: University of Minnesota Press, 2000), 140.

with positive facts, Semprun reminds us that he is incontrovertibly a survivor and a witness" (157). And so, Suleiman concludes, "continuous revision is the literary performance of the working through of trauma, a performance that Semprun's Buchenwald memoirs enact brilliantly" (158).

Suleiman's reading is based explicitly and exclusively on Semprun's testimonial memoirs. The question remains of whether the same can be argued of those of Semprun's works that are presented explicitly as novels. Is novelistic fiction just an extended version of the "artifice," which Semprun judges to be necessary and Suleiman finds acceptable in testimony? The novels themselves give plenty of encouragement to interpretation in the light of Semprun's experiences. There is a family resemblance between many of his principal characters. They share the same cultural and historical references, effortlessly spotting and elaborating on each other's quotations and allusions. Many of them also share aspects of Semprun's past: Rafael Artigas in *L'Algarabie* (1981) and Juan Larrea in *La montagne blanche* (1986), for example, are both Buchenwald survivors and writers with Spanish origins.[11] Despite differences between them, characters sometimes seem to merge with one another, so that after the death of Artigas in *L'Algarabie*, his friend Carlos finds that he is invaded by the private memories of his dead friend.

The novels can, then, be regarded as being populated by Semprun's *alter egos*, living out the lives and deaths that could have been his own. The fact that many of them are killed or commit suicide can also be understood through the Freudian lens of acting out and working through. In *La montagne blanche*, Juan Larrea kills himself after recounting his experiences of Buchenwald. He thereby illustrates the alternative posited and perhaps finally overcome in *L'écriture ou la vie* between forgetting and surviving on the one hand, or remembering and dying on the other. When Larrea is overwhelmed by his memories of Buchenwald, he can no longer carry on living. It is only a small step from here to conclude that, if so many of Semprun's *alter egos* are condemned to die, it may be so that their author can survive. They die in his place, or perhaps part of him dies with them and their death conveys something of the survivor's sense of never fully return-

11. Semprun, *La montagne blanche* (Paris: Gallimard, 1986); *L'Algarabie* (Paris: Gallimard, 1997).

ing from the camps; but at least for the time being their death allows him to continue.[12]

The temptation to read Semprun's novels in the light of what is well known about their author is, then, strong. Moreover, the lack of a substantial body of criticism devoted specifically to the novels effectively relegates them to a secondary position in Semprun's *oeuvre*. *Le grand voyage* is a revealing exception. It is usually described as a novel but treated as a testimonial text, as if its "autobiographical" element justifies and redeems its fictional form. Lawrence Langer, for example, describes how "Semprun's survivor-narrator [in *Le grand voyage*] acknowledges images rising from the soil of history, not myth, images which he can share with his reader's consciousness, insofar as the reader submits to their promptings. But they are literal promptings, not literary ones."[13] What matters here is the literal, historical truth made available to the reader, which subsists intact through the trial of artifice and fiction. Semprun's later novels are generally not discussed at all; or they are mentioned insofar as they reflect issues from the memoirs and ignored to the extent that they do not. In both testimonial works and novels Semprun's "real" subject, this implies, is himself: the survivor-witness engaged in history, struggling to deal with the aftermath of Buchenwald.

There are certainly strong links between Semprun's fiction and the historical events that marked his life. However, his novels also exhibit a tendency to dissociate themselves from reality as we know it. Most obviously, *L'Algarabie* is set in a counterfactual world in which the events of May 1968 have resulted in the fragmentation of the French state. De Gaulle has been assassinated and parts of Paris are outside government control. The novel envisages what may be a *possible* world, but one that the reader knows full well to be *false*. The liminary note in *La deuxième mort de Ramón Mercader* similarly insists that readers should make no connection between the fiction and the world we think we know: "The events described in this narrative are completely imaginary. Even more: any coincidence with reality

12. See Semprun, *L'écriture ou la vie*, 255/246, where he reveals that Juan Larrea was a pseudonym he had used while involved in clandestine work in Franco's Spain, and that at the end of *La montagne blanche*, Larrea "committed suicide, dying in my place."

13. Lawrence Langer, *Admitting the Holocaust: Collected Essays* (New York and Oxford: Oxford University Press, 1995), 120.

would be not only a matter of chance, but genuinely scandalous."[14] The instruction to the reader could not be clearer: do not attempt to tie this fiction to any pre-existing reality. Fiction is imaginary not real, artifice not testimony. And yet it is hard to escape the sense that Semprun is playing a complex, deadly-serious game here: how can we *not* link his novels, populated as they are by characters marked by the traumas and tragedies of the twentieth century, to a history that we know to be all too true?

The easier reading of Semprun's fiction is implicitly realist and autobiographical, autofictional, or even "autothanatographical."[15] Across these variants, the "auto-" remains constant. Semprun's works are treated as being about his own life and death, however much he may fictionalize them. He pushes us in this direction in *L'Algarabie*, for example, by clear hints that Artigas may in fact be none other than Jorge Semprun. The kind of reading that such hints encourage does not—and does not attempt to—separate the novels from the presence, however attenuated, of their author. In terms of repetition, what is repeated here is the same (Semprun, the author), even if the same is complex, fragmented, and postmodern. It's all about me, even if "me" cannot be simply narrated. To read Semprun's fiction independently of what we know about him and his experience has rarely been attempted to any significant degree. Another way of putting this is to say that so far critics have shown little interest in his fiction *as fiction*; we are concerned with it because, and insofar as, it tells us about the author and his experiences. Semprun's defense of artifice and fiction has been seen, overwhelmingly, only in the context of a broader testimonial project. David Carroll's discussion of Semprun is exemplary in this respect, in that it both gives a place to fiction but limits that place to its role in the service of testimony; "fiction," Carroll writes, "is not a weapon to be used to assassinate memory but rather a means to enrich and complicate it."[16] Fiction plays a part in a literary practice that is understood as primarily, fundamentally auto-

14. Semprun, *La deuxième mort de Ramón Mercader* (Paris: Gallimard, 1969; Folio edition), 9.

15. On Semprun's "autothanatographical" writing, see Ursula Tidd, "The Infinity of Testimony and Dying in Jorge Semprun's Holocaust Autothanatographies," in *Forum of Modern Language Studies* 41/4 (2005): 407–17.

16. David Carroll, "The Limits of Representation and the Right to Fiction: Shame, Literature, and the Memory of the Shoah," in *L'esprit créateur* 39/4 (1999): 68–79 (78).

biographical and testimonial. The text tells us about its author even when it does so by indirect means. The critical reception of Semprun is a glaring refutation of Barthes's claim that the Author is dead.

REPETITION AS REPETITION

To some extent, Semprun's novels invite and demand this kind of reading. But it is not the only possible reading of his work, and other interpretative avenues have barely begun to be explored. In this section, I want to look more closely at *Netchaïev est de retour*, regarding it as an extended reflection on the issues of return and repetition.[17] *Netchaïev* is a detective story that begins with a murder and then uncovers the circumstances that led up to it. The specific perpetrators remain unnamed, but they are vaguely specified as international terrorists, and by the end lots of bad people have been suitably dispatched, even if there is also some collateral damage. So far, so generic. The novel begins with an enigma, which its purpose is then to resolve. Its broader resonance comes from the linkage of the initial murder to post-1968 terrorist movements, and to philosophical and political questions about what measures are justifiable when society is perceived as unjust. This is in turn related to the experience of World War II, since all of the principal characters have connections to the Resistance and the death camps, either directly or through their parents. Across the different generations, the novel poses searching questions about the difference between legitimate resistance and willful violence: what separates those who died in Auschwitz and Buchenwald because they opposed Nazism from those who took to terrorism in the wake of the failure of May 1968 to change society for the better? The strength of the novel, and its moral import, derive from its readiness to take this question seriously, without glib answers.

Netchaïev is, then, resolutely rooted in its historical context, adopting the format of detective fiction to examine links between World War II and modern France, and between Resistance violence and modern terrorism. Three years before the publication of the novel, Didier Daeninckx had used the detective format to similar

17. Semprun, *Netchaïev est de retour* (Paris: Editions Jean-Claude Lattès, 1987; Livre de Poche edition).

effect in his well-regarded *Meurtres pour mémoire* (1984), which connects French state crimes during the Occupation to the deaths of peacefully protesting Algerians in Paris in 1961. What Semprun distinctively adds to the political dimension of his work is an element of uncanniness that both accompanies and unsettles the realism of the novel. This is already implied by the title, *Netchaïev est de retour*. The historical Sergey Nechayev died in 1882, so how can he return? The novel explains this impossible return by the fact that Netchaïev was the codename of a terrorist, Daniel Laurençon. So it is not the "real" Nechayev who returns, but someone who has borrowed his name. Yet Laurençon/Netchaïev was also believed to be dead. His companions in his terrorist cell had decided to abandon their armed struggle in order to return to mainstream society. Since he opposed this decision, he was condemned to death. Years later, he also decides to renounce terrorism, and he returns to France in the hope of freeing himself from the murderous organization to which he has belonged for many years. His return is consistently described in the novel as *a return from death*: it is not that he was *believed* to be dead, but that he *was* dead, and he has come back. Netchaïev dies and returns; Laurençon dies and returns. The murder with which the novel begins may be explained, but the novel raises further enigmas: how can the dead come back? What is the dividing line between the living and the dead?

These questions are further complicated by the interpenetration of the lives, stories, and identities of different sets of characters. The terrorist group that Laurençon forms with his friends in the wake of May 1968 parallels the Resistance group to which his long-dead father and his stepfather Roger Marroux (the detective who investigates the murder with which the novel begins) had belonged during the Occupation. Within the terrorist group, the four male protagonists share the same cultural, political, and erotic tastes, as did the Resistance group of the earlier generation. For the terrorist group, Adriana Sponti becomes a shared love object for the male protagonists, just as Laurençon's mother had been for the earlier Resistance fighters, sleeping both with Laurençon's father, who died before his birth as a result of his deportation to Buchenwald, and with Marroux.

Across generations and across history, the lives of each of the characters echo and repeat the lives of all the others. This is not to say that the characters are identical—the novel resists that implication—but neither do they have discrete identities separate from one another. Each reflects the other without repeating him or her identically.

This repetition-with-difference extends beyond the characters to affect the novel as a whole in its aesthetic dimension. We can see this on a small scale through Pierre Quesnoy, the former militant and photographer who inadvertently stumbles across evidence of Laurençon/Netchaïev's return. One night Quesnoy is awoken by a nightmare in which he participates in the torture of a woman named Thérèse, whom he knows to be the writer Marguerite Duras. The nightmare evokes memories of his time as a soldier during the Algerian War of Independence when he had been present during the torture of Algerian prisoners. It also alludes to his recent reading of Duras's *La douleur*, which had been published in 1985. One of the stories in *La douleur*, entitled "Albert des Capitales," narrates how a character named Thérèse presides over the brutal torture of a presumed collaborator. In a liminary note, Duras writes: "I am Thérèse."[18] For Quesnoy, an incident from the Algerian War reflects one from the World War II; in *La douleur*, Duras claims that her fiction reflects her life. Quesnoy's life repeats the fiction that repeats the life of another. Moreover, within Duras's "Albert des Capitales," the torturers are themselves victims of torture, as is indicated when we are told that they have been imprisoned at Montluc, a prison used by the Gestapo during the war.[19] The victims become torturers, as life and literature become dizzyingly imbricated. Fiction reflects the life that becomes a fiction that in turn reflects the life of another. The first term is lost in a vortex of repetition. In this account, repetition does not preserve the same across the vicissitudes of time; rather, it undermines the autonomy of self-contained identities by exposing them to a process of replication and fragmentation without governing principles.

The appearance of Duras's *La douleur* is by no means the only reference to earlier texts in Semprun's novel. On the contrary, the novel constantly manifests its debt to other works. If, for example, Netchaïev returns from the dead in the figure of Daniel Laurençon, he does so through the mediation of Fyodor Dostoyevsky's *Demons*

18. Marguerite Duras, *La douleur* (Paris: P.O.L. éditeur, 1985), 134; quoted *Netchaïev*, 95.
19. See *La douleur*, 142: "D. selected two of them who had been at Montluc, and who had had a rough time of it."

(1872), which is partly inspired by Nechayev, as well as through Albert Camus's *L'homme révolté* (1951). Camus's work discusses Nechayev and quotes the passage (albeit in a different translation) that forms the epigraph to Part 2 of Semprun's novel.[20] The most important point of reference is Paul Nizan's novel of 1938, *La conspiration* (1938).[21] Nizan's novel describes the lives and loves of five would-be revolutionary students in the years before World War II. *Netchaïev est de retour* references Nizan's work even before *Netchaïev* has even actually begun, since *La conspiration* is quoted as an epigraph to its first part. Nizan's work is quoted again within the opening pages as the friendship of two of the principal characters is inaugurated by a joint recitation of its first lines (*Netchaïev*, 15). Semprun's novel then refers and alludes to Nizan's novel on numerous occasions. It is the "fetish book" (273) and the "bedside book" (311) of the friends. Semprun's novel quotes the description of Lucien Herr from *La conspiration* (312, quoting *La conspiration*, 48). One of Semprun's characters, Marc Lilienthal, gives Nizan's novel to his lover Fabienne so that she can read it on the plane as she flies to an assignation with him.[22] Another character quotes it to his lover, changing the name of Nizan's Catherine to Semprun's Bettina, in order to explain her erotic deficiencies (342, quoting *La conspiration*, 196).

The numerous references to *La conspiration* are not just the acknowledgment of an admired book; they also indicate a more fundamental reliance on the earlier novel as a source of repetition. One of Semprun's central characters, Elie Silberberg, is a novelist. Marroux suggests to him that his works are incessant rewritings of Nizan's *La conspiration*. In Nizan's novel one of the group of five, Pluvinage, betrays his friends by revealing the hiding place of a militant sought by the authorities. According to Marroux, Silberberg's novels reproduce this element of Nizan's plot:

> It's always, whatever the events and circumstances, which may vary, the story of a group and a traitor. Of a presumed traitor, at least. It's

20. Compare the quotations in Albert Camus, *L'homme révolté*, in *Oeuvres complètes III* (Paris: Gallimard, 2008), 198, with *Netchaïev*, 199. Camus's interest in Nechayev is mentioned in *Netchaïev*, 108.

21. Paul Nizan, *La conspiration* (Paris: Gallimard, 1938; Folio edition).

22. Moreover, Lilienthal's name recalls that of Rosenthal from *La conspiration*: one is a valley of lilies (which also alludes to Balzac's *Le lys dans la vallée*), the other a valley of roses.

the same schema as *La conspiration*, in sum. But your Pluvinage is less determined, more ambiguous than in Nizan. You never know if he is really a traitor. (216)

In this account of actual or presumed treachery, we have a model of repetition with variation; and variation brings with it greater ambiguity. In Nizan's novel there is little doubt that Pluvinage is a traitor. Silberberg replicates Nizan's schema but holds back from settling the truth or falsehood of the allegation of betrayal. Semprun's novel recalls that Nizan himself had been accused of betrayal after he left the Communist Party in 1939 (273). Nizan's novel predicts his own fate, which is then repeated again in Silberberg's novels, which are themselves fictional insofar as they do not exist: Silberberg is, after all, a character in a novel rather than a real person.

If Silberberg's fictional novels repeat Nizan's real novel, then so does Semprun's *Netchaïev est de retour*. Like Nizan, Semprun bases his novel on five characters, some of whom are students at the *École Normale Supérieure* and who plot the downfall of bourgeois society. Pluvinage's betrayal is echoed in the more ambiguous story of Laurençon/Netchaïev. The latter is at first *accused* of betrayal by the revolutionary group to which he belongs because the others want to abandon the armed struggle; he does not accept this, and so he must be condemned and killed. Later, though, he *actually* plans to abandon and betray the revolutionary cause when he decides to give up violence: that is why he is hunted by his terrorist associates.

The importance of Nizan's *La conspiration* for Semprun's *Netchaïev est de retour* is so great that the latter can be regarded as a rewriting of the former. Both novels are concerned with five friends who declare war on established society, and both entail betrayal. The social, intellectual, and economic circumstances of the principal characters are similar. Semprun's novel even replicates the casual sexism of Nizan's. However, what is mainly repeated in the later work is not so much the content as what is called, in the passage cited above, its "schema," involving characters and plot elements rather than specific intellectual or political material. Moreover, this repetition operates both in the relation of *Netchaïev est de retour* to *La conspiration* and internally, within the novel itself. The group of five terrorists, of whom one is (doubly) accused of betrayal, reflects the history of Laurençon/Netchaïev's stepfather, who during the Second World War was also a member of a group of friends, one of whom was suspected—rightly, as it turned out—of working for the Gestapo. The lines separating stories and identities become blurred. Repetition here has acquired its own dizzying momentum, coming to govern the lives of the characters, their stories, and the novel in which they are created.

TELLING THE ESSENTIAL

In relation to the *fort-da* game analyzed by Freud, Derrida suggests that what repetition repeats is repetition itself: a movement that endlessly reflects back on itself and in the process propels itself forward, removing itself from interpretability in terms of a hidden but stable kernel of meaning.[23] In a later discussion, Derrida relates this absence of a founding, determinable meaning to literature in its broadest sense. A literary work, he says in *Donner la mort*, may be any text that is:

> consigned to public space, that is relatively legible or intelligible, but whose content, sense, referent, signatory and addressee are not fully determinable *realities* - realities that are at the same time *non-fictive* or *immune from all fiction* [. . .] The reader therefore senses literature coming down the secret path of this secret, a secret that is at the same time kept and exposed, jealously sealed and open like a purloined letter. (175/131)

In this account, the "secret" of literature is not a content to be revealed; rather, it is a fundamental relation of self-withholding in relation to its source, meaning and destination. As Derrida, quoted in the epigraph to this article, succinctly puts it, "who says what to whom in fact?" (175/131).

Given that Semprun was both prolific and loquacious, it may seem surprising to describe his fiction as *reticent*. My point is really that the novels leave one with a sense that something remains unsaid, but that this "something" cannot be identified simply with a specific experience or set of experiences involving, or including for example, the author's incarceration in Buchenwald. On this point, the intense self-consciousness of Semprun's writing may be revealing. His fictional novelist, Elie Silberberg, incessantly rewrites a text by Nizan, another lapsed revolutionary. Silberberg's practice tells us something

---

23. See Derrida, *La carte postale de Socrate à Freud et au-delà* (Paris: Aubier-Flammarion, 1980), 322–25.

about Semprun's, as Semprun also rewrites Nizan's novel. What characterizes fiction, in this process, is that it does not pass quickly to the essential. Marroux, Laurençon/Netchaïev's stepfather, is a detective; his job is to find the truth hidden behind ambiguous clues. But hidden truths are not what he expects from literary fiction. He encourages Silberberg to write fiction because, unlike the essay, the novel does not pass directly to the essential. On the contrary, the novel allows variation and obsession; and, referring to Hannah Arendt, he insists that no theoretical reflection can have "the riches of meaning of a well-narrated story" (*Netchaïev*, 217). The role of the novel is not to say the essential, but precisely *not* to say it, or not to say it too soon. In the novel, then, the duty to state the essential is superseded by the narrative proliferation of meaning. As Marroux discovers first hand when he tries to speak of his own experience, the essential remains unsaid: "So he hadn't even alluded to the essential. It would have been necessary to go further back, to get lost in too many digressions, too many side paths for her to understand what he was talking about" (320). In this version, the essential is not something that is gradually revealed through the infinite patience of the storyteller and listener; rather, it is something *necessarily* absent, an ungraspable Derridean secret that propels and eludes narration.

I am not arguing that there is no relation between the historical, autobiographical context of Semprun's more overtly testimonial works and his fiction. There obviously is. His characters are, like himself, scarred by the experience of the concentration camps and twentieth-century history more broadly. But to reduce his fiction to its author's experience also misses what is *fictional* about it. His fiction is unnerving and engaging not only because it bears witness to the traumas of the last century, but also because it resists explanation purely in terms of history and biography. It permits interpretation in the light of the author's identity and experience while also questioning the very notions of identity and experience. This is, I would venture to say, what has not yet even begun to be explored in any serious way. Semprun's fiction should not and cannot be exhausted by an antiquated realist agenda, however much it has been re-invigorated by Trauma Studies. His novels refer to but are not contained by the figure of the Author; they also enact a *dislocation* of meaning that leaves their sense precisely *unlocated, unlocatable.*

ERAN DORFMAN

In Search of the Lost Gaze

SEMPRUN'S GAZE

"They stand amazed before me, and suddenly, in that terror-stricken gaze, I see myself—in their horror."[1] So begins *Writing or Life*, the great literary work Jorge Semprun drew from his experience as a political prisoner in Buchenwald. For nearly two years, during his imprisonment, he had not seen himself, for there were no mirrors in Buchenwald. Indeed, Semprun had been able to see his body, but his face, his eyes, a glance at his own gaze—never. This was the case until liberation, which brought with it no real mirrors—at least not immediately—but *human* mirrors: the gaze of the other, the gaze of horror.

What is the origin of this horror Semprun saw in the eyes of the other? It is the day after liberation, Semprun is standing before three officers in British uniform. He looks at them and they look at him in return. However, the object of his gaze is not the officers themselves but rather their eyes, which leads him to wonder what these new "mirrors" in fact reflect and reveal. He notices at first horror and panic, but this is only the first step, since he now needs to understand what it is precisely in himself that may provoke such horror:

> The stubble of my head, my worn and ill-assorted clothing—such particulars can be startling, intriguing. But these men aren't startled or intrigued. What I read in their eyes is fear.

1. Jorge Semprun, *Literature or Life*, trans. Linda Coverdale (New York: Viking Penguin, 1997), 3 [13]. I shall use in this paper the more accurate title *Writing or Life*. Henceforth abbreviated LL for the English translation followed by the page numbers, and EV for the French original: *L'écriture ou la vie* (Paris: Gallimard, 1994).

YFS 129, *Writing and Life, Literature and History: On Jorge Semprun*, ed. Razinsky, © 2016 by Yale University.

It must be my gaze, I conclude, that they find so riveting. It's the horror of my gaze that I see reflected in their own. And if their eyes are a mirror, then mine must look like those of a madman. (LL 4/EV 14)

The first chapter of *Writing or Life* is entitled "The Gaze," and these two titles together designate the two main themes of the novel. The first is the relationship between writing and life, conceived as an alternative: *either* writing *or* life; the second is the question of the gaze: the gaze of oneself and of the other, of oneself seeing and seen by the other. In what follows I will investigate the close yet sometimes hidden link between these two themes, showing that it is only by finding his own gaze that Semprun could reconcile writing and life. I will argue that the gaze is a limit phenomenon, and will demonstrate this idea drawing on Sartre's analysis of the gaze in *Being and Nothingness* (a book that Semprun claims to have read with passion upon its release) and Freud's concept of "afterwardsness" (*Nachträglichkeit*) as a mechanism of deferred trauma processing. The gaze of the other, it will be shown, may serve to reactivate and retroact past traumatic events, causing them to be relived, not *in contrast to* writing but rather *through* writing.

THE GAZE ACCORDING TO SARTRE

Sartre states, in *Being and Nothingness*, that when the other looks at me, a sudden transition takes place, which makes me move from the level of unreflective consciousness to the level of reflection. To employ Semprun's terminology, the other's gaze takes me from a tacit lived experience ("Life") toward experience as an explicit object for thought and language ("Writing"). Let us start first with the pre-gaze situation, described by Sartre as follows:

> Let us imagine that moved by jealousy, curiosity, or vice I have just glued my ear to the door and looked through a keyhole. I am alone and on the level of a non-thetic self-consciousness. This means first of all that there is no self to inhabit my consciousness, nothing therefore to which I can refer my acts in order to qualify them.[2]

It may seem strange that Sartre never tells us *what* is seen through the keyhole, but for him the crucial thing is not to see but to be seen.

---

2. Jean-Paul Sartre, *Being and Nothingness*, trans. Hazel E. Barnes (New York: The Philosophical Library, 1956), 259 [298]. Henceforth abbreviated BN for the English translation and EN for the page numbers of the French origin: *L'être et le néant* (Paris: Gallimard, 1943).

In order to know my actions and reflect on them (and on myself) it is not enough that I merely look at something, since such a pure attitude has no "outside." Indeed, if it is jealousy that made me look through the keyhole, I still don't have a reflective access to this feeling or any other, since "I *am* this jealousy, I do not *know* it" (BN 259/ EN 299, italics in the original). Now, according to Sartre's famous formula, I am what I am not, and I am not what I am. The human being appears in the world as a "pure nihilation of being" (BN 549/EN 593); it is a "for-itself" which has no positive predicate and is "like a hole of being at the heart of Being" (BN 617/EN 665). Consequently, in order to overcome my inner Nothingness and acquire some Being, I must transcend my solitary sphere and acquire objectivity: not the objectivity of the utensils that I see and use around me—as the keyhole and the scene behind it—but my very own objectivity, since only the object, according to Sartre, is a being that is "in-itself." But how to become an object? According to Sartre, "I am my own nothingness" (BN 260/EN 299) until the advent of a crucial event:

> But all of a sudden I hear footsteps in the hall. Someone is looking at me! What does this mean? It means that I am suddenly affected in my being and that essential modifications appear in my structure—modifications which I can apprehend and fix conceptually by means of the reflective *cogito*. (BN 260/EN 299)

The gaze of the other upon me makes me immediately move from non-verbal consciousness to a "reflective cogito," namely to an "I" that can know itself by distancing itself from itself. However, this process is not a simple passage from "living" to "knowing," since this reflective "I" is not known from the outset, but rather experienced: "It is shame or pride which reveals to me the Other's look and myself at the end of that look. It is the shame or pride which makes me *live*, not *know* the situation of being looked at" (BN 261/EN 300, italics in the original).

The gaze of the other opens for me the possibility of *both* living and knowing myself as an object. Before the advent of the other's gaze I was one with the situation, with no outside or reflection. The introduction of the gaze now makes me enter a new lived situation, yet one that contains its own exteriority. Moreover, I can now say "I" for the first time, but the paradox is that this "I," from the moment it is discovered as such, is an object rather than a subject: when I discover myself as an "I" it is already "me" which is at stake. The gaze of the other thus opens and reveals in me an inner gap, a *différance* that constantly moves from the "I" to the "me" and back, from interiority to exteriority and back. It is a *différance* that henceforth cannot be overcome, an inner split that I experience, feel, and know from the moment that I find myself being looked at by someone. This is why Sartre talks mainly of *shame* and *pride* as the feelings provoked by the other's gaze: on the one hand this gaze allows me to acquire Being, whence the pride ("I"), but on the other hand this Being is dependent on the Other who objectifies me, whence the shame ("me") (BN 262/ EN 301).

Sartre characterizes shame, the discovery of my being an object to the gaze of the other, as an "abrupt modification" that is "in no way provoked by the irruption of knowledge [. . . .] but which suddenly pushes me into a new dimension of existence—the dimension of the *unrevealed*" (BN 268/EN 307, italics in the original). What is this mysterious dimension of the "unrevealed"? Is it simply otherness, as Levinas, for instance, would say? Curiously, for Sartre, the unrevealed is rather *myself* as viewed by the other. It is a "me" which is "outside my reach, outside my action, outside my knowledge" (ibid); a "me" that the other paradoxically reveals to me as unrevealed: "Through the Other's look I *live* myself as fixed in the midst of the world, as in danger, as irremediable. But I *know* neither *what* I am nor *what* is my place in the world, not what face this world in which I am turns toward the Other" (BN 268/EN 307, italics in the original).

The other's gaze thus makes me know that I know very little of myself. It opens up the possibility of reflection, but a reflection that situates me as alienated to myself in the figure of a "me" that does not belong to me and is taken away from me at the very moment it is given to me. Now, it is precisely this mysterious, unrevealed "me" that Semprun is looking for throughout his novel. The initial shock of the other's gaze upon him makes Semprun aware of the experience of death that preceded this gaze, yet this awareness also blocks his access to this experience.

Indeed, for Sartre the situation prior to the gaze of the other expresses the omnipotence of the "for-itself," but it is nonetheless a for-itself that is on the side of Nothingness, enclosed in a universe with no Being, since the latter can be attributed only through the gaze of the other. The gaze thus stands as a limit situation between Being and Nothingness, revealing their mutual dependency. However, whereas for Sartre the gaze incarnates an existential impasse, Semprun cannot admit as much because he now needs to resume "normal" life while still taking into account the traumatic experience of the camp. So what does the revelation of the unrevealed entail practically? What life and writing does it enable or shut out?

HOW TO TELL A TRAUMA?

Semprun is very critical of those who say that one cannot relate what happened in the camps. The difficulty of telling the story, according to him, does not stem from its bearing on an indescribable experience, but rather on an experience that was "unbearable, which is something else entirely" (LL 13/EV 23). It is an experience of Death and Nothingness, hence the difficulty of integrating it into the world and into the language of the living.

In contemporary trauma theory, as it has been elaborated since the 1990s,[3] the difficulty of recounting the traumatic experience is related not only to its monstrosity, but also to the *absence* of the subject at the moment the trauma took place. One of the hallmarks of this discourse is Lacan's *Seminar XI* and his analysis of *tuché* as an always missed encounter with the real, an encounter that inherently takes place either too early or too late.[4] Lacan relates the real to the gaze of the other, a crude reality that necessitates a symbolic or imaginary screen to protect the subject from its blinding glare. Indeed, it is precisely this screen that Semprun lacks when he meets the three officers in Buchenwald. This is why he does not locate the traumatic real in the long months of his imprisonment in Buchenwald, but rather obstinately focuses on his brief encounter with the three officers and their shocked—and shocking—gaze. It is as if the gaze of the other not only revealed an unreflected trauma that can now emerge, but also provoked a trauma of its own.[5]

3. See Shoshana Felman and Dori Laub, *Testimony: Crises of Witnessing in Literature, Psychoanalysis and History* (New York and London: Routledge, 1992); Cathy Caruth, *Unclaimed Experience* (Baltimore: Johns Hopkins University Press, 1996); Ruth Leys, *Trauma: A Genealogy* (Chicago: University of Chicago Press, 2000).

4. Jacques Lacan, *The Four Fundamental Concepts of Psychoanalysis. The Seminar of Jacques Lacan. Book XI*, trans. Alan Sheridan (New York and London: W.W. Norton, 1981), 53–64.

5. Sartre speaks very rarely of trauma, and always in a very critical way. However, he does refer to "the shock of the encounter with the Other" (BN 352/EN 392). Lacan, in turn, refers to Sartre's theory of the gaze, which he summarizes as follows: "The gaze, as conceived by Sartre, is the gaze by which I am surprised—surprised in so far as it changes all the perspectives, the lines of force, of my world, orders it, from

In order to better understand the role of the other's gaze in trauma, it is useful to return here to Freud's concept of *Nachträglichkeit*,[6] which is commonly translated as "deferred action," "afterwardsness," "belatedness" or "après-coup." This notion was elaborated by Freud in the 1890s, as a part of his conceptualization of the psychic apparatus. The apparatus's main function is to receive stimuli in a controlled way, such that they arrive at consciousness only as bound, that is, arranged in a conceptual scheme. However, some stimuli enter the apparatus in childhood but cannot be fully elaborated into concepts. These stimuli are supposed to be of a sexual nature, since only sexual events, according to Freud, may enter the apparatus without being able to be fully comprehended and discharged. This, he says, happens later, through a *second* event that reminds the child of the first by retroacting it and making it behave "as though it were some current event."[7]

What Freud means here is that early perceptions and experiences, such as suffering an instance of sexual abuse—but also, more simply, seeing one's parents make love—enter the apparatus, pass through some layers, and are then stored as speechless and obscure memories. They are not yet translatable into clear concepts since these do not exist at this stage. This is why a second event is needed at a later period in time, in order for the child to live or re-live what happened retroactively. As Jean Laplanche emphasizes, this mechanism works in both temporal directions: from the past to the present and from the present to the past.[8] I therefore propose that we translate *Nachträglichkeit* as *deferred retroaction*, so that the double temporal movement of the German origin is conserved.

the point of nothingness where I am" (Lacan, *The Four Fundamental Concepts*, 84). But after praising Sartre for his descriptions, Lacan severely criticizes him due to his silence regarding the *desire* that motivates the gaze. After all, Lacan says, I am surprised and looked at when I am watching a scene through the keyhole as a desiring *voyeur* (84–85).

6. Although Lacan obviously had the concept of *Nachträglichkeit* in mind in his analysis of *tuché* and the gaze, it is curious to note that he does not explicitly mention it in this context.

7. Sigmund Freud, "Letter 52 from Extracts from the Fliess Papers" (1896), in *The Standard Edition of the Complete Psychological Works of Sigmund Freud*, 24 vols., ed. James Strachey. Vol. 1, 233–39 (London: Hogarth Press, 1953–74), 236.

8. Jean Laplanche, *Problématiques VI: L'après coup* (Paris: PUF, 2006), 29–32. Laplanche further explained his position in an interesting interview with Cathy Caruth from 1994. See Cathy Caruth, "An Interview with Jean Laplanche," *Postmodern Culture* 11/2 (2001).

Secondly, I suggest expanding the notion of deferred retroaction beyond the field of sexual trauma in childhood, and to conceive it as a structural mechanism of trauma in the broad sense of the term.[9] I therefore adopt Cathy Caruth's notion of trauma as a belated and missed encounter, while taking into account both the reality of the original trauma and the changes introduced into it by its later retroaction.[10] More specifically, I suggest that the gaze of the other—similarly to the gaze of the wolves described by Freud in his famous case study *The Wolf Man*[11]—is precisely the second event that retroacts the first and makes it partly accessible.[12]

Indeed, gazes certainly existed in the concentration camp even prior to liberation. Semprun writes that although most of the prisoners were deprived of their gazes, those who managed to keep them would look at each other quite fraternally (LL 16–17/EV, 26). Their gazes were compassionate in the literal sense of the term (com-passion), but this had precisely to do with the fact that they all shared the same self-enclosed and lifeless world. In a sense, the prisoners had *death* in their eyes, and, paradoxically, the only living gaze in the camps was that, very rare, of the Nazi, "brimming with anxious hatred," which

9. For a further development of this line of thought see Eran Dorfman, *Foundations of the Everyday: Shock, Deferral, Repetition* (London and New York: Rowman & Littlefield International, 2014), 97–126.

10. See Caruth, *Unclaimed Experience*. I thus accept Leys's critique of Caruth (Leys, 266–97), but rather than dismiss Caruth's model I propose to reshape it such that it can explain both temporal directions of *Nachträglichkeit*. This is why, again, I insist on the translation of the term as *deferred retroaction* rather than *belatedness* as Caruth does.

11. Freud, *From the History of An Infantile Neurosis* (1918), in *The Standard Edition*. Vol. 17, 3–122.

12. Susan Suleiman proposes the term *revision* to capture the repetition employed by Semprun in order to return to the experience of the camp in literature. She shows how he repeats and revises the same scenes in different books as a way to revise and re-appropriate the past memory, integrating it into the present (Susan Rubin Suleiman, "Historical Trauma and Literary Testimony: Writing and Repetition in the Buchenwald Memoirs of Jorge Semprun," *Journal of Romance Studies* 4/2 [2004]: 1–19). While I agree with Suleiman that repetition is a key concept in the memory of traumatic experience, I prefer the term retroaction, and, more precisely, deferred retroaction in order to preserve the dual relationship between past and present. Revision is too active and well-controlled a verb, as can be seen by the way Suleiman characterizes Semprun: "Like the narrator of Proust's *À la recherche*, who is perched at the top of a temporal edifice from which he can command the whole sweep of the past, the narrator of *Le Grand Voyage* emphasizes that he is writing many years after the journey and allows himself freedom to roam temporally at will" (3). As I will try to show, deferred retroaction is no less imposed on the author than it is freely undertaken by him or her.

provoked an "insane desire to last, to survive, to survive *him*" (LL 24/ EV 34). And yet, this gaze, too, was the gaze of Nothingness, "a death-dealing gaze" (ibid.).

In contrast, the terrified gaze of the three officers after liberation was quite different: no fraternity, compassion, or even hatred, but rather horror, which is what made Semprun see in it his own gaze and the traumatic experience behind it. The discovery of his own horrified gaze fills him with a sudden anxiety, which—typically—occurs when it is no longer needed. It is this anxiety that, from that moment on, made Semprun feel the experience of the camp as an unbearable burden:

> I find it unjust, almost indecent, to have made it through eighteen months of Buchenwald without a single minute of anguish, without a single nightmare, carried along by constantly renewed curiosity, sustained by an insatiable appetite for life (whatever the certainty of death, whatever the precious and unspeakable daily experience of it may have been), having survived all that—only to find myself from then on the occasional prey of the most naked, the most intense despair, a despair nourished almost as much by life itself, by its serenity and joys, as by the memory of death. (LL 160/EV 171)

Despair and anguish come only retroactively. As long as Semprun remained on the side of the dead or the dying ones—within a self-enclosed traumatic experience—he was able to maintain his thirst for life, which probably served as a phantasmatic screen between him and the traumatizing real. But the new gaze he sees in the eyes of Life brings about a belated recognition of what has just been completed, namely the experience of Nothingness. This blurs the simple distinction between the realm of Life and the realm of Death and opens another dimension, that of the unrevealed:

> I've seen myself for the first time in two years in their horrified gaze. These three jokers have spoiled this first morning for me. I thought I'd made it out alive. Made it back to life, in any case. Guess not. Imagining what my eyes must look like from what I see in theirs, I would say that I haven't left death all that far behind.
>
> I'm struck by the idea, if one can call it an idea (that tonic flash of warmth, that rush of blood, that pride in the bodily knowledge of something vital), struck by the sudden overwhelming feeling, in any case, that I have not escaped death, but passed through it. [. . .]
>
> I have abruptly understood that these soldiers are right to be afraid, to avoid looking into my eyes. Because I have not really survived

death. I have not avoided it. I have not escaped it. [. . .] All things considered, I am a ghost. (LL 14–15/EV 24)

The experience of the other's gaze enables Semprun to tie together two seemingly contradictory feelings. The first is a "feeling of immortality": since he is already dead, he will not die again, whence stems a great feeling of power, a sense of invulnerability that Semprun also qualifies as pride. But as we learned from Sartre, pride is but the other side of shame, and indeed, Semprun simultaneously feels ashamed of his newly revealed status as a ghost, that is, a living dead in both the eyes of the other and his own.

Returning to Sartre, shame, according to him, stems from the division between the objectified "me" and the I-subject: "Thus myself-as-object is neither knowledge nor a unity of knowledge but an uneasiness (*malaise*), a lived wrenching away from the ekstatic unity of the for-itself, a limit which I can not reach and which yet I am" (BN 275/ EN 314). Sartre does not say how to reconcile the two egos, how to reintegrate them either into the "ekstatic unity of the for-itself" or the "unity of knowledge" of the reflected I. For him, the experience of the other's gaze is irreparable and irreconcilable. Semprun, however, cannot accept this almost comfortable fatalism, at least not immediately. He feels an urgent need to reconcile Being and Nothingness, life and death, the I before and the I (me) after the gaze of the other. And not for philosophical reasons but in order literally to survive. He must regain his integrity by *writing* what has happened to him, that is, by somehow returning to Nothingness, somehow reaching again the moment before the gaze, retroacting it in the present. But despite all his efforts he fails time and again to do so, finding himself locked in a repetitive and sterile vicious circle, stressed by the repetitive use of ellipses:

> I can't manage, through writing, to get into the present, to talk about the camp in the present . . . So all my drafts begin before, or after, or around, but never in the camp . . . And when I finally get inside, I'm blocked, and cannot write. Overwhelmed with anguish, I fall back into nothingness: I give up . . . only to begin again elsewhere, some other way . . . And the same thing repeats itself. (LL 166/EV 176)

I wrote earlier that it is not the experience of Buchenwald that Semprun characterizes as traumatic, but the gaze he sees in the eyes of the three officers on the day after liberation. But now we have an important clue regarding the access one might have to trauma that demands exploration: if the camp experience was traumatic, which almost goes without saying, and if trauma is characterized by Semprun as the impossibility to return to it, to live it once more and tell its story, it follows that the only approach to trauma is to be located "before, after or around" and never *inside* the camp. It is as if Semprun tries to encircle the trauma through writing, and the gaze of the other is one of the possible entrances to the self-enclosed past traumatic event.

For Sartre the gaze is a limit case between Being and Nothingness. The for-itself can only be achieved through the in-itself, but this happens at the cost of splitting the ego into two, that is to say, by revealing and creating a new dimension of the unrevealed within myself. The shock of the gaze is thus the traumatic discovery of my own inner otherness, the fact that I am a "stranger to myself." But Semprun shows that the shock comes not only from the discovery of the objectified "me," but also from the Nothingness that *preceded* it, namely the overwhelming solitude of the for-itself. It is this Nothingness that should now be integrated into Being: Nothingness as a self-enclosed dimension with no outside or objectivity. It is indeed a traumatic dimension, but one that can be perceived and felt as such only with the help of the eyes of the other. The gaze of the other is thus both the birth and death (or beginning and end) of trauma.

YOU HAVE TO CHOOSE: LIVE OR TELL

So, how does one repair the trauma revealed and retroacted by the gaze? Semprun is convinced that only writing could save him, but, as we have seen, he cannot yet write. As long as he hesitates between them—Writing or Life—without choosing, he can engage in neither. Moreover, on 5 August 1945, four months after his release (but also, as Semprun stresses, on the eve of the bombing of Hiroshima), he comes very near death after falling from a train in the Parisian suburbs, in what appears to have been something between an involuntary suicide attempt and a simple instance of fainting. Much later, in 1967, Semprun dedicates his second novel, *L'évanouissement* (The Fainting Fit)[13] to this incident, this traumatic encounter with Nothingness.[14]

13. Semprun, *L'évanouissement* (Paris: Gallimard, 1967).

14. It would be interesting in this context to compare Agamben's early descriptions of fainting as a return to the origin of language in *Infancy and History* with his later analysis of testimony in *Remnants of Auschwitz*. This, however, would go beyond the scope of the present paper. See Giorgio Agamben, *Infancy and History:*

But when, twenty-seven years later, he returns to the incident in *Writing or Life*, he manages to tell it no longer in the third but rather in the first person, and this precisely through an emphasis he puts on the gaze of the other as enabling him to say "I":

> There was no possibility of saying "I" in that instant, which was primordial in a way. I did not exist: he, this "I," this subject who would have been looking, did not yet exist. There was the world, a minute fragment of the world making itself visible: that was all. Only then could I look at it. It was the visibility of the world that allowed me to see. Made me a voyeur, too, of course. "Feeling better?" someone asked. [. . .] I saw a man wearing a white coat, observing me carefully. It's at this precise moment that I began to exist. That I began to realize once more that it was my gaze that contemplated the world around me. (LL 214/EV 224)

Indeed, it is tempting to interpret this description in the light of Merleau-Ponty's theory of the Flesh as interlacing together the seer and the seen in a mutual visibility.[15] However, as in the case of the gaze of the three officers, the description of Nothingness is a *retroactive* image, revealed but also created and fabricated by a concrete gaze. It is only through the gaze of the pharmacist, the man in white coat, that Semprun starts, or rather re-starts to exist. For the second time he is granted his own gaze and his own existence through the gaze of the other, and for the second time he retrieves his subjectivity, marked by a profound absence and a trauma that is discovered at the moment it disappears. The "real" trauma thus occurs through fainting, that is, in a retreat of subjectivity and a shutting of one's eyes.

This traumatic accident causes permanent damage only to Semprun's ear. His vision remains intact, and yet something inside him has broken. This double failure—of Writing *and* Life—finally leads him to understand the Sartrean maxim: "you have to choose: live or

---

The Destruction of Experience, trans. Liz Heron (London and New York: Verso, 1993); *Remnants of Auschwitz: The Witness and the Archive*, trans. Daniel Heller-Roazen (New York: Zone Books, 1999).

15. Merleau-Ponty places the accent more on space than on time: "A Human body is present when, between the see-er and the visible, between touching and touched, between one eye and the other, between hand and hand a kind of crossover occurs" (Maurice Merleau-Ponty, "Eye and Mind," in *The Merleau-Ponty Aesthetics Reader: Philosophy and Painting*, ed. Galen A. Johnson [Evanston, IL: Northwestern University Press, 1993], 115.)

tell."[16] But for Semprun this choice is impossible, since it concerns the very possibility of his own life: "That's where I am: I can live only by assuming that death through writing, but writing literally prohibits me from living" (LL 163/EV 174).

So how to live without writing? How can Semprun forget what the gaze of the other has revealed to him, namely the Nothingness that was his fate during his imprisonment? "I chose life. I chose a long cure of aphasia, of voluntary amnesia, in order to survive" (LL 196/EV 205). Survival is finally realized by oblivion, which is more a form of foreclosure than of repression. Semprun gives up writing, trying to put it behind him, but he knows that he is thereby giving up something essential in himself, the most essential thing perhaps. "I became someone else, so that I might remain myself" (LL 226/EV 236), he declares, but this "myself" leaves foreclosed the dimension of the unrevealed, the traumatic experience of Nothingness that Semprun had struggled so much to regain and retroact, alas without success.

Should we conclude that Sartre was right and that Writing and Life are indeed irreconcilable? Semprun, however, did manage to write the book entitled *Writing or Life*, as well as many others. From the moment he began to write, publishing in 1963 *The Long Voyage*, he no longer put down his pen. So what was the solution he found to the allegedly impossible dilemma? The only explicit explanation he offers is a dream in which it was snowing, his first snowy dream since Buchenwald. From this dream he mysteriously awakes with the confidence that he might now be able to write again. Yet more revealing is what he decides to relate in his first novel, focusing on the days *before* the arrival at the camp, recounting the train journey leading to it. His second novel, as we saw, takes place shortly *after* his liberation, describing his fall from a train in the suburbs of Paris in August 1945. "Before, after or around" is thus no longer a curse but the very, and only, access Semprun has to his past trauma. It is the possibility to claim what seemed to be an unclaimed experience, and to do so by starting before, starting after, starting around an event in order to reach it obliquely rather than directly.

This is all the more true when it comes to the gaze. The gaze is a limit case that closes a situation and opens another. Semprun's experience of the other's gaze occurs twice *between* life and death,

16. Sartre, *Nausea*, trans. Lloyd Alexander (New York: New Directions Books, 2007), 39.

between Being and Nothingness, in a place and time that can be characterized as being simultaneously before, after, and around the observed object, the situation to be told.[17] The gaze thus opens the torn/tearing dimension of the unrevealed, retroacting it for the first time which is already the second. The gaze is indeed traumatic, but only to the extent that it paves the way to the trauma that preceded it: the trauma of Nothingness that can be seen only through a reflection of Being.

GAZE REGAINED

For years Semprun wrote in the third person or using fictitious names in order to protect himself, maintaining the distance between author, narrator, and protagonist, between the reflecting I and the reflected "me." But on 11 April 1987, exactly forty-two years after the liberation of Buchenwald, and, as he stresses, on the same day that his much admired alter-ego, Primo Levi, chose to end his life, Jorge Semprun regained his gaze.

He was writing a completely different book, about a French soldier named Marroux who was looking for a deported friend, when, suddenly, and much to the author's surprise, this Marroux happened upon the young Semprun himself. Here is what is written:

> Marroux felt trapped by the icy devastation in those eyes (*regard*) glittering in a bony, haggard face. He felt as though he was being observed, sized up, by a look from the beyond, from outside of life. As though the flat, neutral beam of this gaze were coming to him from a dead star, from a vanished existence. As though this gaze had traveled to him across the steppes of a desolate mineral landscape, reaching him permeated with a savage coldness. With an irremediable solitude. (LL 228/EV 238)

Where do these words, describing Semprun himself in the eyes of the other, come from? It is in writing them that Semprun suddenly recalls what he had hitherto foreclosed: that in fact he had already encountered this gaze in April 1945, a few days after his return to Paris from

---

17. Ross Chambers speaks in this context of a "relation of math and aftermath, as two events on the Ettersberg that are both the same event and not the same event (Ross Chambers, "Memory, Genre, Truth: Lucie Aubrac, Jorge Semprun, François Maspero and the Devoir de Mémoire," *Contemporary French Civilization*, 30/1 [2006], 1–27). However, Chambers does not connect this thematic of math/aftermath to the status of the gaze as a limit situation, but rather relates it to testimonial writing as *fraternal*.

Buchenwald. He had wanted to return a book of poems by René Char lent to him by one of the three officers who had looked at him the day after liberation. He had gone to the officer's apartment and knocked on the door. The officer's wife had opened it. Alas, it was too late: her husband had been killed on the German front just two days before. The woman had then shown Semprun a letter she had received from her husband, in which he recounts his encounter with a young prisoner, describing it in the following words: "He felt as though he was being observed, sized up, by a look from the beyond, from outside of life. As though the flat, neutral beam of this gaze were coming to him from a dead star, from a vanished existence" (LL 232/EV 242).

So it was not in 1987 that Semprun invented the description of his gaze from 1945. Rather, he regained it from the bottom of his unconscious, managing to appropriate what, by definition, is not appropriable: his own gaze. Shocked by this revelation, by the sudden appearance of his past gaze seen by the other *and* himself, Semprun finally starts to write in the first person. He writes: "They stand amazed before me, and suddenly, in that terror-stricken gaze, I see myself—in their horror" (LL 230/EV 240).

Semprun thus comes full circle. Or is this story too incredible to be true? Is it fiction or reality that he tells us? Has Semprun really regained his unrevealed dimension, his lost "I"? The answer to this question would not have much meaning. For yes, he has regained his gaze, the unrevealed, his lost "I," yet only through deferred retroaction, that is, as an I-me, an I and a me that do not entirely belong to me and that are nonetheless me. The gaze of the other is, and must be, a limit case, and any attempt to extract it from this status would be but to miss its sense, that is to say, miss its being an always already missed encounter with oneself.

TSIVIA FRANK-WYGODA

Death Chants: Paradigms and Translations in Semprún's Writing

One of the most striking features of Jorge Semprún's writing is its iterative character. It is, as Quílez-Esteve and Munté-Ramos put it, "obsessive, repetitive and recurring"[1] writing in which basic themes are transformed into leitmotifs, undergoing slight variations from one book to another:

> Obsessive themes [. . .] are used again and again in each and every book; though distributed in a different fashion, they punctuate in the same way the litany of memory: the snowy landscape on the Ettersberg, which the future gusts will irreparably make reappear, the strange smell of burnt flesh, the butt of a Machorka, the latrines of the "Little Camp" or the Arbeitsstatistik offices, Zarah Leander's voice over the camp's loudspeakers on Sundays, or the cap of Nikolai, the young Russian.[2]

Repetition in Semprún's writing does not merely affect discrete thematic units symbolizing the reality of the concentration camps, such as those cited by Jean-Paul Pilorget or Françoise Nicoladzé,[3] but extends to recurring characters and to entire scenes repeating again and again. For example, the first encounter with American soldiers at the liberation of Buchenwald, the registration at the camp as a Student/

1. Laia Quílez Esteve and Rosa-Àuria Munté Ramos, "Autobiography and Fiction in Semprún's Texts," *CLCWeb: Comparative Literature and Culture* 11/1 (2009): http://dx.doi.org/10.7771/1481–4374.1416.

2. Jean-Paul Pilorget, "Écriture et mémoire dans les récits concentrationnaires de Jorge Semprun," in *Les récits de survivance, modalités génériques et structures d'adaptation au réel*, ed. Christiane Klègue (Québec: Presses de l'Université Laval, 2007), 140. My translation.

3. Françoise Nicoladzé, *La deuxième vie de Jorge Semprun. Une écriture tressée aux spirales de l'histoire* (Paris: éditions Climats, 1998), 80 (recurring motifs from the camps); 143–44 (auditive memory); 200–203 (colors in Semprún's writing).

YFS 129, *Writing and Life, Literature and History: On Jorge Semprun,* ed. Razinsky, © 2016 by Yale University.

Stukkateur,[4] the shooting of the German soldier and many other narrative units. The leitmotif poetics and iterative character of Semprún's writing create a thread that links the various Semprúnian narrators and merges texts, whose generic status is very heterogeneous, into a coherent—or at least cohesive—corpus.

However, it is clear that corpus homogeneity itself is not a purpose, but rather the by-product of a deeper force shaping Semprún's writing. In fact, this iterative writing has been variously addressed by scholars: some saw Semprún's repetitions as a consequence of the never-ending testimonial duty of survivors, or as a quest for accuracy of memory. Bruno Gelas interprets Semprún's poetics of "proliferation and return" as a writing haunted by ghostly revenants (literally, "those who come back"), analyzing the obsessive iterativity of Semprún's narrative technique as the literary form of this ghostly life: "When death is not an event anymore, life ceases to be a story."[5] As Ursula Tidd puts it in similar fashion, "the tricks played by Semprún with narrative time serve to elude the end of the story and history, for there is in effect no end, no death, but only dying and repetition."[6] Finally, scholars account for this "écriture du ressassement" (writing of endless repetition) – that is, a writing that is "a form of return but with a shifting, a tiny variation, [. . .] an obsessive repetition which belongs to melancholy"[7]—by terming it the literary form of traumatic memory. As Brett Kaplan writes:

> Semprún's structure of memory thus recalls the model of traumatic memory wherein, as Cathy Caruth claims, "trauma is not locatable in the simple violent or original event in an individual's past, but rather in the way its very unassimilated nature—the way it was precisely *not known* in the first instance—returns to haunt the survivor later on."[8]

4. Susan R. Suleiman, "Revision: Historical Trauma and Literary Testimony. The Buchenwald Memoirs of Jorge Semprun," in *Crises of Memory and the Second World War* (Cambridge, Massachusetts: Harvard University Press, 2006), 132–58.

5. Bruno Gelas, "Jorge Semprun : Réécrire sans fin," in *Ecrire après Auschwitz : mémoires croisées France-Allemagne*, ed. Karsten Garscha (Lyon: Presses Universitaires de Lyon, 2006), 103–104. My translation.

6. Ursula Tidd, "The Infinity of Testimony and Dying in Jorge Semprún's Holocaust Autothanatographies," *Forum of Modern Language Studies* 41 (2005): 413.

7. Éric Benoit, Michel Braud, Jean-Pierre Moussaron, Isabelle Poulin and Dominique Rabaté, *Écritures du ressassement (Modernités 15)* (Bordeaux: Presses Universitaires de Bordeaux, 2001), 6 (my translation).

8. Brett A. Kaplan, *Unwanted Beauty: Aesthetic Pleasure in Holocaust Representation* (Urbana and Chicago: University of Illinois Press, 2007), 75.

Ferrán argues, in her analysis of narrative breakdowns and shake-ups in *The Long Voyage*,[9] that traumatic memory, which "keeps re-appearing in an indirect form through an uncanny repetition of events in the individual's life that recreates the traumatic experience," generates a particular status of speech, one that does not "[refer *back* to something that occurred before but [relives] the experience in the present."[10] In other words, survivors' literature and specifically Semprún's writing create a performative discourse that allows one to re-live the traumatic event, while also trying to "gain some mastery over a situation which, by its very nature, robbed one of any sense of control over one's life."[11] Similarly, Susan Suleiman's analysis of different versions of one unique event (the registration at the camp) shows that "continuous revision is the literary performance of the working through of trauma."[12]

In the present study, I shall try to challenge the traditional, syntagmatic approach to Semprún's iterative writing. Beginning with the recurring appearances of a childhood song, "La Paloma," I will show that it triggers a series of iterations: repetitions of an almost identical event. Then I will argue that the structural comparison of these scenes reveals deep invariable elements. These invariants are the key that unlocks a new, synoptic reading of many more narra-tive units that, in spite of their differences, appear to belong to the same paradigm. This poetics of paradigms and translations calls for new approaches, unexploited by the understanding of repetitive writ-ing as literary expression of trauma, and reaching beyond the parallel reading of recurring stories in search of flaws of memory or proofs of fictionalization.

"LA PALOMA": LEITMOTIF AND
RECURRENT SCENE

In many of Semprún's books, an old song named "La Paloma" appears, either played or sung, sometimes by the narrator and sometimes by

---

9. Jorge Semprun, *The Long Voyage*, trans. Richard Seaver (New York: Grove Press, 1964).

10. Ofelia Ferrán, "'Cuanto mas escribo, mas me queda por decir': Memory, Trauma and Writing in the Work of Jorge Semprún," *MLN* 116/2 (March 2001): 266–94; 270.

11. Ibid., 273.

12. Suleiman, *Crises of Memory*, 158.

others, in Spanish, German, or French.[13] Acknowledging the iteration of "La Paloma" in Semprún's writing, Nicoladzé writes, "[Its] music links characters belonging to different books, thus revealing the melancholy in the narrator's past, the angst of death which was weighing upon his future, by means of a hallucinatory reminiscence."[14] A close reading of the seemingly monolithic leitmotif shows that there are, in fact, two different "La Paloma" songs: the first, sung by the German soldier in *L'évanouissement* and later in *Literature or Life* ("*Kommt eine weisse Taube zu Dir geflogen*": "Here comes a white dove flying to you"), is the translation of the Habanera song called "La Paloma," a nineteenth-century internationally popular song by Sebastian Iradier.[15] The other one, appearing in *La montagne blanche*,[16] is an old poem by eighteenth-century Spanish poet Juan Iglesias de La Casa "*Una paloma blanca come la nieve*," ("A dove, white as snow"). This internal splitting of the leitmotif itself will prove to be meaningful.

The original, loosely autobiographical "La Paloma" scene depicts two young members of the Resistance about to kill a German soldier, "the absolute embodiment of the German ideal."[17] In *L'évanouissement*, Semprún describes the soldier turning toward the hidden Resistance fighters whom he cannot see, and beginning to sing:

> The soldier started singing, and he [Manuel] identified the tune and only after identifying the tune of this song did he understand its lyrics. It was funny to hear "La Paloma" sung in German. [. . .] Back in The Hague [. . .] there was a record. [. . .] thus he was in Chatillon's region with Hans, watching a German soldier, and the memory of The Hague had come back to him.[18]

In this scene the "enemy," unexpectedly incarnate, is too full of life to be assimilated into an Idea. This "boy, singing 'La Paloma,' bareheaded, who is barely older than us" is also threateningly similar to

13. Inter alia, in *L'évanouissement*, *Le grand voyage*, *La montagne blanche*, *L'écriture ou la vie*, *Adieu vive clarté*.

14. Nicoladzé, *Deuxième vie*, 69–72; 72.

15. Semprun, *L'évanouissement* (Paris: Gallimard, 1967); *Literature or Life*, trans. Linda Coverdale (New York: Penguin, 1997).

16. Semprún, *La montagne blanche* (Paris: Gallimard, 1986).

17. Semprún, *Literature or Life*, 32.

18. Semprún, *L'évanouissement*, 163; 166.

the narrator and his fictional Jewish friend. It is only when the soldier turns away, becoming a *"shadow* with a cask, the *ghost* of a soldier, a future *corpse,"*[19] that he fuses with death, making it possible for the Resistance fighters to kill him.

This scene undergoes two crucial variations in *Literature or Life.* First, the Proustian telescoping of memories does not lead the narrator back to The Hague, where his father worked as a diplomat, but rather to the lost paradise of his Spanish childhood:

> Perhaps he didn't even know that it was "La Paloma." Even if he'd known that, perhaps the song wouldn't have brought back any memories for him. Childhood, the maids singing in the pantry, music from the bandstands in shady village squares . . . "La Paloma"! How could I not have started when I heard that song? The German went on singing, in a lovely blond voice. My hand began to shake. It had become impossible for me to shoot at that young soldier singing "La Paloma." [. . .] "La Paloma" is happening to me, that's all: my Spanish childhood, right in the face.[20]

Interestingly, the replacement of the memories triggered by the song is accompanied by a grammatical shift: the distanced third-person narrative of *L'évanouissement,* alternating with a solidary—even comforting—first person plural, becomes in *Literature or Life* a distressing first-person singular emphasizing the threat that lies in the memories awakened.

In the (pseudo-) fictional novel *La montagne blanche,* "La Paloma" awakens two kinds of memories: for Larrea and Franca Castellani, the song heard in a hotel in Merano functions as a secret code for their love, thus triggering memories of their romance. But the song also reminds Larrea of "another music, also diffused by loudspeakers, in a totally different place"[21]: "La Paloma" brings back the memory of Zarah Leander's voice over Buchenwald's loudspeakers. Although Larrea tries to hold himself together, despite the threat of internal scission the song casts upon him, he acknowledges that his lost unity lies in that noxious past he has forced himself to forget. Eventually,

19. Ibid., 167 (Italics are mine). My translation. This description echoes Pierre Halbwachs' depiction as "a body of shadow, of possible smoke, in the long Russian greatcoat floating around his ghost."

20. Semprún, *Literature or Life,* 33–34.

21. Semprún, *La montagne blanche,* 79.

the memories awoken in Merano by "La Paloma" compel Larrea to share *"his death"* with Franca.[22]

Contrary to the two great icons and metonymic symbols of the camp—snow and smoke—that haunt the memory of Semprún's survivor characters and inevitably superpose the vision of Buchenwald on every snowy landscape or power plant's smoke,[23] the twofold song, Semprún's equivalent to Vinteuil's sonata, brings back forgotten memories of the narrator's or the character's lost paradise, and also repressed images of the dark shades of Buchenwald. At first glance, "La Paloma" conflates two symbols—symbols of childhood present elsewhere in Semprún's writing (azaleas, for example) and symbols of Buchenwald (snow and smoke). It functions therefore as a double-layered memory-trigger, resuscitating either the childhood self or the Buchenwald prisoner self (or both). The process of remembrance is so violent that it threatens the subject exposed to this assault of either traumatic or delightful memories with internal splitting and eventually with death—metaphorically or literally.

The "La Paloma" leitmotif and scenes thus explicitly deal with the theme of deadly memories. There is, however, a pseudo-associative thread that weaves a web of parallel stories in *Literature of Life*: the "resurrection" of the "Christ of the Kaddish"; the death of Maurice Halbwachs and Diego Morales; the lullaby sung to the little Cecilia, and eventually the story of the survivor from the *Sonderkommando*. At first loosely connected to "La Paloma," they soon appear to be *structurally* similar to the original scene. Indeed, the telescoping of different times and episodes in *Literature or Life* is less the literary form of a compulsive memory writing driven by the uncontrollable need to say everything, than a series of translations of a hidden paradigm, transforming, as I hope to show, the thread of scenes into a variation on one deep-structure narrative.

"LA PALOMA" IN *LITERATURE OR LIFE*: FROM RECURRENT SCENE TO PARADIGM

In *Literature or Life*, the scene of the German soldier singing "La Paloma" is a *mise en abyme* within another story, the story of the Jew found alive among the corpses in the Little Camp. A few days

22. Ibid., 80.
23. Semprún, *La montagne blanche*, 35–36.

after the liberation of Buchenwald, the narrator and his Jewish friend Albert are patrolling near the blocks of the Little Camp when they hear a death chant:

> It was death that was humming, no doubt, somewhere amid the heaps of corpses. The life of death, in other words, making itself heard. The agony of death, its shining and mournfully loquacious presence. [. . .] Two minutes later, we have extracted from a heap of corpses the dying man through whose mouth death is singing to us. Reciting its prayer to us, actually. [. . .] I have never seen a human face that more closely resembled that of the crucified Christ.[24]

The connection between this story and the German soldier's does not take place solely in the author's mind and memory; rather, it is presented as an "intradiegetic" (in Gérard Genette's terms), an involuntary memory of the narrator himself:

> What is it you think I should do for him? We could have a little chat? How about if I sing him a song? "La Paloma," maybe? [. . .] I turn back toward the man. Eyes closed, he lies there, still singing faintly. [. . .] I had mentioned "La Paloma" just like that, out of nowhere. The beginning of the song pops into my mind . . . and strange as it may seem, the words are in German. [. . .] Now I know what story I could remember.[25]

The trigger of the associative memory is the song: the death chant sung by the dying Jew calls for a "replica" that, by a lapsus, triggers the memory of the German soldier's "La Paloma." In fact, the sudden conflation of two apparently different scenes is the real motivation for this associative pseudo-digression. In other words, whether the narrator-in-Buchenwald involuntarily remembers "La Paloma" or not, matters less than the superposition of two scenes, which in a reading focusing solely on their surface or on their narratological structure would have seemed antithetical (killing a German soldier vs. saving a dying Jew), into a single paradigm.

Indeed, the structural reading of both stories reveals many invariants: both "others" (the German soldier and the Christ of the Kaddish) are, in Semprún's account, hybrid beings; one is a young man full of life but nevertheless caught by the shadows of death, "a future

24. Semprún, *Literature or Life*, 29–31.
25. Ibid., 31. The original text (*L'écriture ou la vie* [Paris: Gallimard, 1994], 41) has "gisant," i.e., "recumbent statue," where the translation has "the man [lies] there."

corpse"; the other one, a dying man chanting the prayer of the dead to himself, is a living "recumbent statue" "extracted from a heap of corpses." Both are altogether a metonymy for others and the impossibility of a perfect metonymic embodiment: indeed, as the narrator puts it, the German soldier is too incarnate to serve as an "Ideal" enemy. As for the Jew, although he was physically with the corpses (he almost *is* one), he is the survivor, the one who is still alive and keeps singing, for himself or for the dead. In both scenes, the narrator is threatened by the assault of forgotten memories of himself-as-other (himself in long ago times), but also by the threatening likeness between himself and the hybrid beings, symbolized by the look in the eye.

In the paradigmatic reading of the scenes, the song plays a double role, both functional and symbolic: on the one hand, it is an anchor to life—that is why the soldier cannot be killed as long as, facing the two Resistance fighters, he keeps singing; that is why the narrator sings a song to the dying Jew in order to keep him alive. But on the other hand, the song marks the very possibility of a substitution, the metaphorical substitution of the dying being and his living alter ego. While the narrator negotiates between life and death, he is inescapably confronted with the "life of the death": a Medusa glance that threatens him with being "swallowed by the ancient death." [26]

This deep-structure unit—where a character faces someone caught between life and death, while a song or a poem symbolizes the danger in witnessing the death of the other—recurs throughout the rest of *Literature of Life* and beyond it. In two other scenes, the narrator accompanies Halbwachs and a year later Diego Morales through their last moments with Baudelaire's and Cesar Vallejo's poems serving as a modern Kaddish.[27] Although Halbwachs and Morales are depicted as closer to death and thus less hybrid than both the German soldier and the dying Jew ("He had gone even farther into death than that unknown Jew over whom I am now bending,"[28] says the narrator of Halbwachs), witnessing their agony—chanting a prayer for the dead for them—forces the narrator to confront his own hybridity once more, as someone who, by living the death of someone else, has

26. This is how Semprún refers to death in concentration camps. See *La montagne blanche*, 37; *La deuxième mort de Ramón Mercader* (Paris: Gallimard, 1969), 64, 196; *Literature or Life*, 276.
27. Semprún, *Literature or Life*, 41–43.
28. Ibid., 41.

in some way outlived his own death too. The narration of Morales' death blurs once again—through Vallejo's verse—the frontiers between living and dead: "*Pero el cadáver ¡ay! siguió muriendo*," ("But the corpse, alas, kept dying") writes Semprún. There are two cadavers here, that of Morales—the dying man, who cannot be saved even by the force of fraternity and love, in contrast to the optimistic resurrection concluding Vallejo's poem—but also that of the narrator, whose tale is the tale of a corpse "who keeps dying."

The transformations that the paradigmatic structure undergoes in each one of these stories do not neutralize the deep, inner, almost iconographic similarity of these scenes. The discovery of an unchanging paradigm in turn allows the reading and interpreting of more scenes as variants of this paradigm. For example, *Literature or Life* includes a scene in which the narrator holds the little Cecilia as she falls asleep in his arms, and recites the same last verses of Baudelaire's poem.[29] Explicitly mirroring Halbwachs' death, this scene features the death chant, the ghostly singer, the look in the eye. However, in this translation of the paradigm, Cecilia's full of life figure is stable enough to cast off the spell of the deadly incantation: in Semprún's narrative, oscillating between "writing or life" and "writing or death," the presence of this redemptory moment is very meaningful.

However, long before this moment of serenity and reparation, at the end of the "Kaddish" chapter, Semprún writes about the terrible tale of the *Sonderkommando* survivor in Buchenwald. I claim that despite the many differences between this scene and the other ones (the German soldier, the Christ of Kaddish, Halbwachs and Cecilia's scenes), the story from Auschwitz is but one more translation of the paradigm:

> I no longer remember the name of that Polish Jew. [. . .] I do remember his eyes. They were an icy blue [. . .]. He sat on a chair, absolutely straight, absolutely rigid, his hands on his knees, motionless. [. . .] I do remember his voice. He spoke in German, fluently, in a rasping, meticulous, insistent voice. [. . .] He spoke for a long while; we listened to him in silence, frozen in the pallid anguish of his story. [. . .] We had sunk body and soul into the night of that story, suffocating, without any sense of time. [. . .] The survivor of the *Sonderkommando* at Auschwitz, this Polish Jew who had no name because he could have been any Polish Jew, even any Jew from anywhere at all, really—the

29. Semprún, *Literature or Life*, 276–77.

survivor of Auschwitz remained motionless, his hands spread out flat on his knees: a pillar of salt and despairing memory. We remained motionless, too. [30]

This scene features, once again, someone speaking/chanting (the description of the survivor's voice as the last remnant of life in his body, as well as Semprún's remarks about its sound and intonation, are essential) from beyond death: someone whose statue-like immobility symbolizes his being halfway between the survivor and the dead. Once again, those who are listening to the deadly story are threatened with capture by the deadly memory: the petrification of the audience parallels the immobility of the survivor compared to a "pillar of salt." The Medusa-curse of whoever has stared death in the eye threatens not only the teller but also the listeners. Moreover, Semprún physically underscores the danger the tale brings to its audience by locating the story in the contagious diseases' room, "a lazaretto within a lazar house."[31] By doing so, he also clearly alludes to the character of Saint Lazarus, the dead man who rose from the grave: the *Sonderkommando* survivor, like the narrator and his companions, the Christ of the Kaddish, and pseudo-fictional alter egos (Gérard, Juan Larrea) are modern Lazaruses, ghostly survivors rising from the threshold of the gas chambers, from heaps of corpses or from any camp, to tell their terrible story. Finally, the speaker has no name: at first presented as a fault of memory ("I cannot recall if Jürgen Kaminski mentioned his name to us"[32]), the teller's anonymity becomes a metaphor for his transformation into a symbol. Like the German soldier, with whom he shares the blue eyes and the language, and the Christ of Kaddish, he is swallowed up by the only identity—one both metonymic and symbolic—that remains to him: "the Auschwitz survivor."

TRANSLATIONS IN *LE MORT QU'IL FAUT* AND *LA MONTAGNE BLANCHE*

This paradigmatic structure, projecting itself throughout *Literature or Life*, becomes the core of *Le mort qu'il faut*, a story that is all about enacting the dangerous possibility of the substitution of two alter egos: at first it seems the substitution is nothing more than living

30. Ibid., 49–51.
31. Ibid., 47.
32. Ibid., 49.

"a new life under a fake name," in Semprún's words. "A name that is not your name, right. The life, however, will be yours. A true life despite the fake name!" says the German Communist Kaminski to the narrator.[33] In fact, *Le mort qu'il faut* transforms an event particularly common both in Semprún's life and in his writings—assuming a pseudonym[34]—into a mythical parable that deals with the essential experience of Semprún's survivor: can one survive the death of his alter ego(s) back there?

The hovering substitution between the narrator and his French companion, François L., is hinted at from the beginning: they are the same age, they arrived in the same convoy, their numbers are almost identical, both are students and love the same poems. But the text does more than underline the narrator and François L.'s likeness: through structural elements borrowed from the other scenes belonging to the same paradigm, Semprún minimizes the factual, referential dimension of a story that could easily feature in an adventure fiction book, and gives it an allegorical turn. The first motif taken from the scenes originally appearing in *L'évanouissement* and in *Literature or Life* is the motif of looking the dying alter ego in the eye. The narrator recalls that, instead of lying head to tail as prisoners would do in the camps, he decided, on that fatal night at the end of which destinies would be exchanged, to lie face to face with François L. Looking his alter ego in the eye not only allows for a fuller awareness of the process of his agony, that is, an accented, conscious witnessing of his death, but, as in the German soldier and the Christ of the Kaddish scenes, the direct look creates a fusion between the two selves—the one about to die and the one about to survive. In his agony and death, François L. becomes another kind of alter ego. He is no longer the living Doppelgänger, but "myself as another" whose life, dreams, loves, and stories the narrator will appropriate (loving Jacqueline B. as François's love, for example), and also, inevitably, "myself as dead." In the economy of Semprún's story, the narrator's falling asleep after his alter ego's death represents an immediate, actual threat since he

33. Semprún, *Le mort qu'il faut*, in *Le fer rouge de la mémoire* (Paris: Gallimard, 2012), 984. My translation.

34. Semprún, *Literature or Life*, 292; Semprún and Lila Azam Zanganeh, "The Art of Fiction no. 192," in *The Paris Review* 180 (Spring 2007). Of course, Semprún's literary use of pseudonyms and heteronyms is never insignificant: "Semprún's excess of identities remains by contrast the indelible mark of his final condition: the stateless 'walking cadaver'" (Quílez Esteve and Munté Ramos, "Autobiography and Fiction.")

could have been mistaken for a corpse and taken to the crematorium, therefore becoming the needed "dead man"; but it is also a metaphor for this surrogate—or maybe shared—death.

That is what the death song motif (i.e., song about death, sung by death, song to the dead) is about. François L.'s enigmatic last words, barely heard by the narrator—structurally the exact equivalent to the Jew's Kaddish, but also to the German soldier's "La Paloma" and, as I have claimed, to the *Sonderkommando* survivor's tale—are the funeral chant by which the hybrid being accompanies his own death. But in Semprún's narrative, they also cast doubt on the survivor's own survival.[35] The alter ego's message from the threshold of death, unsolved for years, is deciphered by accident when Semprún, working on a translation and adaptation of Seneca's play *The Trojan Women*, comes across the Latin verse: "*Post mortem nihil est ipsaque mors nihil*," "There is nothing after death, death itself is nothing." While for the dying self these words negating death contain a message of serenity, for the surviving alter ego—that hybrid self, who has taken the dead man's name, has absorbed his life and has to testify as to his death—they are an expression of his ghostly existence.

Earlier, I addressed the presence and function of "La Paloma" in *La montagne blanche* as a threatening memory trigger. I shall now demonstrate that *La montagne blanche* is essentially a variant of the broader, deeper "death chant" paradigm.

Translations, substitutions, and replacements constitute the narrative dynamics of Semprún's (pseudo-)fictional novel. First, they are the external dynamics of a performative writing that displaces the threat of suicide from the writer to a surrogate character (Juan Larrea), as Semprún writes in *Literature or Life*;[36] second, they constitute an internal dynamics where characters act as substitutes, duplicates, and surrogates of one another. Although *La montagne blanche* is, on the surface, a story of intricate love affairs where characters' substitutions seem mainly motivated by sexual games, the omnipresent Ettersberg and its dark smoke, and eventually Juan Larrea's suicide, prove that this novel is not as much a libertine fable as it is a tale about the deadly memories and deadly stories of a character who has outlived his own death.

<hr/>

35. Suleiman interprets these words as a comforting message for the aged survivor as well. Suleiman, *Crises of Memory*, 158.
36. Semprún, *Literature or Life*, 292.

The key to this seemingly unending game of substitutions lies in two characters, Laurence and Nadine, and their relationship to Larrea and his deadly memories. Laurence, the woman who gave the narrator Faulkner's *Sartoris* during the war, is the one who brings him back to life after his return from Buchenwald by absorbing his story and his deadly memory.[37] At first, writes Semprún, the ghostly teller and his lover-listener become "recumbent statues,"[38] prefiguring the *Sonderkommando* survivor and his audience, as well as the Christ of the Kaddish: the deadly story petrifies them and transforms them into hybrid beings caught between life and death. Later, Laurence, victim of a car accident, literally becomes a statue: forced to stay home, she totally disappears from the world, and her voice, like the Auschwitz survivor's and the dying Jew's, remains the only sign that she is still alive.[39] Nevertheless, Larrea constantly acknowledges Laurence's existence and the necessity of preserving her, as if he can live only by virtue of the substitution that occurred between them.

Nadine Feierabend, a young Jewish woman "from after the massacres," symbolizes the Jewish victims. Because she bears the potential of the ancient death on her body, she functions in the narrative as a trigger of deadly memories, like snow, smoke, and "La Paloma":

> But he couldn't see Nadine, he would see nothing but death. He would see nothing but this dreadful, derisory image: naked women, shorn, shaven, running in the mud toward a squat building, at the end, under the laughing gaze of a few S.S. guards. [40]

But she is also a reminder of Larrea's "deadly" survival: unlike those —Nadine's relatives—who had "gone up in smoke," he is the one who has gone through death and remains with a "memory full of ashes."[41] Symbolically, she also shares the German soldier's and the *Sonderkommando* survivor's blue eyes[42]: her gaze, like so many others in Semprún's writing, sends the narrator "back to death."

---

37. About the character of Laurence/Odile, see Nicoladzé, *Deuxième vie*, 129–31.
38. Semprún, *La montagne blanche*, 102; 100–103.
39. Ibid., 257–58
40. Ibid., 169. See also 97: "One could also notice that he was touching the golden, soft skin precisely where the bluish tattoo of Auschwitz could have been." My translation.
41. Ibid., 37.
42. The color blue is one of the most powerful leitmotifs in *La montagne blanche*, and inherently connected to the theme of death and substitution: blue paint, blue

While Laurence succeeded in literally resuscitating Larrea by absorbing his deadliness and his story, Nadine's metonymical embodiment of the "ancient death," similar to Cecilia's ("in whose heart flows Czernowitz blood," writes Semprún) involuntarily pushes him back into his hybridity, therefore forcing him to "repair his forgetfulness." Eventually, Semprún's fictional alter ego unleashes the deadly memories: in a monotone, even voice paralleling the *Sonderkommando* survivor's tone, he shares the "memory of his death"; a few hours later, at dawn, he drowns himself in the dark waters of a river. In *La montagne blanche*, translation allows Semprún to concretize, within the limits of writing, the threat of substitution.

Death chants: these are songs, poems, and tales, sung by ghostly beings, at the threshold of death, but still clinging to life. Chants that are heard by Death, too: listeners who are experiencing or have experienced death. The encounter between the ghostly singer and the petrified listener, or even the memory of it, offers a danger of substitution. Witnessing the death of one's alter ego, living with deadly memories and testifying for the "ancient death"—that is, speaking for the dead—are essentially about blurring the limits between oneself and the other, life and death. The figure of the dying-resurrecting Jew, this Christ-like, Lazarus-like figure singing Kaddish for himself but also speaking for the dead, becomes the symbol of Semprún's writing. Literature or Life, Literature or Death: Semprún's writing is the tale of a man "[who is] not a survivor," "[who] will never speak as someone who has survived the death of his comrades."[43]

Semprún's paradigmatic writing moves beyond mere iteration of leitmotifs, characters, and scenes, beyond compulsive memory or working through trauma. It superposes different events into a similar structure, through the use of identical symbolic units: the ghostly alter ego, the song, the look in the eye, the petrification. The core of the paradigmatic writing is not the specific occurrence, but rather the invariants in the design and their translations, which hints at an essential experience under the variety of its actual forms. The concept of "paradigm" thus enables the understanding that Semprún's iterative writing is not entirely uncontrollable memories—or rather, that uncontrollable memories and trauma-writing are both inalienably

---

nude, blue sky, "April blue," "blue lizard of the Faraglioni," and eventually the blue waters of the river where Juan Larrea drowns himself.

43. Semprun, *Quel beau dimanche!* (Paris: Gallimard, 1980), 281.

connected to the presence of a deep structure, a paradigm, constantly shaping the events processed through memory and narration.

This study of Semprún's writing does not resolve the aporia of truth and fiction; the literary and fictional reconstruction lying at the core of any attempt to "tell" undermines the reliability of testimonial writing. Nevertheless, the analysis of paradigms in Semprún's writing offers us an alternative way of reading testimonial literature that does not simply focus on the presence of inaccuracies, false information, fictional construction, and conflicting versions of a nuclear story, all of which are often pointed out by the author himself. Reading with a focus on deep structures takes us beyond the explicit iterations (identical characters, books, places, scenes, etc.) to reveal otherwise hidden connections between lines, chapters, or books. It reaches beyond the unsolvable question of factual and fictitious, to the deepest connection between memory and textuality: as interest grows in double, overlapping, or repetitive testimonies, paradigmatic reading can be a vital analytic tool for addressing not only the various rewritings or retellings of identical episodes, but the very shape of the traumatic tale.

RICHARD J. GOLSAN

Spanish Memories and Francoist Nightmares: *Le bourreau*, Torture, and the Meaning of Resistance in Jorge Semprún and Michel del Castillo

In his book *Franco's Crypt: Spanish Culture and Memory since 1936*, Jeremy Treglown observes that fictional "memories" of the Spanish Civil War outside of Spain have until fairly recently been shaped primarily by Spanish writers living in exile rather than by those writers who stayed behind at the war's conclusion.[1] This is due in large part, Treglown writes, to (often-justified) suspicions of Francoist sympathies on the part of writers who remained in Spain, although some of these writers have received international recognition despite their conservative or reactionary views. Most notably, the conservative writer Camilo José Cela was awarded the Nobel Prize for Literature in 1989.

In France, arguably the two most prominent Spanish exile writers who have shaped French memories of *la guerre d'Espagne* over several decades are Jorge Semprún and Michel del Castillo. Born a decade apart—Semprún in 1923 and del Castillo in 1933—the two men nevertheless share crucial and transformative life experiences as well as historical interests. Both were born to Spanish Republican parents: del Castillo's mother was a Republican activist, while Semprún's father, José Maria Semprún Gurrea, was civil governor of Toledo under the Republic and briefly served as the Republic's ambassador to Rome. Both went into exile during the Civil War, either at its outset in Semprún's case or, in del Castillo's, in the chaotic final

---

1. Jeremy Treglown, *Franco's Crypt: Spanish Culture and Memory since 1936* (New York: Farrar, Strauss, and Giroux, 2013), 8.

YFS 129, *Writing and Life, Literature and History: On Jorge Semprun*, ed. Razinsky, © 2016 by Yale University.

months of spring 1939. Both ended up in France, where Semprún became a student at the Lycée Henry IV and later at the Sorbonne. Del Castillo, by contrast, arrived in Marseille as a six-year-old in the care of his mother. Lacking resources, del Castillo mother and son lived in a series of cheap hotel rooms, primarily in the *midi*, until both were arrested by the Vichy regime in winter 1940 and sent to the internment camp at Rieucros. These experiences, along with del Castillo's frequent abandonment by his mother, are the subjects of much of his fiction, especially his first novel *Tanguy*, published in 1957.[2]

Both writers also experienced and wrote about the horrors of the German concentration camps, although if the evidence of their "autobiographical fictions" is telling, Semprún's experience in Buchenwald marked him much more profoundly than del Castillo's time spent in Nazi Germany between 1942 and 1945. In fact, del Castillo refers to his German experience only occasionally, in *Tanguy* especially but also in the 1987 novel *Le démon de l'oubli*.[3] As the majority of his fictional works confirm, most of the writer's youthful memories focus on the traumatic conclusion of the Spanish conflict and the terrible hardships of the early years of Franco's dictatorship.

Finally both Semprún and del Castillo launched their literary careers in France and have written most of their important works in French. Moreover, despite periodic returns to Spain—Semprún as a leader and agent of the Spanish Communist Party until his expulsion from the party in 1964, and later as Minister of Culture under Felipe González, and del Castillo in his youth as an internee in a Catholic school, then as an impoverished worker, and later as a traveler—both have resided principally in France. Semprún died in Paris in June 2011. Del Castillo divides his time between Paris and the *midi*.

These similarities aside, there is also much that separates Semprún and del Castillo. In biographical terms, Semprún led a politically active and committed life, first in the French Resistance, then in the Spanish Communist Party, and then as a minister in the post-Francoist Spanish Republic. By contrast, del Castillo has remained generally aloof from formal political *engagements* of this magnitude.

As writers, both men show a marked predilection for *autofictions* in their work, but their novelistic visions and narrative techniques are very different. Del Castillo's vision is profoundly pessimistic and

2. Michel del Castillo, *Tanguy* (Paris: Julliard, 1957).
3. Del Castillo, *Le démon de l'oubli* (Paris: Seuil ,1987).

even tragic, and his narrative technique straightforward and traditional. By contrast, Semprún's novelistic vision is generally less fatalistic. His narratives are also more baroque in their complexity, occasionally confusing in their leaps and jumps from character to character, from place to place, from past to present (and present to past), and disconcerting in their sudden shifts in narrative voice. As Régis Debray has written recently, Semprun's texts can give the impression of "turning in circles in the fog."[4]

Del Castillo's and Semprún's respective attitudes toward history and memory, and toward the historical and even metaphysical meaning of the Spanish Civil War, Francoism, and totalitarianism, also diverge, often sharply. These differences in perspective evident in many of their works to which Treglown alludes suggest in the first instance that despite the broad political distinctions between Spanish exile writers and those who remained in Spain, exile writers were (and are) hardly uniform in their outlook on the conflict and on Francoism. They also raise the possibility, in del Castillo's case, that the writer's views can and do change over time. Specifically, del Castillo's fascination with and apparent sympathy for the figure of the *bourreau*, the perpetrator, most evident is his recent work, has resulted in a troubling revision of the Civil War and of Francoism itself. By contrast, Semprun's many years of political *engagement* and especially the brutal realities of that experience have provided a kind of moral, ethical, and political compass that keeps his views on Spain and especially Francoism constant.

Which works, then, are most representative of the writers' views, their divergent perspectives, and in del Castillo's case, his apparent recent reassessment of Francoism? In del Castillo's case, three works are most apposite. These are the 1981 novel *La nuit du décret*, winner of the *Prix Renaudot* and perhaps del Catillo's most highly regarded novel; the 2003 play *Le jour du destin*, in which del Castillo recreates and recasts crucial episodes as well as characters from the 1981 novel; and the 2008 *récit*, *Le temps de Franco*, a revisionist portrait of El Caudillo and his regime.[5] These works bridge the gap between fact

---

4. Régis Debray, "Semprun en spirale," Introduction to *Exercices de survie* by Jorge Semprun (Paris : Gallimard, 2012), 12. Translations, here and throughout, are mine unless noted otherwise.

5. Del Castillo, *La nuit du décret* (Paris: Seuil, 1981). *La nuit du décret* was also the runner-up for the *Prix Goncourt*; del Castillo, *Le jour du destin* (Paris: Collection des quatre-vents, 2003); del Castillo, *Le temps de Franco* (Paris: Fayard, 2008).

and fiction. More importantly, they focus most centrally on the person of the *bourreau* and his most recent avatars in del Castillo's work.

In Semprún's case, three works are also most appropriate for our purposes here. First, the 2004 novel *Vingt ans et un jour*, written in Spanish and published in French translation, stands out as perhaps Semprún's most sustained and *direct* fictional engagement with the Spanish Civil War and its Francoist aftermath.[6] Two posthumous works, the incomplete *récit Exercices de survie* published in 2012, and the series of lectures *Le métier d'homme: Husserl, Bloch, Orwell, morales de résistance* also reflect on Francoism, the Spanish Civil War, and resistance, contextualizing and amplifying the writer's observations in *Vingt ans et un jour*.[7]

MICHEL DEL CASTILLO, LE BOURREAU, AND THE REVISION OF HISTORY

Although early novels like *Le colleur d'affiches* (1958)[8] evoke the figure of the *bourreau* in the context of the Spanish Civil War, it is only with the character of Avelino Pared, the Nationalist policeman and interrogator in *La nuit du decrét*, that the *bourreau* assumes center stage in del Castillo's meditations, fictional and nonfictional, on the Spanish tragedy. Described as an "ideal" policeman on numerous occasions in the novel, Avelino Pared fascinates and repels colleagues, political enemies, and victims alike, firstly, for his remarkable skills as political interrogator during the Civil War and its aftermath. These skills are richly and forcefully described in the novel. But Pared also disturbs and unsettles because his humanity, such as it is, seems to border on the inhuman, even the demonic. Indeed, as the novel gradually reveals, Pared's "mineral dream" of a utopic future political order requires stripping people of their own humanity and reducing them to will-less, child-like creatures with no secrets and no dignity.

That Pared is a Nationalist and in his youth a militant supporter of Franco and the extreme right, and that his victims are for the most part Republicans, anarchists, or Communists, is, as the novel shows,

6. Jorge Semprun, *Vingt ans et un jour*, trans. Serge Mestre (Paris : Gallimard, 2004).

7. Semprún, *Le métier d'homme: Husserl, Bloch, Orwell : morales de résistance* (Paris : Climats, Flammarion, 2013).

8. Del Castillo, *Le colleur d'affiches* (Paris: Julliard, 1958).

of secondary importance. In political terms his "mineral dream" is indiscriminately totalitarian, ultimately neither right nor left. It is rather apocalyptic in religious and biblical terms.[9] Pared is portrayed in crucial scenes in *La nuit du décret* as a kind of Antichrist, capable of inspiring holy terror in the general population as well as among his prisoners and fellow policemen. Moreover, his vision of the future of humanity is ultimately neither nationalist, nor racist, nor class-driven in inspiration. In fact, it is perversely egalitarian and "moral," since it aspires to strip all humanity equally of the destructive passions that make Pared's ideal of order impossible—and that also make one human. As the younger policeman Santiago Laredo describes it, Pared's "delirious fantasy of order imagine[s] a humanity of automatons who only preserve the appearance of being alive, [they are] without memory, living under the frozen glare of [an] immense and empty eye" (317).

In many ways the most powerful scenes in *La nuit du décret* are those in which Pared interrogates and ultimately breaks the resistance of his prisoners. The consummate *bourreau*, Pared's methods of interrogation consist not in physical abuse or torture, but rather in turning that quality that is at the core of his victim's humanity and that motivates his resistance to Francoist tyranny against him. A representative episode focuses on Pared's breaking of Ramon Espuig, an Anarchist agent and professional art historian whom Pared befriends after arresting him. He furnishes the anarchist with books to read and visits with him daily, not in the latter's cell, but in Pared's own office, where Espuig sits without handcuffs and smokes cigarettes provided by Pared. All the while, Espuig is ostensibly awaiting transfer to Madrid to face certain death.

After several months, Pared abruptly breaks off contact with his prisoner, leaving him alone in his cell for weeks, even months. Espuig is allowed no human contact. When the jailor informs Pared that Espuig wishes to see him, everyone in the police station understands the anarchist has been broken. Unable to survive without human contact, without some form of human *solidarity* and the exchange of ideas essential to his being, Espuig is at Pared's mercy. The latter soon releases him. Eventually Espuig betrays his entire underground network, whose members are arrested and shot. His convictions and

<hr>

9. For a fuller discussion of the theological dimensions of *La nuit du décret*, see my "Visions of History, Versions of Apocalypse in Michel del Castillo's *La nuit du décret*," *Romance Notes* 35/3 (Spring 1995), 303–14.

will destroyed, Espuig is reduced to precisely the kind of automaton Pared seeks to create universally.

That this episode in *La nuit du décret* is emblematic of what the "ideal policeman" represents, especially for the novelist himself, is confirmed by the fact that more than twenty years after the publication of the novel del Castillo wrote a play, *Le jour du destin*, which reprises the episode, albeit with subtle but significant changes. First, Ramon Espuig—renamed Ramon Puig—is also broken by Pared, but in different circumstances: he is seen in Pared's company at a restaurant by a fellow anarchist and denounced. But the result and motivations are the same. Seduced by Pared's apparent humanity, he allows himself to be compromised, thus forfeiting the one thing that kept him going: his political *engagement*. He tells the policeman: "I have ceased to be a man. I am dead, Pared."[10]

But the more significant change in *Le jour du destin* is that Pared, the ideal policeman who destroys the humanity of others, is himself made more sympathetic, more *human*. He becomes a father figure of sorts to the younger policeman Laredo, now "Miguel" instead of "Santiago." More importantly, his own cruelty and inhumanity are accounted for in human terms by the fact that, as he tells Laredo, he had witnessed his father's death at the hands of the Republicans, and his mother's death shortly thereafter from sorrow. He adds: "You did not experience the war, Miguel, you do not know the things men are capable of" (67). Even Pared's victim Puig is sympathetic to the older policeman. He tells Pared that he understands that he could not have acted differently. And in words reminiscent of what the Jew Albert Horne says to the young collaborator who betrays him in Louis Malle's classic film *Lacombe Lucien*, Puig adds: "After all that has happened, I just can't make myself detest you" (85).[11]

At the end of both *La nuit du décret* and *Le jour du destin*, Santiago/Miguel Laredo kills Avelino Pared. But the motives for the two crimes are strikingly different. In *La nuit du décret*, Laredo kills his aging superior because he recognizes himself, his own vocation as an "ideal policeman" in the older man: his crime is intended to forestall

10. Del Castillo, *Le jour du destin*, 83.
11. Horne's comment to Lucien is: "It's strange, I cannot bring myself to loathe you entirely" ("C'est curieux, je n'arrive pas à vous détester tout à fait"). In Louis Malle and Patrick Modiano, *Lacombe Lucien* (Paris: Folio Plus Classiques, 2008), 84.

the advent of Pared's "mineral dream" in his own soul and in the world around him.

In *Le jour du destin*, by contrast, the motives for Laredo's crime are less metaphysical than they are psychological and specifically *human*. Laredo kills Pared to avenge Puig, and also because Pared is an "imposter" who has not lived up to the ideal Laredo had seen in him. Pared, for his part, admits to being afraid of Laredo at the moment of his imminent execution because he fears the memory of his own youthful idealism that he recognizes in Laredo. Here, the mirror of self-recognition is reversed. Finally, whereas the Pared of *La nuit du décret* embodies a metaphysical menace that threatens all mankind, the Pared of *Le jour du destin* embodies only the more mundane dangers of political fanaticism. The gunshot that kills Pared is heard in a darkened theater, and is followed by the playing of *Cara al Sol*, the hymn of the *Falange*.

What are the implications of the changes undergone by the character of Avelino Pared and the story of Espuig/Puig in *Le jour du destin*? What does the *humanization* of the fictional *bourreau* in the 2003 play signify? It is important to stress that, as other works by del Castillo confirm, there is not necessarily a concise "evolution" to the character of Pared because the real person who inspired his creation, Don Pedro Rodrigo, has remained for the writer a constant source of meditation and rumination over many years. By extension these reflections on Don Pedro enrich and render more complex the character of Pared. In the 1977 essay *Le sortilège espagnol*, del Castillo devotes an entire chapter to him, and characterizes him ultimately as "the quintessence of the Spaniard. His uprightness, his honesty, his rigor, and his impassibility at the hour of doling out death sentences . . . ."[12] Like the fictional Pared, don Pedro had been a Falangist and policeman during the Civil War. And despite his brutality, del Castillo adds, what distinguished Don Pedro from a fascist or a Nazi was his "high moral conscience."[13]

But if the portrait of don Pedro in *Le sortilege espagnol* and in other works like *Le crime des pères*[14] enriches our understanding of the fictional Pared, and especially his "Spanishness," they do not account for the kind of "humanization" Pared undergoes in *Le jour du destin*. Nor do they address what this transformation might mean in

12. Del Castillo, *Le sortilège espagnol* (Paris: Julliard, 1977), 146.
13. Ibid.
14. Del Castillo, *Le crime des pères* (Paris: Seuil, 1999).

moral and historical terms for del Castillo himself. Given the constant interplay between fiction and history in del Castillo's *oeuvre*, his biography of Franco, *Le temps de Franco*, offers some answers.

When *Le temps de Franco* appeared in late 2008, some critics and historians praised the work on historical grounds.[15] But others were deeply troubled by it. In *Les séductions du bourreau*, Charlotte Lacoste expresses dismay over del Castillo's characterization of the Spanish dictator in an interview he gave to *L'express* in which del Castillo announces at the outset that Franco "was not a fascist."[16] In that interview, del Castillo also claims that Franco's brutality hid an "inner fragility" (*"une grande fragilité intérieure"*) attributable in part to the "disdain of his father." Moreover, Franco being a "chemically pure *militaire*," intellectuals were at the time and are now incapable of understanding him or appreciating his talents. Far from being "limited" as del Castillo's interviewer suggests, Franco was, del Castillo responds, a man of real intelligence: how else could he have remained in power so long and died in his bed? For Lacoste at least, the *Express* interview reveals del Castillo's complicity in a dangerous cultural trend bent on the rehabilitation of the *bourreau*.

Leaving aside Lacoste's broad claims in her book concerning contemporary culture's fascination with the figure of the *bourreau*, she is correct in detecting a certain *complaisance*—tolerance or sympathy—on del Castillo's part for the former dictator. That *complaisance* is echoed and in fact amplified in *Le temps de Franco*, especially in the Afterword. Here, del Castillo restates his belief in El Caudillo's intelligence: the latter kept Spain out of World War II while deftly balancing conflicting interests at home. He also reaffirms his belief that Franco was no fascist, and cites the fact that he emasculated the *Falange* after the war. In the place of ideology, Franco substituted "pragmatism" (384).

Del Castillo's claims become more troubling, still, when he addresses Franco's reputation for brutality and the repressiveness of his

15. The historian Edouard Husson praised the writer's courage for exposing the "myth" of the Spanish Republic ("Le Temps de Franco," *Le blog d'Edouard Husson* [blog], 27 December, 2010, http://www.edouardhusson.com/Le-Temps-de-Franco _a217.html) and in *La République des livres*, Pierre Assouline lauded the writer for offering a corrective to the overly-demonized and widely accepted (at least in France) image of El Caudillo ("Castillo y va Franco," *La République des livres* [blog], September 4 2007, http://passouline.blog.lemonde .fr/2008/11/16/castillo-y-va-franco/).

16. Charlotte Lacoste, *Les séductions du bourreau* (Paris : PUF, 2010), 380–81. The interview with del Castillo appeared in *L'express* on 16 October 2008. In fact, earlier in his career, del Castillo had labeled Franco a fascist on several occasions.

regime before and after the war. In discussing El Caudillo's "regal" power to condemn to death or to grant a pardon, del Castillo notes that this power is shared by "most heads of state" and even "governors in the United States" (383). He does not specify that in democratic nations and American states that power is restricted to granting pardons, not to ordering summary executions. As for the repressiveness of Franco's regime, del Castillo is content to point out that while it was repressive, it was nothing compared to the regimes of Hitler, Stalin, and Mao. He adds; "This [Franco's repression] was a violent military repression, it was not a mass extermination or a genocide" (377). If crimes against humanity were committed in Spain, del Castillo concludes, this was done by the Communists, not the Nationalists (379).

In his recent book *The Spanish Holocaust* Paul Preston challenges many if not all of del Castillo's claims concerning Franco and the regime he created. During the war and afterward, Preston writes, Franco "was engaged in an investment in terror."[17] After the Republic's defeat he had no interest in national reconciliation in the form of amnesty, which he dismissed as "monstrous and suicidal" "fraud[s]" dreamed up by "liberals" (472). And while Preston does not accuse Franco of being a "fascist," he notes his praise for Hitler's anti-Semitic policies and his statement to the effect that the war was carried out against a "Jewish-Bolshevik-Masonic" conspiracy in his end-of-the-year message in December 1939. If Franco was not a fascist, his mindset, as his year-end message suggests, was not far removed from Nazism.

Preston adds that in carrying out their reign of terror in post-Civil War Spain, Franco and his minions repeatedly sought to promote the idea that those who had defended the Republic against the Nationalist uprising were themselves the "rebels." And thousands were tried in kangaroo courts whose legal framework, imposed *ex post facto*, was based on this "fiction" (473). Moreover, both during and after the war, the victims of Francoism far outnumbered those of the Republic, and Preston does not shy away from using expressions like the Nationalist "extermination" and "annihilation" of its enemies.

In light of Preston's remarks, del Castillo's assessment of Franco, his regime, as well as the Republican side seems all the more troubling: if it is not overtly revisionist, it borders dangerously on being so. That the Communists committed "crimes against humanity" and

---

17. Paul Preston, *The Spanish Holocaust: Inquisition and Extermination in Twentieth-Century Spain* (New York: Norton, 2012), 471.

the Nationalists apparently did not is but one example of numerous historical (legal?) distortions and indeed factual reversals. These also include statements, in the interview in *L'express* to the effect that "one never speaks of Republican crimes." And, more shockingly, that "[t]he responsibility for the civil war does not belong to Franco, but to the revolutionary left." In the Afterward to *Le temps de Franco*, del Castillo makes much the same claim, stating that "the Republican governments never ceased flaunting the Constitution, [and] trampling on legality and, in 1934, with the insurrection in Catalonia and in the Asturias, the far left stabbed the Republic in the back, making the [Nationalist] uprising inevitable" (374). In this scenario Franco, the reluctant rebel, the "Rastignac of the Barracks" (382) is forced by History to play the role that he did. Neither in France nor in Britain, del Castillo explains, was the nation forced to deal with a Communist revolution on its soil, and if Franco was brutal and cruel, it was because he had been "traumatized by the Republic, which had stripped him of all illusions" (380).

It is not difficult to detect in del Castillo's discussion of the Spanish dictator the same troubling tendency to "humanize" and even justify the *bourreau* that one detects in the evolution of Avelino Pared from *La nuit du décret* to *Le jour du destin*. That El Caudillo is cast as a "Rastignac of the Barracks" in *Le temps de Franco* constitutes a strange—and misplaced—fictional analogy that suggests that Franco, like the hero of *Le père Goriot* in particular, is a fundamentally sympathetic and empathetic figure who is ultimately forced to throw down the gauntlet in the face of a corrupt world. Except that the corrupt fictional world of Paris in Balzac's novel is replaced by a very complicated, controversial historical moment that del Castillo frankly distorts, whether deliberately or not, to make the *bourreau* that Franco was, and the actions he took, more palatable. The writer's revisionism in this instance marks a strange and sad epilogue of sorts to a novelistic career that despite its fixation on the figure of the *bourreau*, has also paid moving tribute to history's victims, and those of the Spanish tragedy in particular.

JORGE SEMPRÚN: HISTORY, TORTURE, AND THE MEANING OF RESISTANCE

If Michel del Castillo's recent works dealing with Spain and Franco-ism point to a strong linkage between the writer's fascination with the figure of the *bourreau* and troublingly revisionist views, a very different nexus can be detected in the later works of Semprún. Whereas in del Castillo's case, history is read in relation to, and through "the seductions of the *bourreau*," to paraphrase Charlotte Lacoste, for Semprún it is the experience and insights of the *bourreau*'s *victim*, the *resistant*, that ultimately shape the writer's historical vision and the need to engage with History itself.

Toward the end of his life, Semprún was working on a new volume of memoirs, the aforementioned *Exercices de survie*, in which he reflected once again on his experiences in the Resistance and Buchenwald and in the postwar years as a Communist agent in Franco's Spain. As he told an interviewer in 2010, the theme around which the new memoir would be constructed was one that he said he had rarely discussed previously: torture.[18]

In fact, *Exercice de survie*—or the unfinished version of it that we have—addresses a number of topics in addition to the announced theme of torture. But it is the discussion of torture, and the lessons gleaned from that experience, that constitute the most compelling and eloquent part of the memoir.

What is most striking and arguably original about Semprún's reflections on torture in *Exercices de survie* is that torture is both a *solitary and solidary* experience, and ultimately a fraternal one as well (51):

> For it [torture] to have meaning, to be fecund, one must postulate, in the abominable solitude of one's suffering, a surpassing "We," a shared history, a history in common to prolong, to rebuild, to be perpetually reinvented. (34)

Implicit in this statement is that torture does not, or should not break the will to resist, but rather reaffirms the latter's continuing necessity. And while the victim of torture suffers unspeakable agonies, it is not the victim who is ultimately isolated, separated from the world, but rather the torturer:

> My personal experience teaches me that it is not the victim but the torturer—if the latter goes on to a different life, to a later existence,

---

18. This information is contained in the *Avertissement de l'éditeur* in *Exercices de survie*, 16. For an earlier, somewhat different but also powerful meditation by Semprún on the experience and meaning of torture, see the 1967 novel *L'évanouissement*, 42–46. I am grateful to Van Kelly for calling this passage to my attention.

even an anonymous peaceful one—who will never again be at home in the world, no matter what he says, no matter what face he puts on. (57–58)

But as subsequent passages of *Exercices de survie* reveal, Semprún's recognition of the existential isolation of the *bourreau* does not breed sympathy, or even tolerance on the part of the writer, as it does ultimately for del Castillo, but rather the opposite. He describes an incident when, while serving in Felipe González's government, he encounters the famed police commissioner "B."; the latter reminds Semprún that he had previously been pursued by him when Semprún was an underground agent of the Spanish Communist Party. The encounter is described as cold, and although in the same passage Semprún lauds Spain's efforts at reconciliation, its desire for amnesty and amnesia, he himself is in no mood to share in these sentiments with a man who had arrested and to all appearances tortured and killed some of Semprún's former comrades: "At that moment, I wished to forget nothing. Nor did I wish to forgive" (81).

By contrast, the experience of resistance—to the Nazis, to Francoism—is described as a "privilege," as belonging to a "kind of Knighthood" (82). And the only difference between these two experiences of resistance is that Semprún was never arrested or tortured in Spain, and therefore was never directly responsible for the lives of his Spanish comrades, as he had been for his French comrades. But this difference only serves to remind him that in Spain, others were tortured and saved *his life* by not giving in to the methods of the *bourreau*.

As other passages in *Exercices de survie* make clear, the experience of resistance and the fraternity it creates serve at once to remind Semprún not to lose faith in the struggle against tyranny, despite the disappointments and even betrayal of the Communist Party, and also not to lose sight of the meaning and cost of the Francoist tyranny in historical terms. Borrowing from Malraux's vocabulary in *L'espoir*, Semprún argues that even though the "lyrical illusion" was fading, the one certitude that remained during his Spanish underground days was "the necessity, the rightness of the struggle against Franco's dictatorship, even if the struggle did not result in a revolutionary epiphany" (83). By the same token, his commitment to the struggle against Francoist tyranny prompts him to recall in another passage that the erection of statues of El Caudillo "almost everywhere" in postwar Spain was purchased at a terrible price: "many hundreds of thousands of lives" (64); and to recall as well Franco's exceptional cruelty, even among a host of Nationalist generals noted for this characteristic, in putting down the revolt of the Asturian miners in 1934, a repression Semprún labels "undoubtedly unjustified" (64).

If torture serves as the central theme and the springboard for Semprún's reflections on solidarity, fraternity, and the historical cost and meaning of Francoism in *Exercices de survie*, in another posthumously published work, *Le métier de l'homme: Husserl, Bloch, Orwell, morales de résistance*, it is the related themes of resistance to tyranny and the defense of democracy that inspire the writer's reflections. As the subtitle of the book suggests, the work focuses on three key figures of intellectual resistance to Nazism and totalitarianism. But it is of course Semprún's essay on Orwell that most directly concerns us here.

Semprún begins his essay on Orwell by recalling the tragic end of the Spanish Civil War when Republican forces, divided between Socialists and Anarchists who wished to quit the fight, and the Communists, who wished to continue the defense of Madrid, fought each other. Semprún rightly observes that, even though the conflict is often forgotten by younger generations, it "weighed on the history of anti-Francoism like a festering sore" (89).

Why begin with this sad episode? Because it marked the dramatic and traumatic conclusion of the conflict between the Communists and other groups on the Republican side that created tensions, and much worse, from the outset. At the core of this conflict was the painful conundrum that plagued the Republic from the beginning: "Are we faced with a revolution or a war? Is it necessary to complete the revolution to win the war, or to win the war to complete the revolution?" (96). The issue, Semprún continues, was decided by the Communists, who opted for the second approach. In the abstract that approach was "a perfectly coherent and defensible strategy." But in the hands of the Communists it became a brutal repression using Stalinist police methods, a repression that sought the liquidation of all groups and parties that wished to complete the revolution first. The most brutal act of repression was the destruction of the Trotskyist *POUM* in 1937, which Orwell experienced directly and that he chronicles in *Homage to Catalonia*.

But Communist brutality and divisions in the Republic itself should not, Semprún argues, obscure the fact that many groups and parties, including even the anarchists who opposed all forms of government, rose up in support of the Republic when the latter

was confronted with the Nationalist uprising. And, Semprún continues, the Spanish Republic was fundamentally democratic, and not
revolutionary.

Nevertheless, Semprún writes, what fascinated Orwell and others
was what he describes in *Le métier d'homme* as the "reality of the
élan of the popular and working-class masses in the first months of
the war" (100). And this popular wave of support was directed at those
who would later become *Francoists* but who were at the time unquestionably *fascists*. While this fact should not be lost in understanding
the history of the war, neither should the fact that the methods used
and the violence wreaked in Spain by the Communists were essentially imported into Spain from the Soviet Union, which, Semprún
recalls, was experiencing the horror of the Moscow trials at that time.

At the conclusion of his essay on George Orwell, Semprún turns to
Orwell's views on the conflict at the conclusion of the Civil War, and
also to his views on the justification of Britain's struggle against Hitler. While Orwell's hostility to British colonialism had earlier led him
to speculate if British democracy in India was not worse than Hitler's
regime (109), by the time of Britain's solitary struggle against Nazi
Germany he believed that the struggle, that resistance, was totally
justified, even if one were ultimately defeated. Therefore there could
in fact be a "democratic and revolutionary patriotism" (113), and Orwell's "evolution" up to 1941 and the publication of *The Lion and the
Unicorn*, culminated with what Semprún describes as Orwell's "re-
discovery of democracy" (118). That discovery confirms absolutely
the premise that, looking back, "whatever the Republican atrocities
he had himself occasionally witnessed . . . [n]othing was comparable
to the systematic, organized atrocities of Francoist terror" (119).

In their clarity and forcefulness *Exercices de survie* and Semprún's
essay on George Orwell in *Le métier d'homme* construct a vision and
an ethics of history, and specifically the history of the Spanish Civil
War and Francoism, that is based on an absolute and unbending commitment to resistance to tyranny. In the novel *Vingt ans et un jour*,
that vision and ethics are reaffirmed, albeit in more convoluted, and
decidedly more "novelistic" ways.[19]

19. In an interview in *The Paris Review*, Semprún expresses his admiration for
Faulkner in the following terms: "I have always been drawn to the Faulknerian style
of writing, where an old lady starts off telling a story and then the story segues into
another story, which sends us back to the distant past and then loops around to the
present." Readers will certainly recognize this "Faulknerian" style in *Vingt ans et un*

Vingt ans et un jour focuses primarily on the wealthy Avendaño family, the murder of the youngest of the three Avendaño brothers, José Maria, by farm workers at the outset of the Civil War, and the commemoration surrounding that crime twenty years later. As Semprun has stated in interviews, the story is based on real events, and features cameo appearances by real or historical individuals including Ernest Hemingway, Semprún's friend the bullfighter Domingo Dominguín, and the author himself, who appears in the novel as his former real life Communist alter ego Federico Sanchez (and briefly under another alias, Augustín Larrea).[20] Other characters besides Semprun-Sanchez also take on alternative identities and role-playing, and there are ritualistic reenactments of historical crimes and other moments, as well sexual theatrics, that furnish many of the most striking and significant moments in the novel.

As *Vingt ans et un jour* opens, the most significant of these rituals, the annual re-enactment of the murder of the younger Avendaño by the peasants, is discussed at a luncheon where Larrea, Dominguín, Hemingway, and the fictional American historian Michael Leidson are present. As Dominguín explains, each year following Franco's victory the local peasants are obliged to re-enact their original crime, as a way of reaffirming their own guilt, and thus their responsibility for the violence of the Civil War that ensued. In Girardian terms, they are re-enacting the violent sacrifice that founds and justifies the Francoist new order. According to this scenario the younger brother, Jose-Maria, the representative of the aristocracy, becomes sanctified, even deified, as his sacrifice, in principle at least, eliminates internecine violence while also preserving the political and social status quo.

But as the novel unfolds, problems and complications of all sorts emerge, calling the function, meaning, and efficaciousness of the ritualized sacrifice, or modern *auto da fé* into question. The original victim, José-Maria Avendaño is an entirely inappropriate representative of the privileged classes that Franco's revolt and victory sought to defend. Before his murder he is an enlightened progressive and republican, opposed to the privileges of his own class. It also appears that his murder or sacrifice is accidental. And now, twenty years after

jour, as in so many of Semprún's works. (Semprún, "Interview with Lila Azam Zanganeh, *The Paris Review, The Art of Fiction* 192 [2007]. http://www.theparisreview.org/interviews/5740/the-art-of-fiction-no-192-jorge-semprun. Accessed April 4, 2015)

20. See the interview in the *Wikipedia* entry on *Vingt ans et un jour, http://fr.wikipedia.org/wiki/Vingt_ans_et_un_jour*. Accessed April 10, 2015.

his death, the younger peasants who work on the estate, are restive at the thought of re-enacting the crime, a re-enactment that makes them accomplices to a murder with which they have no connection. At this moment, in order to put the past to rest, members of the Avendaño family, José-Maria's widow and son, along with the second brother, conceive the notion of burying the man supposedly responsible for the murder, Chema or "El Refilon" who fought for the Republic during the Civil War, in the family crypt along with José Maria. The gesture is violently opposed by the older brother and family patriarch, José Manuel, who personifies all the arrogance and abusiveness of a class whose interests Franco has served.

To the extent that virtually all members of the Avendaño family, even those with republican and democratic views, are in one way or another perverted or depraved, as depictions of explicit sexual encounters in the novel confirm, *Vingt ans et un jour* sets itself up as a kind of latter-day *roman-à-thèse* condemning Francoism and the wealth, privileges, and corruption of the ruling class. Even the martyred José-Maria and his wife Mercedes are fond of *ménages-à-trois* with servants and underlings. Their two children, Lorenzo and Isabel, are incestuous lovers, and José-Manuel regularly exercises his *droit de cuissage* by having sex with his brother's widow. Discovering their mother's sexual victimization at the hands of José-Manuel as well as photos displaying her lasciviousness when indulging in the earlier threesomes with her husband, the two children commit suicide together after making love in the abandoned estate.

But if the abuses and indeed decadence of the aristocracy are neatly invoked in the sexual excesses of the Avendaño family, and the necessity of a national reconciliation that embraces all in the ritualized interment of José-Maria and Chema, where in the novel is the theme of resistance to Francoist tyranny and its inherent brutality played out? For readers of del Castillo's fiction discussed earlier, there is a shock of recognition in reading *Vingt ans et un jour* when the character of the police commissioner Sabuesa is introduced. To all appearances based on the famed commissioner "B." mentioned in *Exercices de survie*, in his fictional evocation in *Vingt ans et un jour* Sabuesa strongly resembles the figure of Avelino Pared in important ways. Legendary and feared for his relentlessness, efficaciousness, and fanaticism in the novel, Sabuesa is introduced in language reminiscent of del Castillo's language in describing Pared; "His gray look crystal[izes] an inhuman and despairing hatred. How could one forget this look?" (103). Throughout *Vingt ans et un jour*, Sabuesa never varies in his fanaticism. Even though Franco has won, he announces to his principle victim in the novel, José Juan Castillo, that as long as Communism exists, he will not relent (125). Given the historical perspective of the time, Sabuesa's pursuit of his political commitment and his own desire to be an "ideal policeman" border on the metaphysical, as they did for Pared.

If Sabuesa resembles Pared in the novel, Castillo himself eerily resembles Pared's victim Espuig/Puig. He is broken by Sabuesa, not through torture but by Sabuesa's revelation that other comrades have in fact cracked under torture. And Sabuesa attempts to gain complete control over Castillo by telling him that he will launch the rumor that he, Castillo, has in fact cracked and betrayed his comrades. As Sabuesa informs him, echoing Pared's intentions if not his words: "I will have finished with all that you respect the most, and with that which constitutes the very substance of your life: your Communist ideal" (122). He concludes: "You will be alive, but you will be a dead man" (123).

It is at this point in the novel, however, that Semprún's depiction of his own version of Franco's "ideal policeman" distances itself from del Castillo's—and where Semprún's historical vision diverges sharply from del Castillo's vision as well. In subsequent episodes in *Vingt ans et un jour*, Sabuesa visits Castillo after he is released from prison after the war. The former's sadism and cruelty, the real motors for his actions, are underscored by his dropping in unannounced at Castillo's home in order to frighten his wife, also a former Republican operative, and to, in effect, hold the sword of Damocles over his erstwhile prisoner's head.

But on one of these visits Sabuesa encounters Castillo's young daughter, Nieves. The description of the encounter is revealing. On seeing her, Sabuesa:

> is overwhelmed by a strange feeling, violent, irrepressible. Suddenly, everything had a bitter taste in his mouth, a bilious taste of hatred, of bitterness, of murderous impulses. Of discouragement. As if the apparition of such a relaxed, harmonious, and beautiful young girl with the allure of a silhouette—she stood up immediately, walked away from the table, toward a corner of the dining room, with a distant look on her face and an expression of disgust—as if this apparition of Nieves, graceful, young, uncontestable mistress of the future, was the signal, sibylline but no less disquieting, of his failure. Of the failure of chief

commissioner Roberto Sabuesa, of his First Regional Brigade of Social investigation, in its struggle against the residues, the dross, and the embers of communism, endlessly reborn and relighted. (131)

For Sabuesa, the future may be a Communist nightmare, but what Nieves represents and announces in the novel is simply a brighter future, and the end of the Francoist nightmare. And rather than elicit any form of sympathy or empathy on the writer's part, as Pared does for del Castillo, Semprun's *bourreau* in *Vingt ans et un jour* does not ultimately shape or inflect his own vision of history. In fact, like the torturer he describes in *Exercices de survie*, Sabuesa is unalterably alienated, removed from history, and also from other humans as well. His destiny is not a tragic one, and barely, if at all, deserving of pity.

To conclude: In his Afterword to *Le temps de Franco*, Michel del Castillo writes: "at the end of my already very long life, I believe that what one refers to nowadays as 'the duty to memory' is often for the most part a morbid rehash of the past that prevents memory from contributing to fashioning collective hope" (389). But in reflecting on the Spanish Civil War, Franco, and Francoism in the Afterword and in other recent pronouncements noted earlier, del Castillo seems to apply his own version of "the duty to memory" to recalling—and exaggerating—the abuses and failings of the Spanish Republic in order, if not to rehabilitate Franco and his regime, at least to diminish their abuse and crimes. By contrast, in his commitment to memory, to his own version of the "duty to remember," Semprún restores and in fact celebrates resistance to precisely the kind of tyranny that Franco and his regime created and imposed. In historical as well as in moral terms, Jorge Semprún's is to all appearances the more judicious approach.

URSULA TIDD

Jorge Semprún and the Practice of Survival

Jorge Semprún's posthumously published *Exercices de survie* (2012) offers its readers insight into his narrative approach to remembering the past as a form of survival.[1] Throughout his postwar life, Semprún struggled with how to represent his incarceration in Buchenwald from January 1944 until April 1945 as a "passing through death" because his concentration camp experience constituted an absolute breach in his life and his understanding of the parameters of the human. This thanatographical project initiated in *Le grand voyage* (1963)[2] has its roots both in his Buchenwald experience and in his career of clandestine political activism in which political commitment entailed the perpetual risk of torture and assassination.[3] Being "bound to death by a surreptitious friendship," as Blanchot terms it,[4] was a feature of Semprún's life and intrinsically linked to his practice of survival.

In the present discussion, I will analyze what light *Exercices de survie* sheds on torture and Semprún's subsequent survival. Further, I will explore the intertextual connections that the narrator makes with the work of Jean Améry (also tortured by the Gestapo) and with

---

1. Jorge Semprun, *Exercices de survie* (Paris: Gallimard, 2012). Further references to this work are given in brackets in the text.
2. Semprun, *Le grand voyage* [1963] (Paris: Gallimard, 2001)
3. *Qua autothanatography*, as Jacques Derrida and Louis Marin have explored the term, Semprún's texts challenge generic assumptions concerning autobiography and circumnavigate the unknowable experience of death as an encounter with alterity. See Derrida, *Otobiographies: L'enseignement de Nietzsche et la politique du nom propre* (Paris: Galilée, 1984) and Marin, *L'écriture de soi: Ignace de Loyola, Montaigne, Stendhal, Roland Barthes* (Paris: PUF, 1991).
4. Maurice Blanchot, *The Instant of My Death*, trans. Elizabeth Rottenberg (Stanford, CA: Stanford University Press, 2000), 5.

YFS 129, *Writing and Life, Literature and History: On Jorge Semprun,* ed. Razinsky, © 2016 by Yale University.

Henri Alleg's *La question* (which exposed the victim's experience of torture by French paratroopers during the Algerian War) in his philosophical reflections on the parameters of political commitment and survival.[5]

Exercices de survie was published by Gallimard as a 110-page incomplete fragment in 2012, less than a year after Semprún's death in June 2011. The previous year Semprún had explained to Franck Appréderis that he planned the text as the first of a series of thematic autobiographical volumes entitled *Exercices de survie.*[6] This initial volume would relate to his youth and experiences in the Resistance and be structured according to the theme of torture about which he had so far spoken little. Semprún intended to relate his personal experience and reflect on the broader philosophical question of torture. In fact, torture occupies approximately thirty pages (or less than a quarter) of the published text. However Semprún's statement about its thematic importance to this first volume, viewed in the context of the text's epigraph ("comparing everything unintentionally to torture"), a phrase cited from Louis Aragon's poem, "Chanson pour oublier Dachau,"[7] suggests that he was intending to write more on the subject had the volume's completion not been interrupted by his ill health. The planned series comprised a second volume that would focus on the extermination of the Jews in Europe (a topic about which Semprún had already written in essays included in *Une tombe au creux des nuages*[8]) and a third volume on his experience of commitment to, and later renunciation of, Communism (about which he had already written in several texts including *Autobiographie de Federico Sánchez*[9]). It is not clear when Semprún began working on *Exercices de survie*, since he often worked on several projects at once. However, as the text's narrator indicates, he had written approximately sixty pages by July 2005 and continued to work on the text in the years until his death.

5. Henri Alleg, *La question* (Paris: Minuit, 1958).

6. Semprun, *Le langage est ma patrie. Entretiens avec Franck Appréderis* (Paris: Libella, 2013), 35–36.

7. My translation of Louis Aragon, "Chanson pour oublier Dachau" in "Le cri du Butor," *Le nouveau crève-coeur* (Paris: Gallimard, 1948).

8. Semprún, *Une tombe au creux des nuages : Essais sur l'Europe d'hier et d'aujourd'hui* (Paris: Flammarion, 2010).

9. Semprún, *The Autobiography of Federico Sanchez and the Communist Underground in Spain*, trans. Helen R. Lane (New York: Karz Publishers, 1979).

The implicit acknowledgement of Raymond Queneau's *Exercices de style* in Semprún's choice of title,[10] *Exercices de survie*, is significant in terms of his approach to autothanatographical testimony. Queneau's text is a famously pre-Oulipian example of re-telling a simple story ninety-nine different ways, in a creative *tour de force*. In Semprún's case, he is similarly interested in narrative experimentation as an aesthetic "exercise" yet it is no aesthetic game since its purpose is to facilitate the engagement of his reader who is unlikely to have experienced incarceration in the camps. However, and more importantly here, Semprún is interested in the ethical and spiritual exercise of undergoing a fundamental life-changing experience (such as intense commitment to Communism and subsequent expulsion from the party; torture; incarceration; the witnessing of genocide) and how one can continue to live afterwards rather than to live in spite of those experiences, as the term "survival" is sometimes understood. In this respect, the title further resonates intertextually with the *Spiritual Exercises* (1548) of fellow Spaniard, Saint Ignatius of Loyola (1491–1566) (which consisted of meditations, prayers, and exercises designed to deepen the believer's relationship with Christ) and with Pierre Hadot's investigation of Antique philosophy's "spiritual exercises" in both *Exercices spirituels et philosophie antique* and *La philosophie comme manière de vivre*,[11] with which Semprún may have been familiar. As such, then, the richly polysemic title can be interpreted as an aesthetic, ethical, and spiritual indication that survival after torture and incarceration in Buchenwald entailed practices of survival elaborated by Semprún throughout his postwar life.

The question of survival was complex for every prisoner who returned from the camps. In Semprún's case, he experienced severe internal conflict in relation to writing about his experience, initially as a prisoner of the Gestapo in Auxerre, then in the Compiègne transit camp and in Buchenwald. His survival required him to engage repeatedly with the infinite task of "telling the story of that death right through to the end."[12] In *Quel beau dimanche!* he qualifies his position as a Buchenwald survivor as a precarious one, informed as it is by his experience of having passed through this death, which leaves

10. Raymond Queneau, *Exercices de style* (Paris : Gallimard, 1947).

11. Pierre Hadot, *Exercices spirituels et philosophie antique* (Paris: Albin Michel, 1981); *La philosophie comme manière de vivre* (Paris: Albin Michel, 2001).

12. Semprun, *L'écriture ou la vie* (Paris: Gallimard, 1994), 45; *Literature or Life*, trans. Linda Coverdale (Harmondsworth, UK: Penguin Books, 1997), 35.

him uncertain as to whether he is in fact dead or alive and whether he consciously experienced Buchenwald or not:

> Had my life at Buchenwald been a dream? Or, on the contrary, was my life since I had come back from Buchenwald just a dream? Had I quite simply died, fifteen years ago and was all this [. . .] just a dream of grey, premonitory smoke on the Ettersberg?[13]

For Semprún, as for other Holocaust survivors such as fellow Communist Charlotte Delbo and Primo Levi, the nightmare of having lived through Buchenwald leaves him isolated with his memories, speculating about what exactly he might have experienced. The title of Delbo's first volume of her Holocaust trilogy, *Aucun de nous ne reviendra* (1970) (*None of us will return*) and its closing line: "none of us was meant to return" suggest that prisoners did not or perhaps should not have returned from the camp, an ethical catastrophe that profoundly dislocated any post-concentration camp existence.[14] Acknowledging Primo Levi's observation that the true witnesses are the "*sommersi*" or "the drowned" who were annihilated in the camps, in *Le mort qu'il faut* Semprún asserts his lack of guilt and the random situation of the survivor, separated only by luck from those annihilated:

> I should feel guilty to have been lucky, especially insofar as I survived. Although I am not especially inclined towards that feeling even though it has a considerable literary currency. One should, it seems [. . .] display a certain shame, a guilty conscience, at least if one claims to be a respectable and trustworthy witness—a survivor worthy of the name.[15]

Semprún continues:

> For sure, the best witness, the only true witness, in reality, according to the specialists, is the one who has not survived, who went to the end of the experience and died from it. But [. . .] can the true witnesses, in other words, the dead, be invited to their conferences? How can they be made to speak?[16]

---

13. Semprun, *Quel beau dimanche!* (Paris: Grasset, 1980), 67; *What a Beautiful Sunday!*, trans. Alan Sheridan (London: Sphere Books, 1984), 36.
14. Charlotte Delbo, *None of us will return* in *Auschwitz and After*, trans. Rosette C. Lamont (New Haven and London: Yale University Press, 1995), 114.
15. Semprun, *Le mort qu'il faut* (Paris: Gallimard, 2001), 16. My translation.
16. Ibid.

In *Quel beau dimanche!*, the narrator refutes the redemptory aura of the term "survivor" and its eschatological promise:

> Survivors? The word doesn't mean anything. Well, nothing specific or accurate. What has one allegedly survived? Death? That would be amusing for one never survives one's own death. It is always there, crouching, lying in wait like a patient cat, biding its time. Does one survive the deaths of others? That won't get us very far: we don't need camps to know that it is always others who die.[17]

Semprún's focus on torture in *Exercices de survie* engages the debate running throughout his work on the parameters of survival. Both parts of the text open with a wartime site of memory, Hôtel Lutetia in Paris, located at the crossroads of the boulevard Raspail and the rue de Sèvres. Since Semprún lived in the same *quartier*, he would frequently walk past the hotel. Built in the Art Deco style in 1910 and home to illustrious writers and artists at various times, Hôtel Lutetia housed refugees at the start of the World War II but was later taken over by the German counter-espionage and housed high-ranking Nazi officials in charge of the Occupation. During the Occupation as a young *résistant*, Semprún naturally avoided being in the locality of the Hôtel Lutetia as well as the Hôtel Majestic on avenue Kléber, which was the wartime headquarters of the German armed forces and center of interrogation. Immediately after the war Semprún worked in the Spanish language section at UNESCO, which was, ironically, temporarily located in the Hôtel Majestic. Since his office adjoined a bathroom formerly used by the Gestapo to torture prisoners, the Majestic also became a "lieu de mémoire" of his own Resistance past (53).

Semprún's archaeological technique of revisiting the Lutetia and the Majestic to evoke his wartime past echoes that of Alain Resnais (although he was not himself interned by the Gestapo) when he revisits the ruins of Auschwitz in 1955 at the start of *Nuit et brouillard* (1955) and Jean Améry, who opens his discussion of torture in *Par-delà le crime et le châtiment* (1966) by revisiting Fort Breendonk in Belgium where he was tortured before being deported to Auschwitz.[18]

---

17. Semprún, *Quel beau dimanche!*, 154 ; Semprún, *What a Beautiful Sunday!*, 94.
18. *Nuit et brouillard*, directed by Alain Resnais. France, Argos Films 1955. Jean Améry, "La torture" in *Par-delà le crime et le châtiment*, trans. Françoise Wuilmart (Arles: Actes Sud, 1995), 51–52; "Torture" in *At The Mind's Limits*, trans. by Sidney Rosenfeld and Stella P. Rosenfeld (Bloomington and Indianapolis: Indiana University Press, 1980).

In the narrative present of *Exercices de survie*, approximately sixty years after the Liberation, the Hôtel Lutetia acts as a mnemonic device for Semprún in his bid to summon the ghosts of his past, including his younger existentially available self as a fledgling member of the Resistance. In 1943 Semprún had begun working for Jean-Marie Action, one of the British Buckmaster Resistance networks operating in France. The Jean-Marie Action network was responsible for parachute drops and weapons distribution in various regions such as the Côte-d'Or and the Yonne in Bourgogne. Semprún and his friend Michel Herr had been recruited in Paris by Henri Frager, who led a network as part of the Special Operations Executive's Resistance work in France and whom Semprún would meet again as a prisoner in Buchenwald. Semprún (under the Resistance alias of Gérard Sorel) and Herr (alias Jacques Mercier) worked to supply weapons to various *maquis* groups.

Early in *Exercices de survie* (30), the narrator recalls that Henri Frager asked him in 1943 if he was prepared to be tortured if captured. The shared experience of torture would form the core of Semprún's relationship with him until Frager's execution in Buchenwald in October 1944. "Tancrède," a Resistance acquaintance, was delegated by Frager to explain to Semprún what he could expect and he enumerated various forms of torture: beatings with truncheons of various sorts, reverse hanging (strappado), sleep deprivation, immersion in water, nail extraction, and electricity. Although terrifying in their detail, Semprún also found his descriptions abstract. As he would later experience in the Auxerre prison where he was interrogated and tortured by the Gestapo for fifteen days, torture was a material reality and one that he could not anticipate corporeally or psychologically. In one of several reflections on torture, the narrator of *Exercices de survie* observes that remaining silent under torture involves imposing upon oneself an endless resistance to infinite suffering. This necessarily exceeds the human condition morally and physically since the body aspires to life and survival. Hence to resist surrender under torture is, in Semprún's view, a transcendental act that, from the victim's situation of radical isolation, envisions a collective ideal, removed from the current dire circumstance, and one that can be perpetually renewed. Resistance consequently aspires to the perpetuation of the human species as a collective project. This view of resistance to torture as a microcosm of collective resistance is a feature of Semprún's commitment to collective praxis that I will explore below.

In Buchenwald, Semprún met Frager again, after the latter's betrayal and arrest by the Gestapo in August 1944. In the course of his work in the *Arbeitsstatistik* (labor records office), Semprún had spotted Frager's name on the list of arrivals and had the task of recording his name on the central card index. Frager was among a newly-captured group of high-ranking Resistance leaders who had resisted torture and for whom the Gestapo's plans were initially unclear. The Communist underground in Buchenwald sought to save several of these Resistance leaders and Stéphane Hessel (of the Bureau central de renseignement et d'action), Forest Frederick Edward Yeo-Thomas, and Harry Peulevé (both of the British Special Operations Executive) survived by having their identities switched with deceased prisoners in the sanatorium in Buchenwald, a strategy described by Semprún in relation to his own situation in *Le mort qu'il faut*. Frager, however, was shot by firing squad on 5 October 1944. In the preceding months Semprún had met with him regularly on Sunday afternoons and they had discussed their experiences of torture. Frager told Semprún that he viewed the experience of torture as a crucial memory that would unite survivors in the postwar period. Yet they both agreed that resistance to torture is no absolute moral criterion on which to base the potential humanism of humankind (48). Semprún and Frager recalled the infamous "butcher of Lyon," Klaus Barbie, who had interrogated Jean-Marie Soutou (Semprún's friend, brother-in-law, and rescuer of many Jews in his work for Amitiés judéo-chrétiennes) and Jean Moulin, the emblematic Resistance leader. Moulin resisted speaking under torture to the point of refusing to supply his own name. He then corrected its misspelling when Barbie triumphantly supplied it after some investigation, a gesture which Semprún applauds in *Exercices de survie* as a sublime example of a man transcending his own mortality in the midst of a wretched human situation (50).

Citing the example of Moulin in *Exercices de survie* paves the way for Semprún to articulate further his own perspective on torture. Consonant with his commitment to socialist praxis, he again represents torture as an experience of fraternity, rather than one of solitary suffering. In the Heideggerian terms in which Semprún describes it in this part of *Exercices de survie*, torture may be a 'being-towards-death' (*Sein-zum-Tode*) but it is also a being-with-others (*Mitsein*). Despite its apparent targeting of the individual, torture is not, in his view, a narcissistic experience since it is not directed at the individual; it is as much concerned with fraternal solidarity as with solitude.

Like Henri Alleg in *La question* (1958), Semprún's stance on torture is a humanistic one in which he refuses to capitulate to the sadistic psychology of the torturer and see himself as a victim. In *Le grand voyage*, the narrator recalls how he and his Spanish Communist underground comrades had read Alleg's book eagerly in 1959 as a manual of how to survive various forms of torture.[19] Characteristic of the existential phenomenological emphases of his writing, which foregrounds the embodied "lived experience" of remembering, Semprún explores how torture has affected his embodied sense of "being-in-the world" with others. In so doing, he initially agrees with Améry's statement in *Par-delà le crime et le châtiment* (*At The Mind's Limits*) that "Whoever is overcome by pain through torture experiences his body as never before. In self-negation, his flesh becomes a total reality."[20] Semprún explains in *Exercices de survie* that torture similarly caused him to feel fully aware of his body, which functioned at odds with his mind and volitions. His body became a hostile "for-itself" suffused with varieties of pain hitherto unexperienced and shot through with terror and a bestial desire for capitulation as he experienced different forms of torture in Auxerre prison: truncheon beatings, hanging by hand-cuffs, reverse hanging, and water torture (56).

Torture, however, does not only entail a painful experience of embodiment. Bodily experience is one of four mutually dependent elements that are present in the theater of intensified oppression from which torture is constituted: body, speech, mind, and the relationship with the other as torturer. The sufferer's resistance may require a witholding of speech, the disidentification of habituated sense impressions with corporeal experiences, and a sustained and intensified commitment to the political ideology and comrades at risk of betrayal. In short, it is a concentrated exercise in survival that, for Semprún, acted as a prelude to his experience of incarceration at Buchenwald. Resisting torture in 1943 involved an initiation into a form of silence that infused his subsequent writing: "silence populated by fraternal shadows." He explains further that "you both cling to and brace yourself against silence by gritting your teeth and trying to escape from your own body, your wretched body, by flights of imagination and memory and this silence is enriched by all the voices and all the lives which it protects and enables to continue to exist" (50). Later, during

19. Semprún, *Le grand voyage*, 202–203.
20. Améry, "La torture," 69; "Torture," 33.

his clandestine existence as a high-ranking Communist politician in Madrid, Semprún found himself protected for over a decade by the silence of others. It is from this fraternal, well-proven silence that his literary testimonies emerge as he now speaks in the name of others who did not have his luck to survive: "speak in the name of the drowned. Speak in their name, in their silence, to give them back the power of speech."[21]

Yet Semprún differentiates his position from that of Améry when the latter says that the experience of torture irredeemably disrupts any confident sense of being at home in the world and that it leaves the sufferer with an indelible trace. Semprún disputes this since he contends that it is the torturer who is radically dislocated from the world, whereas the victim, braced in his own silence, is able to multiply his connections, sense of purpose, and rootedness with the world (58). In affirming this, Semprún draws on his own experience of torture at Auxerre, during which each hour of silence gained over the Gestapo enriched him and his sense of being-in-the-world, whereas his persecutors became weakened, feverish, and dulled by their actions. He offers a classic Hegelian account of the process insofar as according to the master-slave dialectic, the master is ultimately enslaved by his own need to maintain tyranny over the slave from whom he cannot obtain the free recognition that he desires. In this way, Semprún refused to occupy a subjugated position or to be *personally* wounded by the experience. His response to his situation was pragmatic and highly political: occupying the stance of the victim would only sabotage the urgency and efficacy of collective praxis. His unshakable commitment (at that time) to the Communist cause, and his identitarian confidence due to his privileged social class and gender contributed to his ability to sustain himself under torture and during its aftermath.

While Améry is unable to ascertain in *Par-delà le crime et le châtiment* why some resist confession under torture and others do not, a key difference between his situation and that of Semprún is that Améry had nothing to divulge to his torturers at Breendonk, although he confessed to a variety of political crimes that he readily invented. Semprún did, however, have information to divulge to the Gestapo

---

21. Semprún, *L'écriture ou la vie*, 149; Jorge Semprún, *Literature or Life*, 137, from which I have changed the translation of "naufragés" as "missing" to "drowned" in order to preserve Semprún's intertextual reference to Primo Levi's *The Drowned and The Saved*.

but remained silent. Améry's own observations on torture draw on Georges Bataille's discussion of sadism as best understood in the light of existential psychology insofar as it seeks to eradicate the world and the other in order for the torturer to be able to establish his own total sovereign power. Améry contends that "whoever was tortured, stays tortured" and that the experience of torture is alienating because it entails an encounter with a unique form of power that enacts both physiological and psychological dominance.[22] In the asocial world of the torturer, according to Améry, it is the torturer who is the survivor: "the power of the torturer, under which the tortured moans, is nothing other than the triumph of the survivor over the one who is plunged from the world into agony and death."[23] By contrast, as noted above, Semprún refuses to concede any victory to his torturers (be that construed by their "survival" or by his own psychological distress).

In Semprún's discussion of torture in *Exercices de survie* what counts is the ideological worldview that drives his political commitment to reject a world in which torture and oppression triumph. The question and practice of survival in relation to torture implicitly alludes to a question posed by a Resistance fighter, Henri, who was incarcerated and tortured by the French milices in Jean-Paul Sartre's *Morts sans sépulture*: "Do you still feel alive while men beat you until they break your bones?"[24]

Here, as in Semprún's writing, torture and survival are linked to the parameters of the human: how and even why does one continue to live in a world in which human beings torture each other? The question posed by Henri in Sartre's play was specifically taken up by Theodor Adorno as a crucial metaphysical question insofar as it broached "the possibility of any affirmation of life" after Auschwitz.[25] For Semprún such an affirmation becomes possible through a political commitment to change the world as illustrated by a maxim from F. Scott Fitzgerald's 1936 essay, "The Crack-Up," which Semprún cited as a personal ethic and one that encapsulated, in his view,

22. Améry, "La torture," 70; "Torture," 34.
23. Améry, "La torture," 78; "Torture," 40.
24. Jean-Paul Sartre, *Morts sans sépulture, Théâtre I* (Paris: Gallimard, 1947), 263; Jean-Paul Sartre, *Three Plays: Men Without Shadows*, trans. Kitty Black (Harmondsworth: Penguin, 1962), 225.
25. Theodor Adorno, *Metaphysics: Concept and Problems*, ed. Rolf Tiedeman, trans. Edmund Jephcott (Cambridge: Polity, 2000), 111.

the finest definition of the dialectic: "One should be able to see that things are hopeless and yet be determined to change them."[26]

In *L'écriture ou la vie*, in a section that alludes to Kant's theory of radical evil and Hannah Arendt's notion of the "banality of evil," Semprún links torture to the parameters of the human and the freedom to do good as well as evil:

> Everything is human: nothing of what is called inhuman in our superficial moral language, which renders everything commonplace, is beyond man. [. . .] In Buchenwald, the SS, the *Kapos*, the informers, the sadistic torturers all belonged to the human race just as much as the best and purest among us, among the victims . . . The frontier of Evil is not that of inhumanity, it's something else altogether. Hence the necessity for a moral philosophy that transcends this original foundation from which spring both the freedom of Good and the freedom of Evil . . . An ethics, therefore, that has broken free forever of theodicies and theologies, since God, by definition [. . .] is innocent of Evil.[27]

In this plea for an atheistic ethics, Semprún rejects not only the mystification of "Holocaust piety" that refuses to face what humanity may not dare to understand in itself, but also the piousness of any belief system that aligns morality with certain social groups since it will fail to account for the parameters of the human in all human beings in which the freedom to respect or to abnegate the other person exists at every moment.[28] This "impiety" on Semprún's part is born of a bitter political and moral experience that revealed to him that all ideologies and belief systems must be subject to question on a continual basis in order to assess if they respect human freedom in their practices and in their theoretical elaborations. In that sense, torture as an abnegation of human freedom and a subjugation of the other is never justified in the service of any ideology or belief system. Semprún's courage, like that of Améry and Alleg, in broaching "the question" in *Exercices de survie* from the perspective of the victim exposes it as an intensified practice of survival that both tests and exemplifies the parameters of human connection and solidarity.

26. My translation. Semprún, "Prélude," *Le langage est ma patrie, Entretiens avec Franck Appréderis*, 16.
27. Semprún, *L'écriture ou la vie*, 174–75; *Literature or Life*, 164.
28. For an explanation of "Holocaust piety" as a mystificatory retreat to the ineffable in the face of the Holocaust as something that we dare not understand for fear of it being only too human, see Gillian Rose, *Mourning Becomes the Law : Philosophy and Representation* (Cambridge, Cambridge University Press, 1996), 43.

MARCUS COELEN

"*Travelling arrière et circulaire*": Jorge Semprun's Script Writing

A film script is a challenging entity for criticism. Its destiny is to disappear, its function to contribute to a screen production in which it dissolves and is forgotten behind image, music, and voice.

Film scripts can nevertheless become "objects" of literary criticism. And when they do, they can remind criticism of its own peculiar place in the "economy" of forgetting and remembering, of memory and the vanishing of the past. As a presence contrary to the intent of its function, the movie script captured by criticism reveals it to be more of a "construction" than an "interpretation." It is helpful to recall here Freud's distinction between the two, although it was made in a totally different context, for it applies to history in a general sense. "Construction" is understood by Freud as directing attention to that in the past which almost necessarily had to be forgotten; and, being neither remembering, nor fiction or pure invention, construction is thus an attempt at grasping a "historical truth"[1] that reveals at the same time a truth about history itself. Neither reducible to positivistic facticity nor to an abstract historical meaning distilled out of the traces of the past, this type of historical truth embodies its own need to be forgotten, the attempts and effects of its being suppressed, or simply the transient nature of events. Only a construction of a specific type can come close to both the forgotten truth as well as to the truth that forgetting is part of history. It reminds us that rewritings are by no means accidental to a history that could in principle be free of them but that they are, on the contrary, essential to it.

---

1. Sigmund Freud, "Constructions in Analysis" in *The Standard Edition of the Complete Psychological Works of Sigmund Freud*, ed. James Strachey, vol. 23 (London: Hogarth Press and the Institute of Psycho-Analysis, 1953), 255–70.

YFS 129, *Writing and Life, Literature and History: On Jorge Semprun,* ed. Razinsky, © 2016 by Yale University.

One is also reminded here of one of Jorge Semprun's most quoted sentences, in *L'écriture ou la vie,* concerning the possibility of testifying to the experience of the death camps: "Only the artifice of a masterly narrative will prove capable of conveying some of the truth of this testimony."[2] This sentence expresses an idea underlying all of Semprun's writing: the opposition of an artifice (of literary nature) to a truth (of historical essence)—in which the former serves as privileged vehicle or even sole form of manifestation of the latter—organizes his entire endeavor of inscribing his productions into the texture of historicity.

A similar dichotomy is presented to the viewer in the written words that appear on the screen at the beginning of Alain Resnais's movie *Stavisky* (1974),[3] for which Semprun composed the script. After the opening credits, among which the name of screenwriter appears, a short text tells us that the "events" that the movie is said to render as "exact" have nevertheless been supplemented and altered in such a way so "imagination" can play its part in historical apperception. At the outset of the movie, we might feel invited, thus, to perceive a strong and direct desire on the part of the "authors" to produce writing, literally on the screen; but at the same time, it is the idea of construction or artifice in the guise of "imagination" that is given to be read, thus shaping the moving object in the making.

From this point on, Semprun's scripts can be seen as a focal point for a multiple *mise en abyme:* Semprun's historical "constructivism" and "fictionalism" are intensified by the artificial, almost "virtual" nature of the film script in relation to the movie that was shot and projected; this intensification in turn reflects the act of critical reading, whose job it is not to only analyze or comment on what is "given," but to construct, paradoxically, the conditions of appearance of that very material it set out to read , inventing it more than remembering it. The following fictitious example helps render the complexity of this *mise en abyme* as object of criticism: imagine a movie, beyond the confusing and complex layers of which an artwork would have to be virtually constructed, that is somehow "about" this very movie production—not as an effort of producing images to *see,* but rather as the means to make the viewer *think* and *invent* that which cannot be seen in it. The viewer produces all the stratifications of time lost

2. Jorge Semprun, *Literature or Life,* trans. Linda Coverdale (New York: Penguin, 1997), 13–14.
3. Alain Resnais, *Stavisky* (1974).

in the images that are "present"; the unheard and unknown words spoken off-screen by characters as well as uttered on the set by those contributing to the making of the movie; the gestures, techniques, and machines that are not visible on the screen but that nevertheless are the condition of the film's possibility; the appearance "in" the cut, not of what is edited and assembled together during the editing process, but rather of what has been *cut out*, i.e. an entire, not total and virtual world or non-world, by far more complex and undetermined than the indeterminacy and complexity of the picture itself. This virtual dimension outside the movie, cut out by it, can be seen as an equivalent to what can be appreciated in "Jorge Semprun's screenwriting," beyond that which can be read in the actual scripts.

But isn't this comparison an exaggeration of the artifices necessary for critical appreciation? And don't movies like the one just imagined indeed exist, including Resnais's *L'année dernière à Marienbad*,[4] and perhaps his *Stavisky*? But are we not, on the other hand, with the type of memory produced in these movies, a memory the modality of which is a "productive negative," very far from Semprun, the author of recollection, of the possibility, however complicated and painful, of appropriation, conservation, and just appreciation of the historical and personal past as well the social promises of a political future based on memory?

These three questions must be answered affirmatively. For Resnais, one of the appealing elements in both Semprun's work and personality perhaps was their opting for positive—psychological, cultural, and linguistic—memory, their tendency toward preservation and rendering a present that can be seen in *Le grand voyage*[5] and, time and again, in *L'écriture ou la vie*, as well as in many of Semprun's essays. Resnais's own work was, on the contrary, devoted to research into the anti-psychological and a-personal or multi-personal time and memory of the movies; not *about* history, but rather as *part of* history's open horizon.

One might object here that the gravity of the historical events Semprun refers to when he speaks of the "double task" to "master the past in a critical manner" and to build "principles for a [. . .] future that allows us to avoid the mistakes of the past,"[6] should be

    4. Resnais, *L'année dernière à Marienbad* (1961).
    5. Semprun, *Le grand voyage* (Paris: Gallimard, [1963] 2001).
    6. Semprún, "Ni héros ni victimes. Weimar-Buchenwald" (1995), in *Le fer rouge de la mémoire* (Paris: Gallimard [Quarto], 2012), 939. Translations, here and throughout, are by the author unless noted otherwise.

considered on an entirely different level from that of the film script as writing that vanishes in the production of a visual that itself disappears in a virtual image of which no one can claim to be the master. But that would mean not taking seriously the author Semprun, who quotes Maurice Blanchot at the beginning of *L'écriture ou la vie*: "Whoever wishes to remember must trust to oblivion, to the risk entailed in forgetting absolutely, and to this wonderful accident that memory then becomes."[7] And it would mean not taking seriously the writer who acknowledges the gravity of literary choices. Writing is even understood to threaten life: "Professional writers, whose lives are bounded and consumed by writing itself, who have no other biography than that of their texts, would be incapable of bringing it off."[8] Making only "literary" choices would thus be choosing death.

One of the most "professional" ways of writing then, a type of writing determined by the impersonal mechanisms and constraints of cultural production like no other—screenwriting, in other words—must have had a particular and complicated status for the author Semprun. Perhaps the film script, bound to disappear, had to disappear in a particular manner lest life disappear with it. The theme of the double life—serious in *La guerre est finie*,[9] frivolous in *Stavisky*; the topic of the violent interruption of life and its painful projection into an entirely altered environment for a "second life"—as in *L'aveu*[10]; or the literary attraction of a mere letter indicating life itself—as the Greek "z" also means "he is alive" in the movie *Z*,[11] all draw virtual figures on the screen where the movies homonymous to them are projected and thus give shape to the peculiar destiny of the life of a script.

The movie *Stavisky* gives a peculiar twist to the question of the reanimation of the past. One could go as far as to affirm, with Gilles Deleuze, who talks about "the strangeness of *Stavisky*," that in this movie a specific, image-linked spatiality occurs, not easily reducible to the "space" in which stories can be narrated: "The image no longer has movement as its primary characteristic but topology and

7. Semprun, epigraph to *Literature or Life*.
8. Ibid., 52.
9. Alain Resnais, *La guerre est finie* (1966).
10. Costa-Gavras, *L'aveu* (1970).
11. Costa-Gavras, *Z* (1969).

time."[12] Even if one did not agree with this interpretation one would easily understand its basis in the succession of non-chronological and non-narrative sequences and illustrative shots in that movie. And in the same way, one would not understand, or accept, an interpretation similar to the one offered by Deleuze concerning *Stavisky* of Semprun's *Le grand voyage*, a work in which the fragmentation of temporal linearity and spatial homogeneity always leads to making memory and narrative representation more complex, rather than leading us to imagine time itself, or to deduce the topological space of images. Whereas Resnais revolutionized cinematographic creation and contributed to giving cinema a genuine questioning of the possibilities of truth, Semprun deployed, skillfully yet restrictively, the modernist techniques of the novel in order to represent what was true to him in history, politics, and biographical experience.

A conflict, a discrepancy, or at least a tension has thus to be hypothesized at the heart of the collaboration between Resnais and Semprun, and it is one of the most important elements in a critical appreciation of the latter's work as screenwriter. In order to restrain the artificial exaggeration necessary for such a claim, it might be useful and sufficient simply to pay particular attention to some of those moments where traces of this hypothesis become more clearly visible or more explicitly readable. Some examples: in a 1966 conversation between Semprun and the film critic Jean-Louis Pays about *La guerre est finie*,[13] Semprun talks at length about his work as screenwriter for Renais's movie; in the book published in 1974 under the title *Alain Renais's "Stavisky"*[14]; and in the similar publication *La guerre est finie* that followed the making of the movie of the same name in 1966.[15] Furthermore, and without a systematic "comparison," it is by means of creating constellations of elements from movie and script— for both *La guerre est finie* and *Stavisky*—that we can to retrace some of the ways in which script writing's destiny to disappear marked parts of Semprun's work. A more thorough examination of what can be perceived and analyzed in the work of the screenwriter Semprun

12. Gilles Deleuze, *Cinema 2. The Time-Image*, trans. Hugh Tomlinson and Robert Galeta (Minneapolis: Minnesota University Press, 1989), 125.

13. Jean-Louis Pays, "Un film experimental. Entretien avec Jorge Semprun," (1966), in *Alain Resnais, Positif, revue de cinema* (Paris: Gallimard, 2002), 187–206.

14. Semprun, *Le "Stavisky" d'Alain Resnais* (Paris: Gallimard, 1974).

15. Semprun, *La guerre est finie: scénario du film d'Alain Resnais* (Paris: Gallimard, 1966).

would present similar conclusions. (Recent publications have well documented the work of Semprun the screenwriter, laying out their subjects and offering a framework for their hermeneutic appreciation, and the reader is referred to these works.[16])

In the 1966 interview with Pays on the occasion of Semprun's collaboration with Resnais in the making of the movie *La guerre est finie*, Semprun conceives the function of authorship in its relation to a filmmaking and to movie production as a peculiar one: "Even if Resnais does indeed not write a single word or put a single comma in the text, one has still to underline that there is no colon in the script either that would have been put in without a discussion preceding it."[17] As if Semprun had been a scribe of sorts: the scrivener of a text produced by a multiple voice called "discussion." Even if Semprun is the most dominant personality in it, script writing is nevertheless alluded to as the action and product of a certain impersonality. To the extent that Semprun is, in a strong sense, the author of anything in *La guerre est finie*, he would most likely have authorized the surrendering of his words to the filmmaker who, in turn, only uses them as elements along with the mechanisms, framing, turning, and tracking of the camera, as the substance of diminishment, the shrinking nerves of memory for the presence of forgetting in the guise of images on the screen.

The voiceover, a prominent feature of the movie, does not undermine the neutralization of linguistic elements in Resnais's cinematography. On the contrary, the voiceover or language spoken off screen is, as in other films by Resnais, important for what is not said, or rather for what can in principle never be said by it: it diverges not from any particular image, but rather functions as the negative reminder of the divergence itself, of movements and turns, as well as objects and apparatuses of shifts, transpositions, and separations. In one sequence, for example, where the main character, Diego, is on his way to a meeting of the clandestine committee of the Spanish

16. See *"Cinéma et engagement: Jorge Semprun scénariste," CinémAction* 140 (2011), as well as Esteve Riambau, "The Clandestine Militant Who Would Be Minister: Semprun and Cinema" and Txetxu Aguada, "Dissidence, Citizenry, and Witnessing: Three Screenplays by Jorge Semprun," both in *A Critical Companion to Jorge Semprun. Buchenwald, Before and After*, ed. Ofelia Ferrán and Gina Hermman (New York: Palgrave Macmillan, 2014), 71–88, 187–201. See also the "Introduction" to this volume by the editors, 1–37.
17. Semprun, *Entretien*, 188.

Communist Party in the outskirts of Paris, the voice from off screen, addressing Diego as well as "us," viewers, in the informal second person singular "*tu,*" names the places and metro stations Diego has to pass by or stop at: "You know these outskirts . . . you know this landscape with your eyes closed," the voice affirms after having listed well-known toponyms of the greater Paris region. The images first are loosely related to those names—subway entrances, steps, street corners, Diego meeting someone in front of a building, and so on— as if to illustrate the repetitive nature of these clandestine encounters. The rapid succession and superposition of extra-short shots of Diego passing posters, graffiti, or billboards on no longer localized Parisian walls, however, projects these images out of the narrative time and into an undetermined dimension of the film image itself: in frames not mastered by writing, but ones that expose printed letters in their relative impossibility to be read. For the rapid cuts only show us that there is writing on the wall in these posters behind the passing character, but do not allow us enough time to read the words; we might just be quick enough to conjecture that one poster invited us to "Learn How to Dance." In a moment like this—a flash of cinematographic apperception—the movie no longer has an illustrative function in relation to the language we hear or the story we imagine is unfolding; rather, it allows us to see and think its own independence, the disconnectedness of the movie image jumping away from its narrative domestication. The published script does not mention the urban scenery, focusing instead on the two characters, Diego and his comrade: "They perform gestures, movements of their arms, hands, void of meaning."[18] Yet the text of the script contains the very resources for the dynamics by which it veers away from itself while the images follow their own path. The encounter of script and image is twisted and seems to turn into a commentary on their very independence from each other.

In this same sequence, Diego, on his way to one of the meetings and accompanied by his comrade, briefly turns around at the moment the voice from off screen mentions his "return" from his country, Spain, to his exile in France. His gaze follows a group of school children walking in the opposite direction, as if it is attracted by the staffage and voiceless or murmuring decor of the moving image. On the one hand, these divergences can be seen as mere ironic commen-

18. Semprun, *La guerre est finie,* 108.

taries by the visible on the story being told by the script in form of the voiceover. On the other hand, it is difficult not to perceive the detachment from narration or other modes of language that is performed by the cinematographic elements in *La guerre est finie*, the independent choreography of the tracking shots (called *"travelling"* in the anglophile French idiom of cinematology), cuts, and crystal-like clusters of fragmented flashes of diverse temporal layers that are difficult to categorize with stale terms like "flashback," "flashforward." All these elements drift away from the textual which then, retrospectively and belatedly, becomes less the basis for their production, rather appearing as an invitation to be declared a part of history that is, if not "finished," then at least to be "detached from." Another sequence that occurs near the beginning of the story, in which Diego tries to find the meeting place of his clandestine group in one of the housing projects in the Parisian outskirts, makes this movement of separation very explicit. We see Diego approach the buildings, and we can quote the script's version as an approximate description of the sequence that follows:

> He walks toward the block of buildings closest to him. In a dark colored relief the letter "E" is set apart from grey concrete in the entrance hall. . . . There is the letter "D" in the entrance hall of the first tower and this is not yet where he is. . . . The second tower shows the letter "G" and here he enters. . . . He stops in front of the door 107 and rings the bell.[19]

After an unknown woman opens the door, denying that the Madame Lopez Diego he had asked for lives there, he repeats from memory: "Building 'G,' tenth floor, door 107."[20] The female stranger inhabiting this spot confirms that this is accurate and eventually, after an exchange of smiles, closes the door. "He sees, at the door, the three numbers that do not mean anything anymore: 107."[21] The sequence is a remarkable condensation in which a micro-narrative dynamic or movement through space and time is organized by an alphabetic mini-series with a cipher attached, to which a fractured section of the plot telling of the disappearance of comrades over the span of a year is added, the two levels joining in both forming and illustrating the character's experience of loss of continuity and consistency in the

19. Ibid., 45–46.
20. Ibid., 47.
21. Ibid.

network of memories and experiences called life, as well as hinting at the break with party communism. When the door is shut, a biographical and historical dynamics is closed down, and "107" does not mean anything anymore. The war is over. The story is told. And yet, the succession of images has occurred and their "space" and "time"—or, in psychological terms, the "memory" they form in the viewer, or, in more philosophical terms, the "thought" they become—seem to belong to a different order as well. It is precisely the visual insistence on the literal inscription that makes those ciphers "E," "D," "G," "107" hard to ignore or forget, without giving them, however, a different or even precise meaning. As if they had been thrown into a cinematographic existence in which they move from writing to image, and on into drawings or even scribbling, together with the geometries of indifferent edges and corners, shifting frames and gyrating shots, the contingencies the stuff of which history is made and that matters in a different way than in only being told. And it is the virtual side of the script, the one to be reconstructed, that will have written it down.

From here on, the historical and biographical conflicts presented in the plot—the war is over, party communism is over, this idea of the past has to be left behind, a man is changing his life—turns into just one of the elements in a struggle of images and words, of perception, memories, and thought, a struggle that cannot be reduced to questions of aesthetics or form. For what is at stake is the nature of historical existence itself, instantiated not only *in*, but *as* cinematography. And the published script takes this stake very seriously, stating the following from the very first line, as if feeling threatened in its existence and having to stand its ground in a battle with the moving image: "From the first image on, perhaps even a split second before the first image shoots forth, the Voice of the Narrator makes itself heard."[22] In this script published post-factum, the direct, second person singular address of the narrator in the film—"*You* came to see Juan, a year ago. Building 'G,' tenth floor, door 107, at Mrs. Lopez's. *You* think *you* remember"[23]—is synthesized in the clearly constructed main character. This is done by means of its alignment with the third-person narrative in those long sections of the text that are neither dialogue nor the "Voice of the Narrator," but that form the even more tran-

---

22. Ibid., 11; in the quote "la Voix du Narrateur," both terms are indeed capitalized; the following paragraphs repeat the beginning: "It (the Voice) makes itself heard . . ."
    23. Ibid., 48 (my Italics).

scendental voice of the omniscient literary narrator who is both a distant and at times summarizing observer of the movie's images: *"He looks around, disconcerted. . . . He sees the three numbers on the door . . ."*[24] Yet in the movie, "he" does not see, that is, on the screen his seeing is not visible. Whereas the linguistic mechanism of pronouns binds the "he" with "his" verbal actions and "us" to it as readers to a character, on the screen this mechanism is neutralized. Here, "he" does not see alone—a "he" is seen, a door is seen, a number is being read or rendered visible, etc. And the whole is a movie being thought. Because onto the screen an image is projected and reflected to eyes and ears that are equally addressed by *"you."* Because it is addressed to the person thinking the movie, rather than attributed to a character, the image is undetermined in both its belonging to and targeting the viewer, who has both a virtual and essential role to play. He or she has to form hypotheses concerning the "belonging" of what is seen. The point-of-view shot—the character sees the door—is just one of these hypotheses.

The disjunction and multiplicity at the heart of the movie are classified and put into narrative in the script as "mental images"[25] belonging to the character, in an effort to present the film as a sequence of psycho-graphical snippets of memories, dreams, perceptions, imaginations, and so on. Semprun's script, in its reappropriation of cinema's a-personal and anti-psychological movement, of the image drifting away from the mental and into thought and history, releases at the same time—with a generosity not always accounted for by itself—its writing from the realm of the novel into what it cannot master as creation on the screen. Pays, in his interview, underlines in *La guerre est finie* that the main character belongs more to the world of cinematography than to the world of representation: "Trains, suitcases, borders, travels, as well as all which he is haunted by, the fear of the telephoto lens, dodging, false contacts, etc. make up his true environment."[26] Semprun agrees with Pays and thus recognizes that the film critic sees in a movie first of all its cinematographic essence, which depends on the way a film's moves, frames, shots, angles, contacts, and cuts are laid out for temporal and spatial apperception. Not that the language of a script does not have a role to play in this,

24. Ibid., 47.
25. Ibid., 38.
26. Semprun, *Entretien*, 198.

but only in as much as it enters the essential techno-graphics of the movie.

Through this insight into screenwriting, an additional layer of complexity is added to the already complicated question of the autobiographical dimension of *La guerre est finie*. For not only does the party-sanctioned activist, the one whose decisions and maneuvers are accounted for by the organ of dramatic consequences called dialectical materialism, recede from the stage of history—this is true for Semprun as well as for Diego—but so does the writer recede from the scene of production. To the dichotomy of *L'écriture ou la vie* is added, probably inadvertently, the peculiar life of cinematographic writing that does not easily concede to either writing or life, nor to their dialectic or supplementary relation. The journey of Semprun the screenwriter that had its first major stop with *La guerre est finie* leads to a space-time where writing also does not stop ending and where life begins reanimating death as image, in the ghostly world of cinema.

A hint to spectral living can be heard in the penultimate frame of *Stavisky*: "'There are no dead, only drowned people.'"[27] This quote from Jean Giraudoux, spoken by a ghost in the play *Intermezzo*, is repeated here by Baron Raoul, a friend of the late Stavisky and *paredros* to the one who calls himself "Alexandre the Great." Under the name Serge Alexandre, Stavisky is the owner of the *Théâtre de l'Empire*. As scriptwriter, actor, and director of a fraudulent plot involving the French *monde*, he plays the role of a rich entrepreneur to cover up his former life as the impostor he had illustriously been. Toward the middle of the movie this character, Stavisky/Alexandre/the actor Jean-Paul Belmondo, reads the lines quoted again at the end, "[t]here are no dead, only drowned people," aloud on stage. The con artist, impresario, and actor in life replaced a "real" actor on stage in order to help a young actress who had come to an audition at his theater. The woman, a German Jew forced into flight and who alludes to Shakespeare's *The Merchant of Venice* in her audition, will reappear interwoven into the movie's parallel story at a later moment when she has become friends with one of Trotsky's young French followers. True to her family name, "Wolfgang," on which Stavisky will comment, she stealthily but intransigently moves her conspicuously fictional character through the story. The entanglement of quotes, borrowed

27. "*Stavisky*, Alain Resnais." Special issue, *L'avant-scène Cinéma* 156 (March 1975): 51; Semprun, *Le "Stavisky" d'Alain Resnais*, 190.

voices, staged images, the play-within-a-play dimension around the ghostly line from Giraudoux—all of this is nearly infinite, yet condensed at the end in a short moment when the "talking head" Baron Raoul recites the quote, followed by a cut to the image of Belmondo's body who is made up to look like Stavisky disfigured by a bullet to the head, and from which the camera moves backward in a circular tracking shot, "*travelling arrière et circulaire*." A hypertextual and mnemotechnical mirror hall into which thought has to swirl, worthy of Resnais, and with the name of Semprun attached to it. We are being drowned in a sea of cinematography to be sure.

The script of *Stavisky* comes to us in two very different versions. One can be found in the journal *L'avant-scène*, which since 1961 has been publishing monthly *découpages* and transcripts. In March 1975, an issue was published on *Stavisky*, only a few months after an even more indirect publication of the "same" script had appeared: Gallimard presented a monograph by Semprun under the ambiguous title *Le "Stavisky" d'Alain Resnais*. Whereas *L'avant-scene* as always clearly states its referent: the movie seen and meticulously analyzed,[28] the reader of Semprun's book enters a strange, slightly Borgesian fictional world. The author Semprun, whose name could have been seen on screen under the heading "*Scénario et dialogues*," publishes a book on Resnais's movie—the title's possessive construction makes it very clear that "*Stavisky*" is the filmmaker's property of sorts—as if the book were *about* it or a (literary) version *of* it. Then, a peculiar subtitle or indication of genre is added: "*scenario*" (script) is placed where one usually finds "*roman*" (novel) "*récit*" (narrative) or something similar, on the cover and title page of the book. The monograph appears in 1966, as did *La guerre est finie*,[29] in Gallimard's famous *Collection blanche*. Any explanation of the relation between the text in this volume and the words spoken, the images framed, the shots taken, or the decor chosen in Resnais's *Stavisky* is carefully avoided. The book rather employs the rhetoric of allusive notoriety: the movie just came out with great commercial success. But even without this success, the signifier "Stavisky" is supposed to be known by everyone. The

---

28. We read in the "Foreword" of *L'avant-scène* that "the *découpage* has been established, as always, at a viewer *(visionneuse)*, shot by shot" (11).

29. The play of title and subtitle is here less surprising, more explanatory, *La guerre est finie* being followed by "*scénario du film d'Alain Resnais*."

dust jacket is unusual for Gallimard at the time. It camouflages the legendary *NRF* aspect by a variety of fonts, including the one used for the movie credits, and even claims that there is the possibility that our own "era" has begun with this name. Not only that, it warns the reader in an anonymous text on the back cover that *death* is at stake with the book: "Death of an era, thus, in the two senses of the word. One era dies and another one begins: one of death, of a death having become the general rule, rendered banal. Yet have we ever left this era?"[30] Stavisky, the name attached to a political and economic scandal that brought down the government and triggered a fascist uprising in Paris on February 6, 1934, was, on the cover of the book at the time at least, a well-known symbol for history stretching into the "now."

But the "here and now" of this book is difficult to locate. For one thing is certain: the "Stavisky" of *The "Stavisky" of Alain Resnais* is not Resnais's *Stavisky*. It is—if it is anybody's at all—a *"Stavisky"* created by Semprun's readers, and the "script," while loosely reminding cultural memory or contemporaries of Semprun's professional role as screenwriter, provides the script for a construction of the imagination that does not have a proper name. Reminiscent of "Pierre Ménard, author of the Quixote" that Semprun mentions elsewhere,[31] a less extreme though no less original version of an identical yet totally different and thus peculiarly imaginary text is presented with this *"scenario"* that resembles an existing movie while nevertheless being the script of a work that does not exist.

So who is the Jorge Semprun whose name is on the cover of the published script (*scenario*) in relation to the Jorge Semprun, author of the film script? This text conjures up the dead as laughing specters. Baron Raoul addresses us in the final words of *Stavisky*: "Ah, I imagine his laughter if he reappeared among us."[32] But, when he was still a living image, "Stavisky" was deprived of his laughter on the screen animating him: Where the one Stavisky laughs—"he laughs crazily"[33]—in Semprun's book version of the scene in which the impostor's plot crumbles—the other Stavisky on Resnais's screen does not laugh at all. Incarnated in Belmondo, he becomes the correlate of

---

30. Semprun, *Le "Stavisky" d'Alain Resnais*, dust jacket, and back cover text.
31. See Semprún, "Mal et modernité" (1990), in *Le feu rouge de la mémoire* (Paris: Gallimard [Quarto], 2012), 696.
32. Semprun, *Le "Stavisky" d'Alain Resnais*, 190; again, the script based on the movie presents a variant: "Can you image his laughter . . . ?" (*L'avant-scène*, 51)
33. Semprun, *Le "Stavisky" d'Alain Resnais*, 170.

an elaborate and conspicuous camera movement: in the screen version of the same scene, a circular shot is taken around the character, who wears an angry expression. And this disjunction is repeated,
a second *fou rire* is replaced by cinematic gyration: a second time
Semprun's *"scénario"* presents Alexandre "laughing with his crazy
laugh"[34] while Resnais's camera is ordered to take a diagonal pan
shot, and Belmondo is not even smiling. This divergence between literary laughter and a cinematographic movie opens interesting critical
possibilities. Minute and insignificant as these differences may seem,
Semprun will have left us with a script for those gestures, probably
without the intention of writing it. His legacy, to memory and the
though of history, is perhaps not entirely voluntary and all the more
generous in the uncanny displacements between the *grand voyage*
and uncountable instances of *travelling*.

34. Ibid., 172.

EMMANUEL BOUJU

In and Out: The names of Jorge Semprún, between France and Spain

He does not live in the name of his personal life.

—Franz Kafka

A personal imperative is perceptible throughout Jorge Semprún's *The Long Voyage*. The author formulates it in a paradoxical way: "I must not speak in my own name, but in the name of the things that happened."[1] By adopting this principle he places his entire work under the aegis of a specific literary ethic based on the fact of speaking (speaking and writing not being really distinct for Semprún in either letter or spirit) "in the name of" history — meaning the history that a personal name connotes and stands for.

This literary ethic relies on a personalist kind of commitment inspired far more by Paul-Louis Landsberg and the journal *Esprit* than by Sartre and *Les temps modernes*, on an ethical-esthetic choice —a "value model" as Calvino would say[2] —that makes the question of the name fundamental: not only because the name underpins a mandate or act of delegation (in the sense that a surviving witness must "speak in the name of" by adopting an identity lost but entrusted to him), but also because the name embodies a destination (speaking "in" or "to" the name of), an intention, a unique aim that gives rise to it and establishes it definitively "in its own right." In the passage of *The Long Voyage* just cited, the narrative is dedicated to the name of the Jewish children—those whom Nazi persecution meant to erase

---

1. Jorge Semprun, *Le grand voyage* [1963] (Paris: Gallimard, 2000), 193. English translation by Richard Seaver: *The Long Voyage* (New York: Grove, 1964; Overlook Press, 2005; entitled *The Cattle Truck* in some editions).
2. Italo Calvino, "Usages politiques de la littérature," in *La machine littérature* (Paris: Seuil, 1984), 82. English translation by Patrick Creagh: *The Literature Machine: Essays* (New York: Random House, 2011).

YFS 129, *Writing and Life, Literature and History: On Jorge Semprun*, ed. Razinsky, © 2016 by Yale University.

by turning them into things—"things that happened" in that they were slaughtered.[3]

Similarly, elsewhere—indeed everywhere—in Semprún's work, the name is never acquired beforehand, nor is it registered after the fashion of a trademark or set once and for all: it is always assigned by the *history* (or History) to which it belongs and constituted by the *story* that it tells; it is never fully fixed or completely defined save by means of writing, as I will now attempt to show.

1. THE NAME AS PASSWORD

When one considers Jorge Semprún's "proper" or "personal" name, it is apparent that it is always partial, always provisional, and always potentially dual in nature.

It is a name at once French and Spanish with a very slight variation in the way it is written (Semprún/Semprun) that points up the difference between the two languages and their pronunciation: on the one hand the mother tongue, the original language with its accent, namely Spanish, and, on the other, the adopted language, French, which, by virtue of its double "nasalization" of the original surname, its voicing of -*em* and -*un*, incorporates it into a new speech register. The removal of the tonic accent from the second syllable constitutes a remarkably economical way of Gallicizing the original surname. As for the first name, there is no call for modification thanks to the phonetic happenstance that the natural French pronunciation of "Jorge," as written, precisely echoes that of the French "Georges."

This process of naturalization might be compared to that undergone by the name of Georges Perec, where, alongside the "normality" of the pronunciation and spelling of the first name, the absence of an accent on the family name (Perec rather than Pérec) discreetly signals the foreign roots of the paternal genealogy—the very genealogy which, according to Perec's *W, or the Memory of Childhood*, helps define a person's identity.[4]

---

3. In Semprun's novels, "arriver" (happen, occur) is often used as a synonym for "to die." This is the subject of my paper "In the Name of Things that Happened: Jorge Semprún and the Writing of History," in *A Critical Companion to Jorge Semprún: Buchenwald, Before and After*, ed. Gina Herrmann and Ofelia Ferrán (London and New York: Palgrave Macmillan, 2014), 125–34.

4. Georges Perec, *W ou le souvenir d'enfance* (Paris, Gallimard [L'imaginaire], 1993 [1975]), 57.

In Semprún's case, however, we are further confronted by the history of a name reduced to its bare bones by exile, yet capable of re-emerging in its entirety when Semprún's original Spanish identity comes back to the fore, reviving the Spanish double (paternal + maternal) naming convention: Jorge (de) Semprún Maura is a name with a double connotation of high birth (the particle of nobility being eschewed of course by the progressive ideology of direct lineage), as well as a double history figuring by turns in the forefront of Semprún's ethical, political, and esthetic heritage. That heritage is always double, whether José María de Semprún Gurrea and Susana Maura Gamazo, separately and together, evoke the Spanish Republic (the father was a minister in the Second Republic, while the maternal grandfather, Antonio Maura, was several times prime minister of Spain), or poetry and politics, or love and philosophy.[5]

We may go so far as to say that *all Semprún's names*, be they original or adopted, fictional or real, clandestine or official, bespeak this double identity, Spanish and French, which is of historical origin: whenever Semprún assumes a particular name (such as Federico Sánchez or Rafael Artigas), he means to speak "in the name of" the history that it enshrines. For him a proper name is always also a reinvented and collective name, and a fictional name is similarly at once personal and historical.[6]

It is clear, in particular, that the name of the "dead man needed" (*"Le mort quil faut"*) is central to Semprún's experience of Buchenwald, for this is the name that not only allows him to survive (by taking it and thus avoiding execution, leaving his own name for the man who no longer needs a name because he is already dead), but also teaches him once and for all how contingent identity is: "This was otherness acknowledged, existential identity perceived as the possibility of being other."[7] This consciousness of existential contingency, acquired in the thick of his experience of the camps, is precisely what so greatly facilitated Semprún's later systematic embrace of clandestine activity. He was to become one of the Spanish Communist Party's most important leaders and men of action and until 1964 he undertook missions into Franco Spain under the pseudonym

5. Jorge Semprún's father was even a correspondent from Spain of the personalist journal *Esprit* before the exodus of 1936.

6. On this point, see my "In the Name of Things that Happened."

7. Semprun, *Le mort qu'il faut* (*The Dead Man Needed*) (Paris: Gallimard, 2001), 43.

of Federico Sánchez. This is how that pseudonym came to be the "real" personal name of his Spanish identity. Or rather, if you will, the real personal name of his *second* Spanish identity, his strictly anti-Franco identity, subsequent to that of his childhood and prior to that of his life in democratic Spain. Federico Sánchez is the name of all the risks he ran, an assumed name but one that in a way made him "immortal," because, despite all those perils, he who bore it (who donned this pseudonymous identity) had already returned from the camps: Jorge Semprún was already endowed with "the insouciant immortality of the revenant" (so well explained in *Literature or Life*),[8] and therefore Federico Sánchez had barely any need to fear for his life.

Imagination and historicity thus combine throughout Semprún's bilingual oeuvre to construct his history on both sides of the border separating France from Spain and turn a name, in the words of *Le mort qu'il faut*, into "a password, a rallying cry, a gauntlet thrown down to death, to oblivion, to the evanescence of the world."[9] This is an identity, manufactured by means of writing, that makes the name analogous to a password, a means of being recognized and allowed to pass a frontier—exactly what Jacques Derrida, echoing the Old Testament and citing Paul Celan, called a "shibboleth."[10] "Federico Sánchez" functioned as just such a password for the purposes of the anti-Franco struggle: it was more useful, more valuable, during the time of clandestine resistance in Spain than the French "Jorge Semprun," but by the time *Autobiografía de Federico Sánchez* was published in 1977,[11] with democratization underway in Spain, it would serve above all as the borrowed identity whose illusions had eventually to be renounced despite the risk of condemnation and the rifts entailed thereby: a mask, the marker of a clandestine persona the recourse to which in the end turned elevated principles of political action against themselves.[12]

8. Semprun, *L'écriture ou la vie* (Paris: Gallimard, 1994), 257; English translation by Linda Coverdale: *Literature or Life* (New York: Viking, 1997), 248.

9. Semprun, *Le mort qu'il faut*, 89 (my translation [--trans.]).

10. Jacques Derrida, *Schibboleth. Pour Paul Celan* (Paris: Galilée, 1986).

11. Semprun, *The Autobiography of Federico Sanchez and the Communist Underground in Spain* [1977] (New York: Karz Publishers, 1979).

12. This is the theme, expressed in other terms, of the political novels *La deuxième mort de Ramón Mercader* (1969), whose subject is the man who assassinated Trotsky, and, very much later, *Netchaïev est de retour* (1987), which deals with the subterranean collusion between terrorism and raison d'État.

Like the pseudonym of the militant, all Semprún's names in his fiction are borrowed identities used as passwords, identities both contingent and necessary—contingent because they are intentionally artificial and transient but necessary in order to convey, to recount, and to "speak in the name of" the things that happened. This multiple identity is distinctly reminiscent of the well known utterance attributed to the celebrated novelist Pío Baroja as he left Spain during the Civil War: "*Se puede pasar?*" (Can one go through?). Everything suggests that each time he crossed the border, Semprún asked himself that question, which was originally framed in favor of the abolition of the frontier between Franco's Spain and democratic France (that primary frontier of exile and separation), and later to help free other European nations from their authoritarian subjugation.[13] Indeed Semprún never gave up posing this question, the point being to prevent dictatorships from acting with impunity within their territorial confines.

2. PERIPHRASES OF THE NAME

In a sense Jorge Semprún's entire work has a periphrastic relationship to a reversible name, a name with a double (Spanish and French) resonance. But this double identity has not always been either well understood or well received in Spain. Indications of more or less deliberate incomprehension and rejection are legion over the years since the 1960s, when Semprún's aliases were first revealed.

The first such indication is the complete, and astonishing, absence of the name Jorge Semprún from several well known and widely read histories of twentieth-century Spanish literature. It gets not a single mention either in the volume edited by Santos Sanz Villanueva for the publishing house Ariel (even in the third, revised edition of 1988),[14] or in volume 6 ("Época contemporánea") of *Historia de la Literatura Española*, edited by Ángel Valbuena Prat.[15]

13. Semprún is well known as the scriptwriter of such films as *Z* and *The Confession* and a champion of the causes (*¡no pasarán!*) of all anti-authoritarian rebellions.

14. *Historia de la Literatura Española*, vol. 6, part 2: "El Siglo XX. Literatura actual" (Barcelona: Editorial Ariel, 1984); third edition, 1988.

15. Ninth edition, expanded and updated by María del Pilar Palomo (Barcelona: Gustavo Gili, 1983). In this case, almost eight hundred pages contain only a reference to a Moraima de Semprún Donahue, the doubtless admirable author of a book on Blas de Otero, the mention of whom, as part of a list of several others in a simple note, seems almost designed to point up the total absence of his namesake.

Elsewhere Semprún's presence is so minor and ghostly that it implies nothing so much as a polite indifference on the part of editors, a kind of declaration of virtual irrelevance. For example, the eighth volume of Francisco Rico's celebrated *Historia y Crítica de la Literatura Española*, covering the "Contemporary Period, 1939–1980" and edited by Domingo Induráin, makes only two simple and brief references to *Autobiografía de Federico Sánchez*.[16]

It should be noted that Semprún's "return" to public life as a "Spanish writer" with the publication of *Autobiografía de Federico Sánchez*, a novel that won the 1977 Premio Planeta,[17] was not an unmitigated success. The moment even precipitated an (unsuccessful) lawsuit by a disgruntled finalist, Manuel Barrios, against José Manuel Lara, Planeta's famous millionaire owner. The negative reception may be seen as an eloquent expression of the difficulty for a Spain barely emancipated from the Franco era to accept the idea that Semprún was a truly "Spanish" writer and not merely a Spanish-speaking French one combined with a binational political activist.

Ten years later, within a now fully democratic country, echoes of that moment were still perceptible, as can be seen in Javier Goñi's description of Jorge Semprún, in the part of the collective volume *Letras Españolas 1976–1986* entitled *"Crónica literaria,"* as a *"novelista hecho en Francia,"* a novelist made in France.[18] By itself, the term *novelista hecho* would mean an accomplished novelist, but the "made in France" facilitated the drawing of a sharp distinction between Semprún and two challengers described as "Andalusian," namely Alfonso Grosso and Fernando Quiñones, whose regional origin, though all concerned wrote in Castilian, apparently made them more appropriate for consideration in Goñi's eyes. Granted, in the more "literary" portion of this volume, Darío Villanueva conceded that *Autobiografía de Federico Sánchez* makes use of "narrative forms"—meaning more properly literary ones—in support of a political thesis (Semprún's protest against his expulsion from the Spanish Communist Party for "Euro-

16. Francisco Rico, *Historia y Crítica de la Literatura Española* (Barcelona: Editorial Crítica, 1981). Not until the year 2000 and the "first supplement," edited by Jordi Gracia—vol. 9, part 1: "Los nuevos nombres, 1975–2000"—were two new but trivial mentions offset by the generous addition, as an appendix, of a substantial 1966 article on Semprún by Randolph Pope.

17. The award of this prize ensured publication by Planeta and above all wide distribution.

18. *Letras Españolas 1976–1986* (Madrid: Ministerio de Cultura/Editorial Castalia, 1987), 333.

communism"); but in order to justify himself for making this assessment, Villanueva invokes the passage of time: ten years, seemingly,
sufficed to make it arguable that Semprún's writing was not reducible purely and simply to polemical purposes—otherwise, Villanueva
added, implicitly echoing the complaint voiced by Manuel Barrios at
the time, Semprún could have been accused of exploiting the Planeta
Prize "as a commercial, and propagandist platform."[19]

In his *Crónica sentimental de la transición*,[20] published around
the same time, the novelist and essayist Manuel Vázquez Montalbán
(already very eminent in Spain) assigned an equally typical role to
Semprún (whose name he cited just twice): that of a kind of outsider,
present without being present, endorsing the reforms in Spain only
belatedly and without ever understanding them fully because of not
having experienced the trials of the Franco years from within.[21] One
note on *Autobiografía* did appear, and it was quite clear, but Montalbán animadverted very quickly to the picture Semprún draws of
Santiago Carrillo, apropos of which Montalbán in effect accused Semprún of having "waited fifteen years" to criticize Carrillo, and in this
respect quite failing to achieve harmony with the views of "the Spanish people" (from which community he was thus logically excluded).
The one and only direct quotation from Semprún was taken from an
article in *Le nouvel observateur* (signaling both spatial and temporal
distance), only to be instantly dismissed with a resounding "No!"
from Montalbán.[22]

It should be noted, though, that all reference works did not share
this attitude, for the reception was not completely one-sided. A case

19. Ibid., 43. As early as 1978, in a first version of this volume published by Castalia as part of *L'année littéraire espagnole: 1974–1978* (Madrid: Editorial Castalia, 1979).
Darío Villanueva began his discussion of the "the novel" for 1978 by bringing up the
Planeta Prize in order to ask whether *Autobiografía de Federico Sánchez* was really a
novel: "It is a novel in that Semprún prefers to employ the narrative form to communicate his 'truth.'" And he concludes as follows, mixing praise in the shape of the comparison to Baroja with the treacherous characterization of Semprún as a Spanish writer
despite himself: "by looking at the problem from this angle one is inclined to grant that
with this novel Semprún, perhaps despite himself, has integrated himself into Spanish
literature and that *Autobiografía de Federico Sánchez* is further proof of the protean
nature of that 'discipline without rules' practiced by Baroja and by all novelists."
20. Manuel Vázquez Montalbán, *Crónica sentimental de la transición* (Barcelona:
Planeta, 1985).
21. True, differing points of view about the history of the Spanish Communist
Party are involved here.
22. Montalbán , *Crónica*, 208.

in point is the dictionary of the *Centro de las Letras Españolas*, associated with the Spanish Ministry of Culture,[23] where the Spanish translations of Semprún's "French" books are presented as the works of a Spanish author and treated in exactly the same way as those written directly in Spanish.[24] Thus *The Long Voyage* is listed as *El largo viaje* and not under its original French title as *Le grand voyage*, and singled out, moreover, for having won the Prix Formentor in 1964—a prize representative of the anti-Franco opposition in exile that was bestowed just as Semprún was expelled from the Spanish Communist Party for "views diverging from the party line."

But in other instances, as in the recent *Dictionnaire des littératures hispaniques*, Semprún hardly exists as a Spanish writer, and the author of a brief entry on him chooses to concentrate on "what is perhaps his best French novel, *La deuxième mort de Ramón Mercader*."[25] In any event, Semprún is never really looked upon, for generational reasons, as one of the war-exiled writers who returned to their country: unlike Rafael Alberti or Francisco Ayala, he left Spain as a young adolescent with his family and continued his education in Paris until he was deported, so that he never went into exile as a writer. Consequently, in many Spanish eyes, his writing career was quite simply a French affair, regardless of the reasons, and the history of his various periods of antifascist resistance. This may explain the different treatment accorded to a Juan Goytisolo, who left later, already bathed in glory as a "Spanish writer" (despite the fact that Goytisolo's critique of traditional Spanish culture and of the peninsular imaginary was always fiercer than Semprún's).

Regardless of all the reactions to his ambiguous identity that characterize his unique relationship to Spanish history, Semprún was appointed Minister of Culture in Felipe González's Socialist government and served from 1988 to 1991. A witticism in vogue at the time dubbed him "French Minister of Spanish Culture" (a rarer variant being "Spanish Minister of French Culture").

23. *Diccionario de autores. Quién es quién en las letras españolas* (Madrid: Fundación Germán Sánchez Ruipérez/Pirámide, 1988), 242.

24. The same curious procedure is found later too, in 2000, in Jordi Gracia's supplement cited earlier (note 16): Semprún, writes Gracia, "returns to the autobiographical genre with *Federico Sánchez se despide de ustedes, La escritura o la vida/Literature or Life*, and *Adiós, luz de verano*."

25. Jordi Bonells (ed.), *Dictionnaire des littératures hispaniques* (Paris: Robert Laffont, 2009), 1328.

But whatever the nature, extent, and implications of this phenomenon of incomprehension, even hostility, it does not really have the power to overturn the peculiar logic of the Semprunian identity. The witticism just mentioned, for example, whether delivered in an affectionate tone or not, clearly bespeaks the place without a location —the writer's "paratopos" —in which Semprún put himself, involuntarily or deliberately, and which led him to dwell in a country that was neither France nor Spain but a mixture of the two, at once real and imaginary, material and fictional. A utopian country where Semprún wrote his second autobiographical novel, an exercise in distanciation, which was published in 1993 in the two languages simultaneously as *Federico Sánchez se despide de ustedes* and *Federico Sánchez vous salue bien.*[26]

So it scarcely mattered that Semprún continued, like it or not, to be seen in Spain as a "Communist writer," with all that the term implied of ineptitude at the formal level and of inability to get beyond the boundaries of realism—i.e., in effect, beyond the boundaries of the historical anti-Franco era; nor at least that he had long been directly involved, as an official and an intellectual, in the history of the Spanish Communist Party and later in that of the Spanish Workers' Socialist Party (PSOE). Twenty years after the Planeta Prize, he was still being labeled a "Communist writer" in the college textbook *Le roman espagnol contemporain*[27]—and it is true that he was one of those who kept vigil at the death of La Pasionaria (Dolores Ibarruri) — not a small thing in Spanish memory.

And no matter, either, that in France Semprun came gradually to be seen as a writer concerned almost exclusively, because of the critical and public success of *Literature or Life*, with the history of deportation (especially that of the *résistants* sent to Buchenwald), having earlier been chiefly known as a friend of Yves Montand, Simone Signoret, and François Mitterrand, as the scriptwriter of the successful director Costa-Gavras and, later, as a respectable member of the Académie Goncourt —"Jorge Semprun, Member of the Académie Goncourt" was an identifying attribution late in his life that appeared on every one of his novels published by Gallimard.

---

26. Semprún, *Federico Sánchez se despide de ustedes* (Barcelona: Tusquets, 1993); and *Federico Sánchez vous salue bien* (Paris: Grasset, 1993).

27. Jordi Bonells, *Le roman espagnol contemporain* (Paris: Nathan, 1998).

EMMANUEL BOUJU   137

The fact is that this deep Spanish-French dualism and all the mis-apprehensions that went with it are actually a true reflection of the identity of a man who never ceased to present a double face to the world as writer and political activist, novelist and screenwriter, or anti-authoritarian Communist and confirmed Europeanist. A Janus-despite-himself, then, who labored and agitated so that the "or" in "literature or life" should no longer be an exclusive distinction ("either literature or life") but rather an inclusive one ("literature, which is to say life").

CONCLUSION

"In this book," wrote Jorge Semprún some years ago in a copy of *Le mort qu'il faut* as part of a personal dedication to me, "fiction aims to do no more than accentuate reality." At the time I took these words as simply a way of describing his poetic method. Today, however, I also see them as a key to the reading of his name, a key thus discreetly and amiably offered me for later use: accentuating (i.e., accenting) the reality of *Semprun* meant rediscovering the original, Spanish fiction of *Semprún*—the identity that history had deprived him of, and that only literature (or life—the same thing) had allowed him to retrieve by becoming the authentic other face of his action.

The narrator of *Veinte años y un día* (*Twenty Years and a Day*)[28] puts it differently: "at each step, on each page, I collide with the reality of my own life, my personal experience, my memories." Which is what makes Semprún a French writer or a Spanish one, take your pick. As witness, this second major novel written in Spanish and published at the late date of 2003, in which Semprún (who is living in France at the time) chooses to retrace his steps by returning to their Spanish beginnings, recounting the lead-up to the Civil War but from the point of view of a character who is an outsider—a North American historian, Michael Leidson, who comes to investigate the strange celebration, twenty years after, of the murder on 18 July 1936 (the exact date of the outbreak of the Civil War) of a landowner by his day laborers. In this novel Semprún gives a last pseudonym to his autofictional double, the "Narrator," calling him Agustín Larrea

28. Semprún, *Veinte años y un día* (Barcelona: Tusquets, 2003). French translation by Serge Mestre: *Vingt ans et un jour* (Paris: Gallimard, 2004), 357.

(in memory of Juan Larrea, "a truly interesting bilingual writer of the Republican exile") and evokes both Hemingway, who apparently once told him the story, and a painting, Artemisia Gentileschi's "Judith Slaying Holophernes": this painting stands here not only for the bloody and arduous struggle against oppression but also for the power of art and for Semprún's loyalty to literature, since it was Michel Leiris's discussion of Judith and Holophernes in *L'âge d'homme*[29] that first led him, as a student in Paris, to Gentileschi's work.

In this way Semprún rehearses one of the principles of his secret identity, because twenty years, as he has explained, is the length of the prison term meted out to leaders of underground anti-Franco leaders: the sentence that Federico Sánchez risked in the event of his capture, with an additional day for a decision on the possibility of conditional release. Thus from 1936 to 1956 (the symbolic twenty years), to 1986 (when he saw the actual Gentileschi painting), and 2003 (the publication date of the novel that finally confirmed that he really was just as much a "Spanish writer" as a French one), Semprún never ceased to be the same and another, the one or the other—on "conditional release," so to speak, as much from Franco's Spain as from the Nazi Occupation of France or from Buchenwald, repeatedly destined for a return to his native land but summoned every time, from one side or another, to lend a hand to all who seek to throw off the tyrant's yoke.

—Translated from the French by Donald Nicholson-Smith

---

29. Michel Leiris, *L'âge d'homme* (Paris: Gallimard, 1939). English translation by Richard Howard: *Manhood* (Chicago: University of Chicago Press, 1992).

SARA KIPPUR

Semprun in English: Multilingualism, Translation, and American Publishers

In the closing pages of his 1977 Spanish memoir *Autobiografía de Federico Sánchez*, Jorge Semprun reflects on what he calls the "strange" experience of reading himself in translation. After quoting at length a passage from *El largo viaje*, the Spanish translation of his 1963 French novel *Le grand voyage*, Semprun writes:

> That was what I said, years ago now, speaking of Lekeitio, remembering that last night in Lekeitio. No, to tell the truth, I didn't say it exactly like that, because I wrote this book, *The Long Voyage*, in a foreign language, French. It was Jacqueline and Rafael Conte who translated this book into Spanish for me not long ago. It will always seem strange to me to read myself translated into my own language, however well this is done, as it was in this case.[1]

For Semprun, the sentences of *El largo viaje* resonate as unfamiliar because they belong to his translators, and not to him, author of the French version of *Le grand voyage*. In this brief allusion to the strangeness of translation, Semprun characterizes his texts as intimately tied to their original language of production, while also indirectly explaining why, despite a prolific bilingual publication record, he himself rarely translated between his two literary languages (his 1993 memoir, *Federico Sanchez vous salue bien*, self-translated as *Federico Sánchez se despide de ustedes*, being the only exception[2]).

As unfamiliar as translated versions of his texts may have felt to Semprun, they nonetheless constitute one of the principal modes by which he came to be recognized as an international literary figure

---

1. Jorge Semprun, *The Autobiography of Federico Sánchez and the Communist Underground in Spain*, trans. Helen Lane (New York: Kars Publishers, 1979), 257.
2. Semprun, *Federico Sanchez vous salue bien* (Paris: Grasset, 1993).

YFS 129, *Writing and Life, Literature and History: On Jorge Semprun*, ed. Razinsky,
© 2016 by Yale University.

whose writings and experiences captured many of the major political upheavals of the twentieth century. Semprun once defined himself as the quintessential "European man," whose personal background "straddling several countries"—his native Spain, adopted France, and Weimar Germany, where he spent the war years—positioned him well to reflect upon the future of Europe.[3] While as a public intellectual and writer Semprun was indeed most well known in France and Spain, the translations of his books out of the two languages in which he wrote were instrumental in situating him as a leading voice of his generation. This essay uncovers previously unexamined sources in the publication history of Semprun's works in the United States and attends to the choices translators made in rendering his works legible to English-language readers. In so doing, it underscores Semprun's role as a transnational author, whose aesthetic project and literary vision extended well beyond the boundaries of Europe.

GROVE PRESS AND RICHARD SEAVER: SEMPRUN IN ENGLISH IN THE 1960S AND 1970S

In his posthumously published memoir *The Tender Hour of Twilight*, Richard Seaver, renowned editor at Grove Press in the 1960s, who later went on direct his own imprint at Viking and establish Arcade Publishing, recalls the moment when Barney Rosset, publishing mogul and founder of Grove, was invited to represent the United States for the newly established Formentor Prize:

> Barney pulled a crumpled telegram from his pocket, the gist of which was that several leading European publishers were planning a literary prize—Gallimard in France, Einaudi in Italy, Seix Barral in Spain, Rowohlt in Germany, Weidenfeld in England. Would Grove like to be the American partner? It would be a feather in our cap, I said. Barney, justly proud at the honor, totally agreed.[4]

When representatives of these six publishing houses met in Spain later that year, 1961, they envisioned two different prizes: one, the Prix International, was to be a kind of precursor to the Nobel, and the other, the Prix Formentor, would honor an emerging writer demon-

---

3. Semprun and Dominique de Villepin, *L'homme européen* (Paris: Plon, 2005), 9. All translations, unless otherwise noted, are my own.
4. Richard Seaver, *The Tender Hour of Twilight*, ed. Jeannette Seaver (New York: Farrar, Straus and Giroux, 2012), 306.

strating literary promise. The first Prix International was co-awarded to Samuel Beckett and Jorge Luis Borges, and the Prix Formentor went to Spanish author Juan García Hortelano for his novel *Tormenta de verano*. All winners received a financial award, as well as a commitment from participating presses to translate and publish the awarded novels. In this sense, and in accordance with Grove's press release, "The aim of the prize [was] . . . to provide the largest possible international audience for the winning author."[5]

When Jorge Semprun won the Formentor two years later for his first novel *Le grand voyage*, seven additional publishing houses—Arcadia (Portugal), Bonniers (Sweden), Gyldendal (Denmark and Norway), McClelland & Stewart (Canada), Meulenhoff (Holland), and Otava (Finland)—had signed on to participate, further enhancing the international scope of the prize. The power of these new international prizes was such that the winning books and authors would, in Loren Glass's terms, "be immediately catapulted into the realm of world literature."[6] Guaranteed publication in thirteen countries and eleven languages, *Le grand voyage* not only launched Semprun's career, but offered him an immediate presence on the global literary stage. At its very inception, then, Semprun's emergence as an author was the product of close international collaboration and consecration.

Le grand voyage was not Grove Press's top pick for the Formentor that year. Their committee had nominated Driss ben Hamed Charhadi's *A Life Full of Holes*, an episodic novel that, according to one reader's report submitted to the Formentor judges, succeeded in showing "so brilliantly and effectively, yet unemotionally, the condition of the poor in North Africa and the fatalism with which the most appalling injustices and crises are accepted."[7] Despite Grove's loss of their first choice, Seaver happily agreed to take on the task of translating Semprun's novel himself. Seaver had already made a name for himself as a French-English translator. Of the translators charged with quickly rendering *Le grand voyage* into their respective languages so as to ensure a timely publication, Seaver was among

5. Quoted in Loren Glass, *Counter-Culture Colophon: Grove Press, The Evergreen Review, and the Incorporation of the Avant Garde* (Stanford: Stanford University Press, 2013), 57.

6. Ibid.

7. Robert Baldick, *Reader's Report submitted to Weidenfeld & Nicolson / Arthur Barker*, Grove Press Records, Special Collections Research Center, Syracuse University Libraries, Box 190.

the most celebrated, along with Portugal's João Gaspar Simões and Spain's Rafael Conte.[8] One of his chief successes as an American living in Paris in the 1950s was discovering Samuel Beckett and bringing his work to the attention of English-language audiences through his translations in the emergent literary magazine *Merlin*. In publishing Semprun's work, Seaver not only fulfilled the contractual obligations of the Formentor, but continued his tradition of developing close working relationships with the authors he translated. Seaver queried Semprun directly on his translation choices, and in one letter, dated less than a year after the English publication of *The Long Voyage*,[9] announced how much he looked forward to seeing Semprun in his upcoming visit to Paris, signing off with "Jeannette [Seaver's wife] joins me in sending our love to you."[10]

Seaver's personal commitment to Semprun's writing furthered their publishing relationship and enabled Semprun's works to appear in English throughout the '60s and '70s. As part of Grove's overall initiative of publishing inexpensive annotated and illustrated screenplays of avant-garde films—an innovative publishing decision that, as Glass demonstrates, responded well to the budding field of cinema studies in American higher education—Seaver solicited the publication of the screenplay of Semprun and Alain Resnais' film, *La guerre est finie*.[11] Seaver once again translated Semprun's text himself, and his translation accompanies over a hundred stills from the film, interspersed contextually throughout the book—a far more ambitious endeavor, both in terms of cost and layout, than the dozen or so screenshots that precede the original 1966 Gallimard publication.[12] In Seaver's letters to Semprun, he emphasizes just how much his interest in publishing Semprun's screenplays stems from his personal commitment to the author:

> I'm sending you a copy of two or three books we made from films—in other words, the screenplay and a generous selection of images. You're

8. See Rainier Grutmans article "La traduction ou la survie: Jorge Semprún, Carlos Barral et le prix Formentor," *TTR: traduction, terminologie, redaction* 18/1 (2005): 127–55, esp. 143–48, for a careful analysis of the various translators of *Le grand voyage*.

9. Semprun, *The Long Voyage*, trans. Richard Seaver (New York: Grove Press, 1964).

10. Seaver, Private Correspondence to Jorge Semprun, February 16, 1965, Grove Press Records, Special Collections Research Center, Syracuse University Libraries, Box 644.

11. Glass, *Counter-Culture Colophon*, 175.

12. See Semprun, *La guerre est finie*, trans. Richard Seaver (New York: Grove, 1967) and Semprun, *La guerre est finie: scénario du film d'Alain Resnais* (Paris: Gallimard, 1966).

familiar with what we do from your experience with *La guerre est finie*, but since then we've found a better way of doing it. In any case, it occurred to me that we could envision a similar kind of book taken from your screenplay of *Z*. Do you own the rights? In that event, send me a note right away and I will do it. If it's a big movie house that holds the rights, and you won't touch any of the profits, the idea interests me less, but whatever it is, let me know and we'll see what happens.[13]

That Seaver never published an English translation of *Z* suggests that Semprun was likely not the rights owner. Once he had left Grove and had control of his own imprint at Viking Press, Seaver did however publish, in 1975, the screenplay for *Stavisky*,[14] the other film script Semprun authored for Alain Resnais. Interestingly, Seaver prefaced the book in his own name, but attributed the translation to a certain "Sabine Destrée"—the same pseudonym of the American translator of *Story of O*, revealed to be Seaver himself only after his death in 2009. While it is unclear why Seaver would have used this enigmatic pseudonym when translating a fairly uncontroversial text like *Stavisky* (uncontroversial, at least, in comparison to *Story of O*), the fact that he continued to publish and personally translate Semprun years after Seaver had left Grove demonstrates the durability of their professional relationship and Seaver's commitment to Semprun's literary career in the United States.

Seaver recognized his own ties to Semprun's works, and in a letter to Weidenfeld & Nicolson editor Tony Godwin regarding the forthcoming English publication of *La deuxième mort de Ramon Mercader*, attributed it to the fact that he had already been Semprun's translator: "Thanks for your letter of August 20th about the new Semprun. Having translated two of his books, my interest in his work is obviously more than ordinary."[15] Seaver's editorial concern with *The Second Death of Ramon Mercader*—a lengthy novel in the style of the *nouveau roman* that he opted not to translate—concerned the quality of the translation itself. Between July 1969, when Grove acquired the translation rights to the novel, and late 1972, when *The Second*

13. Seaver, Private Correspondence to Jorge Semprun, July 11, 1965, Grove Press Records, Special Collections Research Center, Syracuse University Libraries, Box 644.

14. Semprun, *Stavisky*, trans. Sabine Destrée (New York: Viking Press, 1975).

15. Seaver, Private Correspondence to Tony Godwin, September 2, 1970, Grove Press Records, Special Collections Research Center, Syracuse University Libraries, Box 645.

Death of Ramon Mercader went to press,[16] Grove and Weidenfeld
editors engaged in extensive written discussions about the shortcom-
ings of the translation drafts, and the revisions necessary to make the
novel accord more faithfully with the French original. The British and
American presses worked in close collaboration to ensure that both
sides divided production and printing costs equitably, shared the task
of copy-editing, and found the translation equally satisfactory. The
British publisher had selected Len Ortzen as a potential translator—
a choice Grove approved after careful consideration of a translation
sample. In her report on the sample for Grove, Helen Lane, who would
later translate Semprun's *Autobiografía de Federico Sánchez* into English, noted that "the translation *does* sound very British, but I can
see no harm in that in this case, since Semprun's story intrinsically
has an international flavor."[17] The foreignness of the English translation for the American reader embodied the international character of
Semprun's prose and mirrored, in that sense, the close transatlantic
alliance that was integral to shepherding the novel to publication.
Though the translation would subsequently undergo multiple rounds
of revisions—particularly as both publishing houses lamented the
number of passages cut from the original text—Lane's observation
astutely identified the way a translation itself could reflect the prose
style and publishing history of a text.

Translation is unquestionably an inherently international affair, as
it entails the transposition of a text from one language to another. Yet
the degree and intensity of multilingual partnerships and transatlantic
cooperation involved in bringing Semprun's works to the attention of
English-language audiences in the 1960s and 1970s augured, in an
almost prescient fashion, the increasing internationalism of Semprun's prose itself. What I refer to as Semprun's "internationalism"
encompasses both the transatlantic publishing history I have traced
and his multilingual poetic form, through which the literary text itself functions as a site of contact between languages. Three more of
Semprun's books would subsequently appear in English—*The Autobiography of Federico Sanchez and the Communist Underground*

---

16. Semprun, *The Second Death of Ramon Mercader*, trans. Len Ortzen (New
York: Grove Press, 1973).

17. Helen Lane, Reader Report addressed to Richard Seaver, October 11, 1969,
Grove Press Records, Special Collections Research Center, Syracuse University Libraries, Box 645.

in Spain, What A Beautiful Sunday! and *Literature or Life.*[18] All published by different presses and editors, and undertaken by different
translators, none of these books had the consistent editorial support
offered by Grove and Seaver for Semprun's earlier works.[19] Nonetheless, to the extent that they reflect varying approaches to and concep-
tions of Semprun's writing, the English translations offer a productive
vantage point from which to understand the author's aesthetic project
more broadly. The internationalism inscribed in Semprun's emergent
career and in the production of his English-language publications became even more pronounced in the prose of his later French texts—a
characteristic that, somewhat counter-intuitively, can be most easily
perceived by way of the choices made by his English translators.

SEMPRUN'S MULTILINGUAL
POETICS: FROM 1964 TO 1997

Over thirty years separate Richard Seaver's translation of *The Long
Voyage* (1964) and Linda Coverdale's translation of *L'écriture ou la vie*
as *Literature or Life* (1997). Between the first and last of his books to
be translated into English—at least as of 2014—Semprun refined many
features of his prose style. While there remains a certain consistency
to Semprun's literary voice across time—frequent stylized digressions,
playful temporal shifts, intertextual references to poets and authors
who greatly influenced him—his works find increasingly sophisticated
modes for representing the multilingualism of his environment, particularly in his depictions of Buchenwald. What Semprun refers to in
Le mort qu'il faut (2001), his last Holocaust narrative, as a world characterized by the "colorful mix of Buchenwald idioms"[20] becomes, over
the course of his career as a writer, an image that he attempts to render aesthetically through various means. I refer to this aesthetic practice as "language authenticity," a term derived from Steven Kellman's

---

18. Semprun, *What A Beautiful Sunday!*, trans. Alan Sheridan (San Diego: Harcourt Brace Jovanovich, 1982); *Literature or Life*, trans. Linda Coverdale (New York:
Penguin, 1997).

19. Anne-Solange Noble, longtime Foreign Rights Director at Gallimard, recalls
that Richard Seaver bid on the English translation rights to *L'écriture ou la vie*, but
because the offer was modest, and because Penguin was a much more "powerful publisher" than Arcade, Semprun chose to publish with Penguin. Email correspondence
(February 4, 2014).

20. Semprun, *Le mort qu'il faut* (The Dead Man We Needed) (Paris: Gallimard,
2001), 30.

notion of cinematic "verbal authenticity," in which characters in a
film speak diagetically realistic languages (in contrast, to invoke one
of Kellman's examples, to a film such as Stanley Kubrick's *Spartacus*,
in which Tony Curtis portrays a Roman slave, all the while speaking
English with a Bronx accent).[21] Semprun's literary universe is peopled
with characters who speak various languages and idioms, which Semprun in turn represents "authentically," without recourse to flattening
their speech to conform with the dominant language of his text.

Le grand voyage is filled with an international cast of characters—
the Germans who occupy the camp, the Spaniard protagonist Gérard
and his fellow Spanish and French inmates—and foreign tongues pe-
riodically punctuate its prose. A camp loudspeaker will bark orders
in German, just as Gérard, a fluent German speaker, will engage in
lengthy conversations with Germans and Spaniards in their native
tongues. Semprun models language authenticity through the use of
footnotes: to accommodate French readers unfamiliar with the languages he cites, he includes direct translations at the bottom of the
page. Thus in a conversation early in the novel between Gérard and
a German soldier, the German lines of their conversation are interspersed in the text—"Verstehen Sie Deutsch?"; "Ich möchte Ihnen
eine Frage stellen"; "Bitte schön"; "Warum sind Sie verhaftet?"—
while the French translations are dutifully provided, one by one, as
footnotes ("Vous comprenez l'allemand?"; "Je voudrais vous poser
une question"; "Je vous en prie"; "Pourquoi êtes-vous arrêté?").[22]
Seaver's translation of *Le grand voyage* adheres to Semprun's language authenticity by including passages that, like in the French original, are recorded in German or Spanish. But whereas Jacqueline and
Rafael Conte's Spanish translation of the novel adheres precisely to
Semprun's narrative technique,[23] Seaver opts to forgo footnotes altogether, relying on readers to infer meaning from the text itself. Often
this means that he eliminates the translation entirely, as is the case
with "Warum sind Sie verhaftet?," the meaning of which Semprun's
subsequent sentences, and Seaver's faithful translation, make clear:
"I must say, it's an appropriate question. It's the question which, at
this particular moment, goes further than any question possible. Why

21. Steven Kellman, *The Translingual Imagination* (Lincoln: University of Nebraska Press, 1992), 102, 104.
22. Semprun, *Le grand voyage* (Paris: Gallimard, 1963), 49–50.
23. See Semprún, *El largo viaje*, trans. Jacqueline and Rafael Conte (Barcelona:
Tusquets, 2004), 43–44.

was I arrested?"[24] In other instances, Seaver paraphrases Semprun's footnoted translation in the body of the text. The "Was ist den los?" that another German soldier asks Gérard, which Semprun translated in a footnote as "Qu'est-ce qui se passe?"[25] (161), is paraphrased in Seaver's edition through the third person, "He wants to know what's going on," while also leaving the German intact (135). Seaver makes a similar editorial decision in a long passage in Spanish, interrupting the flow of the conversation to explain the nature of the exchange: "'Has visto?' 'He visto, y qué le vas a hacer?' He's seen what I've seen, but he wants to know what I can do about it" (151).

We can perhaps understand Seaver's translation technique as an attempt to iron out Semprun's clunky stylistic choice of footnotes—a choice that, it bears mentioning, Semprun would never repeat in his later works. Widely reviewed in the United States, *The Long Voyage* featured, for many American critics, a problematic prose style. The *New York Times* bemoaned Semprun's "tendency to overexplain, in rational terms, what could be communicated more forcefully through esthetic means," a sentiment echoed in the *New York Review of Books*: "The book's principal and decisive defect is insufficient artistic ability. Semprun's insight is not deep enough, his emotional power not strong enough, to make us forget that we have seen all these matters more movingly treated before."[26] And in the most damning review, *The New Yorker* claimed that:

> [The novel] reads not as if he [Semprun] has spent 1942 and 1943 in the Maquis and then three years in the world of the concentration camps and genocide but as if he had spent most of his life in a library studying other people's novels and the critical tip sheets that announce what sorts of fiction and technique are "in" and "out." As a result, *The Long Voyage* does not give the impression of being either a work of art or an account of an experience, and it produces abundantly the sense of *déjà vu*.[27]

Seaver may have intuited these potential critiques of Semprun's prose, removing footnotes so as to minimize an overly labored and

<hr/>

24. Semprun, *The Long Voyage*, 42.

25. Semprun, *Le grand voyage*, 161.

26. Leon S. Roudiez, "A Free Man Rode Also in the Boxcar: *The Long Voyage*, by Jorge Semprun," *New York Times* (May 3, 1964), BR5; and Stanley Kauffmann, "New European Fiction," *New York Review of Books* (May 28, 1964), 7.

27. Anthony West, "The Long Voyage: Book Review," *New Yorker* (August 8, 1964), 87.

heavy-handed writing style. He maintains the language authenticity that Semprun would strive to develop further in his later writings, all while deemphasizing the transparent act of translation itself.

In subsequent novels and memoirs, Semprun refined his approach to representing language authenticity and to depicting his role as a translator both within the camp environment and in his relationship to readers. His maturing style, evident in a text such as *L'écriture ou la vie*, allowed him to perform a translator function through more subtle aesthetic means than the stark use of footnotes. In one scene, the narrator recalls a conversation with Lieutenant Rosenfeld, an American officer and fluent German speaker who liberated Buchenwald, and interrupts himself to clarify that they had spoken in German, not French, the dominant language of narration: "Depuis le jour de notre rencontre, nous nous sommes parlé en allemand. Je traduirai nos propos pour la commodité du lecteur. Par courtoisie, en somme."[28] Linda Coverdale's award-winning translation of the Buchenwald memoir, as *Literature or Life* (1997), accentuates Semprun's self-conscious bid to language authenticity. Her translation accurately renders the French original ("Ever since the day we met, we've spoken to each other in German. I'll translate our remarks for the reader's convenience. To be polite, in short"[29]), demonstrating, like in the French original, the author's playful relationship to translation. Instead of simply translating passages from text to footnote, as in *Le grand voyage*, Semprun calls attention to his authorial function as a translator within the body of the text itself—an author who, in other words, reflects on the act of translation between experience and representation. In a fascinating move, Coverdale's translation internalizes this narrative technique, interjecting moments of language authenticity into the English version of the text where they do not appear in the French original. She chooses, for example, to maintain phrases in the original French, followed immediately by her own translation, such as "I shouldn't have ignored the portents of *le malheur de vivre*. The sorrow of living" (154). Coverdale transforms simply rendered passages in Semprun's text—the above example, in the French original, does not call attention to translation whatsoever[30]—into opportunities to foreignize the English version, anchoring the text in its French-

28. Semprun, *L'écriture ou la vie* (Paris: Gallimard, 1994), 108.
29. Semprun, *Literature or Life*, 78–79.
30. See the original passage in *L'écriture ou la vie*, 204.

language origins, placing original alongside translation, and in so doing, rehearsing Semprun's translation strategies. This multilingual play of juxtaposed languages permeates the English text; whenever Semprun cites lines of poems by those who most influenced him— René Char, Louis Aragon, or César Vallejo—Coverdale includes the original passages in their entirety, followed by a bracketed English translation.[31] Where Seaver's *The Long Voyage* inserts only the English verses of Valéry's poem "Le cimetière marin" that the narrator would recite to himself in French,[32] Coverdale's version of Semprun's intertextual references, cited in both the original and English, signals her sense for his aesthetic commitment to a multilingual poetics.

Coverdale's translation conveys generally the prevalent multilingualism of Semprun's literary universe, as well as his specific stylistic feature of calling attention to translation as a self-conscious, playful, and transparent authorial gesture. The English text visually juxtaposes languages on the page—what Coverdale calls one of her express "editorial" decisions to keep original passages in foreign languages[33]—while it also willingly moves beyond the French text to accentuate the translational nature of Semprun's writing. In translating Semprun, Coverdale not only reproduces his prose style—the objective of any translator—but inscribes recursively the translation aesthetic that Semprun proffers in the French original. Her translation gives the impression, in other words, that Semprun's book has already grappled with its future as a translated text.

Despite any resistance Semprun may have had to translation—and especially to the jarring experience of reading himself translated— his works were deeply invested in the *idea* of translation. The evolution of Semprun's literary techniques, as seen through the shift from Seaver's to Coverdale's translations, highlights his central interest in figuring translation discursively, and in articulating a viable model to translators of his texts for how to position languages vis-à-vis one another. The aesthetic that Semprun created and honed over the course of his career concretized, in that sense, the early lesson of the Prix Formentor: that his writings and career could be shaped through the very process of translation itself, even beyond the bounds of his own literary languages.

31. See *Literature or Life*, for example 111, 115, 183–7, and 192.
32. Semprun, *The Long Voyage*, 57.
33. Linda Coverdale, email correspondence, January 20, 2014.

LIRAN RAZINSKY

The Never-Ending Book: On "the dream of every writer" in Jorge Semprun

Jorge Semprun has written more than twenty books and sixteen film scripts. But the Semprun I wish to study here is not the Semprun of many books but the Semprun of one, the Semprun who throughout his life wrote one book.[1]

While studies examining Semprun's Buchenwald narratives from a general autobiographical perspective are not numerous, it is nevertheless widely acknowledged that his work is to be seen through the lenses of both autobiography and testimony. Deferring the discussion of the testimonial aspect of Semprun to the end of this paper, I wish to home in on Semprun as autobiographer, to discuss him under the somewhat abstract perspective of the relationship between author and book. Through this somewhat roundabout path, I will be suggesting a perspective on matters central in Semprun: repetition as a principle of writing, the infinity of writing, and the relationship of writing, life, and death.

In *L'écriture ou la vie* (*Literature or Life*) Semprun famously elaborates on his early decision following the war to abandon writing about his deportation experiences, despite his literary aspirations and initial wish to do so, for fear of being thrown back to those experiences and submerged in them. He chose life over writing. This literary-existential choice is saturated with the dark colors of the Nazi camps and has been amply commented on by almost everyone who has written about *L'écriture ou la vie*.

But perhaps, precisely given Semprun's literary aspirations, we may disconnect this choice from its context of deportation—only

1. My warm thanks to Bruno Chaouat, Sara Kippur, Tsivia Frank Wygoda, and Yogev Zusman for their helpful remarks on this paper, and to Guy Segev and Mark Joseph for their help with preparing it.

YFS 129, *Writing and Life, Literature and History: On Jorge Semprun,* ed. Razinsky, © 2016 by Yale University.

temporarily—and discuss it on a more literary level. The dilemma of writing and life is after all more general, shared as it is by many authors. Should one write, or should one live? Semprun, after all, is telling us that he is afraid that, once he writes down his memories, he will not be able to survive his own autobiography, that there will be no life afterwards. Not to write would be a solution to this problem, but there are other solutions as well.

Writing an autobiography is no easy task. Making a representation of yourself on the written page, one that is both you and different and separate from you, with its own logic that you perhaps do not share, is a complex task. Putting aside the difficulties involved in self-exposure and rendering the intimate public, there is sometimes another problem in play, namely, that of surviving one's autobiography. The published book is sealed. It might be on sale in bookstores, but the writer goes on living and what was supposed to be a true, fitting, and complete representation becomes limited, partial, and fixed, no longer faithful to the life of the author it was supposed to represent. As John Sturrock puts it, "autobiographers want the time that has intervened between the completion of their life-story and the completion of their life to be overlooked."[2] Beyond the lack of correspondence, the threat is also one of petrification: The representation of a life is closed, and has now immobilized the life, perhaps rendering it unnecessary: "to 'evoke your memories,'" asks Nathalie Sarraute in *Childhood (Enfance)*, "wouldn't that mean that you were retiring? standing aside? abandoning your element [. . .]."[3]

There is also a risk, however, in writing but never publishing the book, dying before it is ready. The time of the book, that is, the time encompassed by the writing, and the time of the writer are never completely synchronized. One always has a residue, one always continues after the other. Only if they were to end simultaneously, if there were complete overlap between autobiography and life, could there be synchronization (at least in this sense).

From here arises the fantasy of one author, one book: just one book in the course of a lifetime, a perfect totality, the full coincidence of life and its textual representation. This fantasy is not limited to autobiographical writing. Proust, for example speaks of "this essential,

2. John Sturrock, *The Language of Autobiography: Studies in the First Person Singular* (Cambridge: Cambridge University Press, 1993), 5.

3. Nathalie Sarraute, *Childhood*, trans. Barbara Wright, fwd. by Alice Kaplan (Chicago: The University of Chicago Press, 2013), 1–2.

the only true book" that every writer has to write.⁴ Here and elsewhere, Proust expresses the view that not only does each author in
fact have but a single book, but also that this book is the realization
of the inner life of that author.⁵

Such a project, a book whose writing would span an entire life,
such as, for example, Michel Leiris's *La règle du jeu*, or the *Essays*
of Montaigne who "opted for the obstinate revision of a single book
rather than the production of multiple opuscules,"⁶ is not only an
answer to life's finitude and temporariness. It also expresses (and answers a demand issuing from) a perspective of total self-representation
(especially when the book is an autobiography): Say everything, transmit everything, the whole of oneself and one's life. The requirement
of totality, where the book must contain one's entire life, is even
more antithetical to the existence of a remainder, of unrepresented
life. The one-book-throughout-life model "solves" this. One's self-
representation, one's life-rendered-as-text becomes total. One book
containing everything would be able as such to replace whatever it
represents, give it value, full objecthood, existence in the outside
world: "By writing a work based on my own experience I would re-
create myself and justify my existence," writes Simone de Beauvoir
in *Memoirs of a Dutiful Daughter*.⁷

Here, though, the Golem might turn against its creator: if a written representation justifies the life as lived, what would underwrite
the life lived after publication? The need for justification cannot be
properly met. Therefore the dream: one book, monolithic, a closed
unit without residue, a life folded into a book.

The one-book-throughout-life paradigm also partakes in similar
fantasies of literary totality such as Mallarmé's "Le Livre," or the

4. Marcel Proust, *Time Regained*, vol. 3 of *Remembrance of Things Past*, trans.
C. K. Scott Moncrieff, Terence Kilmartin, and Andreas Mayor (New York: Random
House, 1982), 926; *À la recherche du temps perdu* (Gallimard, *la Pléiade*, 1989), 4: 469.
See also the discussion of "the inner book of unknown symbols [. . .] the only book that
really belongs to us" [*notre seul livre*], ibid., 913–14; 4:458.
5. Consider the following: "[. . .] [T]he raw material of my experience, which
would also be the raw material of my book [. . .]"(Ibid., 953; 4:493–4); "[N]ow that I
seemed to see [. . .] that a life, in short, can be realized within the confines of a book!"
Ibid., 1088; 4:609.
6. Michel Beaujour, *The Poetics of The Literary Self-Portrait*, trans. Yara Milos
(New York and London: New York University Press, 1991), 106.
7. Simone De Beauvoir, *Memoirs of A Dutiful Daughter*, trans. James Kirkup,
(Harmondsworth: Penguin, 1963), 142; *Mémoires d'une jeune fille rangée* (Paris: Gallimard, 1958), 143.

German Romantic notion of the absolute book, or the huge totalizing cycles or *romans-fleuve* of the nineteenth and early twentieth century, such as Balzac's *La comédie humaine* and Zola's *Les
Rougon-Macquart*.

★   ★   ★

In *L'écriture ou la vie*, Semprun describes a strange fantasy. Some
context: Salzburg, 1964. Semprun has been awarded the Formentor Literature Prize for *The Long Voyage*. He receives copies of the
translations of the book from the various publishers. But the Spanish
translation is missing. The book was banned under Franco and had to
be printed elsewhere, in Mexico, and the edition is not yet ready. Instead, the Spanish publisher, Carlos Barral, hands Semprun a special
copy: the book in its jacket, with the right number of pages and correct dimensions but with blank pages.[8] This blank book is interesting
on its own terms and we shall come back to it, but I wish to get to the
fantasy that follows:

> One day, I thought, after that evening in Salzburg, one day I'll rewrite
> this book on the blank pages of that single copy. I'll rewrite it in Span-
> ish, disregarding the existing translation.
>
> "That's not a bad idea," Carlos Fuentes told me, not very long
> afterward.
>
> We were in Paris, in a café on the Boulevard Saint-Germain-des-Prés.
>
> "Anyway, you should have done the Spanish version yourself. You
> wouldn't have simply translated, you would have allowed yourself
> to betray yourself [*te trahir*]. To transform [*trahir*] your original text,
> to try to go farther with it. This would have created a different book,
> which you could have turned into a new French version, a whole new
> book! You say so yourself: this experience is inexhaustible . . ."
>
> His conclusion had made us laugh, on a day of Parisian spring
> showers that might have come from a poem by César Vallejo.
>
> "And so," Carlos Fuentes concluded, "you will have realized
> the dream of every writer: to spend your life writing a single book,
> endlessly renewed!" [*tu aurais réalisé le rêve de tout écrivain: passer
> sa vie à écrire un seul livre, sans cesse renouvelé !*]

---

8. Jorge Semprun, *Literature or Life*, trans. Linda Coverdale (New York: Viking,
1997), 271–74. Further references to *Literature or Life* are given in the text, and all page
references in parentheses are to this book. The French edition I refer to in parallel is
L'écriture ou la vie (Paris: Gallimard [Folio], 1994).

We laughed. The downpour battered the windows of the café where we'd taken refuge. But I didn't carry out this plan. The pages of the single copy Carlos Barral presented to me in Salzburg on May 1, 1964, have remained blank, untouched by writing. (275–76 En, 354 Fr, translation modified)

Of all of Semprun's work, in both French and Spanish, of all his books where the same episodes are worked and reworked, where things keep being rewritten, I wish to deal here with this one episode, this weird fantasy Semprun puts forth through the mouth of Carlos Fuentes, who as Susan Suleiman notes, plays on the well known pun *tradut-tore/traditore*, the translator who is also a traitor.[9]

The circumstances of this fantasy may be concrete—one of the editions is delayed—but the result is abstract: a dream, a fantasy. What interests me is not Semprun's decision to translate his own books, something that he did in only one instance (*Federico Sanchez vous salue bien*),[10] but this to and fro between languages, which in fact renders the book a life project, a never-ending story. One book for one lifetime. In this book, the writer never dies. He never faces the problem of the lack of complete overlap between life and its textual representation. The idea of self-translation (a causa-sui project? a dream of self-containment? an expression of the notion of multiple and un-

9. Susan Rubin Suleiman, *Crises of Memory and the Second World War* (Cambridge, Massachusetts and London: Harvard University Press, 2006), 141.

The scene, in a slight variation, is recounted in the interview with Semprun in the Paris Review. Semprun, "Interview with Lila Azam Zanganeh," *The Paris Review*, The Art of Fiction 192, 2007. http://www.theparisreview.org/interviews/5740/the-art -of-fiction-no-192-jorge-semprun; retrieved April 4, 2015. Fuentes's suggestion, and the idea of being the author of just one book, comes out again, this time more prominently in an interview with Gérard de Cortanze from as early as 1981 (Gérard de Cortanze, *Jorge Semprun, l'écriture de la vie* [Paris: Gallimard, 2004], 218). Semprun also makes concrete reference there to a plan to translate his own *Quel beau dimanche!*, giving us an idea of how the translation would be much more than a translation. He emphasizes that he would use for it sections of the manuscript that he did not include in the French version, and develop certain chapters and characters, thus making it a rewriting (*réécriture*) rather than a translation (217).

10. Sara Kippur, "Translating Semprun," *Michigan Quarterly Review* 52/2 (2013): 195–98. Not only does Semprun very rarely decide to translate himself, he also repudiated the very idea of self-translation. In a chapter in her *Writing It Twice*, Kippur studies Semprun's repudiation of self-translation in the context of his bilingualism and his conception of language. Kippur, "Resisting Self-Translation: Jorge Semprun, Language Authenticity, and the Challenge to World Literature," in *Writing It Twice: Self-translation and the Making of a World Literature in French* (Illinois: Northwestern University Press, 2015).

locatable selves?) is part of Semprun's project here, but it seems subordinate to the similar yet different vision of a single life-long book.[11]

The circumstances described in this anecdote are particularly noteworthy, both in the context of the opposition in *L'écriture ou la vie* between writing and life, and in the context of an idea inherent to the fantasy of one book throughout life, namely the identity of lived life and its literary representations. Beyond the framing scene in which Semprun is awarded a literary prize, surrounded by editors and publishers, and in which he receives copies of his book, the occasion of Semprun and Fuentes talking presents itself in an exaggerated manner as a literary event. Semprun converses with a famous author; they sit, of all places, in a café in Saint-Germain-des-Prés, an iconic backdrop of the Parisian literary world. The spring day is compared for no obvious reason to a poem by Vallejo. Fuentes and Semprun here are like protagonists in a novel, living life as if it were literature, citizens of *La République des Lettres*. Rain batters the windows. It is as if the two are taking refuge from life in the warmth of literature.[12]

THE *PERPETUUM MOBILE* OF WRITING

Let us examine this fantasy, first more generally, then in the context of Semprun's book. I have presented the idea of one book per life from the point of view of totality and closure: the fantasy of capturing life in its entirety in a book. Semprun's version treads a fine line between this notion of totality and closure and that of infinite openness. On the one hand, a dream of totality: "to spend your life writing a single book," and in another version of the story, Semprun talks of "being truly the man of one single book."[13] This is also "the dream of every writer." On the other hand, it is a dream about a text that remains

11. On the actual practice of self-translation see, for example, Rita Wilson, "The Writer's Double: Translation, Writing, and Autobiography," *Romance Studies* 27/3 (2009): 186–98 and Brian T. Fitch, "The Status of Self-Translation," *Texte* 4 (Text/Translatability) (1985): 111–26.

12. The same motifs—literature, an author Semprun admires, bilingualism, and to-and-fro between languages—are all at play in another scene that takes place in a Saint-Germain-des-Prés café, recounted in *Le mort qu'il faut*. There, a young woman brings Semprun a novel by Faulkner, his first encounter with that writer. He ruminates on whether he should describe her in French or Spanish, or both. "I would need bilingual readers [. . .] who could move [. . .] from French to Spanish, and vice versa," he concludes. Semprun, *Le mort qu'il faut*, in *Le fer rouge de la mémoire* (Paris: Gallimard [Quarto], 2012), 1018–19 (my translation).

13. Semprun's interview with Cortanze (*Jorge Semprun, L'écriture*, 218).

forever open. A book that is never settled or closed, but is rather "end-lessly renewed!"[14]

There is a sense in which closure is integral to autobiography. Inasmuch as autobiography is turned toward the past, Lejeune reminds us, "I am always at the endpoint of my story" in this form of writing. It is only in its similarity to a diary, turned as it is toward the future, toward the implications of ever writing anew, that an autobiography can still be unfinishable.[15] Semprun seems to want it both ways.

The link between closure and openness seems to be structural. Because there is an idea of totality involved in many autobiographical representations—the wish for the text to be *the* version of oneself—there is a constant need to rework it and avoid closing it. In a thoughtful paper on "Autobiography and the Problem of Finish," Hannah Sullivan studies the various ways authors from the Victorian age to the mid-twentieth century have sought to avoid the closure of an autobiographical text, by leaving it open, avoiding publication, or, more pertinent to our discussion, interminably rereading and revising it (both pre- and post-publication). "Because the genre aims to present a coherent and totalizing record of past time [. . .] it also presents its practitioners with the fear of incompletion, error and fragmentariness."[16] Accordingly, she concludes, "autobiography is structurally prone to revision,"[17] and specifically, this revision is often carried out through an act of rereading an older version of one's autobiography and rewriting it according to present concerns and afterthoughts.[18] Sullivan notes that the concern with finishing an autobiography that leads to permanent revision is also a more general

14. Mallarmé's vision of *Le Livre*, probably the greatest myth of one book in literature, displays a similar mixture of totality and openness. In terms of totality, Mallarmé's Book is nearly the cosmos itself metamorphosed into book form. This book of everything, however, if we are to follow Blanchot (Maurice Blanchot, *The Book to Come*, trans. Charlotte Mandell [Stanford: Stanford University Press, 2003], 266 n. 15), is envisioned as ever open, not only of course in the sense that it remains a promise, never actually realized, but also and more importantly in the sense of being eternally reshaped through variant readings: its pages are not connected to each other, so that the reader can change their order. Different permutations actually fabricate different books, assuring the book an eternal life.

15. Philippe Lejeune, "How Do Diaries End?" in *On Diary*, ed. Jeremy D. Popkin and Julie Rak (Honolulu: The University of Hawai'i Press, 2009), 191.

16. Hannah Sullivan, "Autobiography and the Problem of Finish," *Biography* 34/2 (2011): 298–325, 298.

17. Ibid., 301.

18. Ibid., 320.

one, that of "closure in literary texts," threatening because it implies the author's death.[19] "To keep on writing [. . .] or to keep revising an already complete draft [. . .] are activities that attempt to keep at bay the anxiety of 'letting go.'"[20]

Michael Sheringham examines the explicit will-to-form, the desire for unity and closure in autobiography such as Leiris's to "gather his life into 'un seul bloc solide [. . .],'"[21] and more specifically, the idea of "self as book," "'Livre consubstantiel à son autheur'"[22] as he cites Montaigne. He sees such desires for "the fetishizing of the self" as merely moments in "a dialectical process."[23] "The lure of form, closure, and definition [. . .] is often in turn countered by [. . .] the appeal of open-endedness and indefinition."[24] Specifically the idea of oneself as book is refracted into the dual nature of the book, on the one hand a solid form of closure, and on the other, "'full of turnings and windings,'" due to the nature of writing, that mirror the self's plurality.[25]

I have already mentioned some of the implications of the fantasy of penning a totality, of writing just one book. If to write might be to stabilize the self, or to cause it to become petrified, if after writing down one's memories nothing is left, if there is a danger that on publication life's sting will be neutralized, we can see the temptation of writing just one book. First, this way one never finishes, and therefore never becomes finalized in a single representation. There is no residue in the writer's life beyond its textual manifestation. No problem of surviving one's autobiography.

Second, when writing just one book, the book becomes the complete and faithful representation of its author's thought. Life and its representation converge in one monolithic entity. Life is put in a box. Although all this is certainly at work in Semprun's dream, it pointedly avoids closing the box, or the coffin, opting rather for permanent change, making clear that the text is at no point finished.

19. Ibid., 299.
20. Ibid.
21. Michael Sheringham, *French Autobiography: Devices and Desires* (Oxford: Clarendon Press, 1993), 5.
22. Ibid., 7.
23. Ibid.
24. Ibid., 6.
25. Ibid., 7–8.

The identification of author and book is compelling but ipso facto renders the book dangerous for its author. In *What a Beautiful Sunday!*, this danger is evident:

> You were sitting at your desk, with all the uneasiness a writer feels when his work is unfinished. [. . .] Perhaps, quite simply, you really didn't want to have done with it. Perhaps it was simply that this unfinished manuscript, forever taken up again, rewritten, forgotten, rediscovered, proliferating through the years with a dangerously autonomous life which you no longer seemed capable of mastering, perhaps this manuscript was quite simply your life. And you certainly weren't going to put an end to your life![26]

So the book, when forever revised, *is* one's life, and it is precisely that identification, the success of putting everything in the book, that dictates that the box should never be closed.[27]

Incompleteness, however, is not only willful, it is also inherent. In Semprun's version of the dream of one book through perpetual retranslation, the dream undermines itself with its emphasis on the impossibility of achieving wholeness, since no version is ever final. The one book aspired to will never be sealed. At some point, death will simply intervene to interrupt the text at a random point, cutting off the story that has no end. There is, therefore, a fundamental openness that undermines the idea of closure. And thus, parallel to the aspiration to totality embodied by this project, there is also a recognition of its inevitable failure. When an author translates her own texts, Fitch notes, she renders the first version incomplete, as if work on it had been suspended, deferring the "final realization" until its completion by the self-translation.[28] In the fantasy of continuous self-translation as hypothesized in Semprun, the deferral and suspension—this fundamental openness—perpetuate themselves. Once the project has been conceived, every new stage that at first seems like an end, every additional translation, only heralds the next translation. Every tempo-

26. Semprun, *What a Beautiful Sunday!*, trans. Alan Sheridan (San Diego, New York, and London: Harcourt Brace Jovanovich, 1982), 288; *Quel beau dimanche!* (Paris: Grasset, 1980), 260.

27. The central narrative characteristic of Semprun's writing, playfulness with chronology, is explained by Tidd as a means to avoid closure: "The tricks played by Semprún with narrative time serve to elude the end of the story and history [. . .]." Ursula Tidd, "The Infinity of Testimony and Dying in Jorge Semprún's Holocaust Autothanatographies," *Forum of Modern Language Studies* 41/4 (2005): 413.

28. Fitch, *The Status of Self-Translation*, 117.

rary state, every present version only suggests its incompleteness, its deficiency that can only be put right with another translation, a new version that will of course, in its turn, be incomplete.

In his essay on the storyteller, Walter Benjamin points out that this structure of otherness, of a deficiency that hints at the future is inherent to every story (and *The Long Voyage* is a story). There is always one more story.[29] At the end of every story, the questions can be asked: What happened next? How did it continue?[30] As Sam Weber puts it: "Stories never simply end; they stop, are interrupted, and thereby invite and provoke re-iteration, a re-telling that is also a transformation. Human beings are finite and mortal but the stories they tell are often not [. . .] they live on in the responses they provoke."[31]

According to Benjamin, the listener asks what happened next, but does something happen next? Does Semprun's imagined story have an end at all? Is there a future involved? Is there progress and change, or is there rather only repetition, the story drawn to old memories and dwelling repeatedly on them? Is there a future or merely an eternal present, the present of Buchenwald that one never steps out of; even when one believes the past has been left behind, one wakes up—by one, I mean Semprun—hearing the shouts *Krematorium, ausmachen!* (153–54 En, 202–203 Fr), and understands that life is a dream and that Buchenwald was never left behind, but is rather the only reality.

Our pendulum then returns again from openness to closure, and not only in terms of content. There is, after all, something absurd in this fantasy of retranslating into French a book written in French in the first place:[32] it seems that what is involved here is not the growth and development of the text but rather a desperate attempt to close it, to close it in the right manner. Something in it persists in being too open and the text needs to be brought back home, brought back to the

29. Samuel Weber, Yuki Maeda, and Takashi Minatomichi, "On the Japanese Translation of *The Legend of Freud*. A Dialogue with Samuel Weber," *Qui parle* 17/2 (2009): 179.

30. Walter Benjamin, "The storyteller," in *Illuminations*, trans. Harry Zohn (New York: Schocken Books, 1969), 98.

31. Weber, Maeda, and Minatomichi, "On the Japanese Translation," 179.

32. Borges' Pierre Ménard rewriting *Don Quixote* comes to mind, a myth of rewriting as renovating a text, although Semprun's project is different in that the rewriting will not produce something identical to the source. In the interview with Cortanze (*Jorge Semprun, L'écriture*, 220), Semprun himself evokes Pierre Ménard in the context of self-translation.

source, to the original from which it all started. Of course, once two languages, two homes, are involved, this can no longer be done, and each translated text yearns for its other home.

A book, in general, we know, is a paradoxical object. It signifies closure, fixity, unity, the full course of a narrative with a beginning and an end, while being written in language whose nature is to unravel rather than to close, to point beyond and aside rather than to hold meaning to the center. In the fantasy of one book throughout life this is even more pronounced: there is a quest for something total and holistic, but through language, a site of unraveling and otherness. The illusion of totality and closure is just that, an illusion, and is always broken by the open nature of language, which never holds one meaning in place, but is open to multiple interpretations and understandings.[33]

In Semprun however, all this has a special nuance, since there are always two languages involved. Two languages whose aliveness and openness, and the gap between them, do not allow for closure. In moving between French and Spanish, the text keeps evolving, is never one with itself. Each language infuses the other with a dimension of foreignness.[34] Thus, over and above the fundamental openness of language, its property of always being given to interpretation and misunderstanding, the illusion of the book's closure faces here a duality, the existence of two poles, such that each of them thwarts the closure of the other. Whenever the text is at one pole, appearing closed and whole, the possibility remains of moving again toward the other pole, the other language, the other identity.

For it is not just the book of Semprun's fantasy that is torn between two languages, but also Semprun himself, torn between his two homelands, and he feels comfortable in neither.[35] Something is

33. See, for example, Jacques Derrida, *Writing and Difference*, trans. Alan Bass (London and New York: Routledge, 2001), 365; Jacques Lacan, "The Function and Field of Speech and Language in Psychoanalysis" in *Écrits. A selection*, trans. Alan Sheridan (London and New York: Routledge, 1989), 62–64.

34. "The synergies established by the 'invasion' of one language by the other," Nikolau Paschalis says about self-translation, "create a certain cognitive dynamic; translation sets off a destabilizing dance of associations that accelerates self-reflexivity [. . .], fosters a sense of plurality, undecidability and ambiguity" (28). Paschalis, "Notes on Translating the Self," in *Translation and Creativity: Perspectives on Creative Writing and Translation Studies*, ed. Eugenia Loffredo and Manuela Perteghella (London: Continuum, 2006), 19–32.

35. Kippur even speaks of Semprun's "multilingual aesthetics" ("Translating Semprun," 195), in which the original French text is full of scattered expressions and citations not only from Semprun's other language (Spanish) but from other languages

always missing and in need of completion. Semprun, or Semprún? Semprun himself is split, harboring an internal plurality. He is always in exile:

> [. . .] a sign of deracination. Suddenly, not only did it become clear that I was not at home, but also that I was nowhere. Or anywhere at all, which amounts to the same thing. From that moment on, my roots would always be nowhere, or anywhere. (151 En, 199 Fr)

This long voyage of text and translation suggested by Semprun's fantasy is actually a voyage of continuous migration without a home. Perhaps the only place Semprun would feel at home on this journey is the text itself, a text, it should be recalled, about Buchenwald. And it is in fact Buchenwald that Semprun qualifies as his only true homeland: "the unquiet sleep of my companions in the crowded bunks, the feeble, raspy breathing of the dying, the flames of the crematory, were a sort of homeland. A place of plenitude, of vital coherence [. . .]" (153–54 En, 203 Fr).[36]

Whose fantasy, in fact, is this, this dream of every writer? Fuentes's? Semprun's, who brought it to us, if not invented it? Semprun could of course have written it in the first person but opts to present it as a dialogue, a dialogue with a Spanish author while he, Semprun, is writing in French. Again, we face this internal split, as in the to and fro between languages, in the very telling of the fantasy that alternates between two sources—Semprun and Fuentes.

In all this the felt presence is that of the translator/author. If ordinarily the writer dissolves into the text-become-independent, were we to trust the French tradition of the sixties, here the true story is not what is written in the book but rather the voyage the text has made, its vicissitudes among languages, the paradoxical move of going back over and over to the same languages, and this process is that of a creator; the presence of this author, this creator, is brought to the

---

as well (German, for example). Such an aesthetic, one can suggest, reflects a struggle against monolithic unity.

36. Klinkert, discussing the episode recounted in *L'évanouissement* and in *Writing or Life* where Spanish and French double each other in a sort of struggle in Semprun's mind as he comes round after having fainted, sees both maternal languages as being replaced, in this metaphorical second birth, by the experience of Buchenwald, the true source of identity henceforth. Thomas Klinkert. "Quand la 'neige d'antan' efface la 'langue originaire.' À propos du bilinguisme de Jorge Semprun," in *Écrire aux confins des langues*, ed. Jeanne Bem and Albert Hudlett, *Creliana*, hors série I (2001): 130–31.

fore. The artistic work, more than the text itself becomes the endless translation that, like some performance art, becomes a life project that cannot be detached from its creator.

The implications of this fantasy go beyond questions of closure and openness. For example, one result of the eternal repetition where the story is told and retold is that the origin is blurred. Fuentes speaks of translating [*traduire*] without treason [*se trahir*]. But what is this original that one ostensibly betrays? The original no longer has any privileged status for in fact it is the most deficient of all versions. The translation here is better and more complete than the original, and every new version renders earlier ones superfluous.

This thought has a further implication having to do with amortization and loss. Semprun's fantasy goes against the laws of nature. We have here an emptying of one vessel into another, and back again, where nothing is spilled and each container is repeatedly filled to the brim. The dream accentuates the unremitting work of elaboration and creation in Semprun that would manifest itself in a continuous enrichment of the texts, perhaps through the new associations and connotations that words have when translated (or through rewriting—see note 9). George Steiner remarks that when an author translates his own work, he "seeks in the copy the primary lineaments of his own inspiration and, possibly, an enhancement or clarification of these lineaments through reproduction."[37] "The self-translator," Rita Wilson writes, "has the possibility of enriching the source text by, for example, 'activating' meanings which were only 'between-the-lines' in the original."[38] But the magic of this fantasy hides the opposite dimension of loss and extinction: the reduction that follows any translation, the fact that something is always lost. In this fantasy nothing is lost. No place of oblivion, petrification, or loss of memories. Do memories, as in a *perpetuum mobile,* keep bubbling up to enrich language, or is there an inevitable loss so that the text is necessarily diminished? Life too diminishes: in this fantasy the text keeps renewing itself, but is its author/translator incessantly renewed, with the flow of time?

If we saw that a continually translated work remains open, it is interesting to note how in another section of *L'écriture ou la vie* Sem-

---

37. George Steiner, *After Babel. Aspects of Language and Translation,* 3rd ed. (Oxford: Oxford University Press), 336.
38. Wilson, "The Writer's Double," 192.

prun recounts how he systematically destroyed his writer's journals, notebooks, and unfinished drafts, since "[o]nly the finished work counts" (170 En, 224 Fr). His fantasy book however will always remain a draft. It has neither a privileged original version nor a privileged final one; it is nothing but continuous becoming.

Remarks about the unity of life and book, and on the repetitive nature of writing abound in *L'écriture ou la vie*. (Uncoincidentally, one of them refers to Proust, another author captive in the dream of one book for one lifetime and whose work is a constantly reappearing intertext in Semprun's. Semprun has read Proust, he tells us, over 40 years, "a lifelong reading" [147 En, 193 Fr]: another book that lasts, in a way, a lifetime.[39]) One of these remarks concerns the very writing of *L'écriture ou la vie*:

> Half a century earlier, [. . .] I'd already recounted that episode to Lieutenant Rosenfeld [Semprun refers to the often-told episode of his entrance into Buchenwald]. [. . .] [I]t was a good beginning [. . .] of this experience and the account I could give of it. [. . .]
>
> Almost a half-century later, I was just telling the end of that same story [. . .]. (297 En, 380 Fr)

It turns out that *L'écriture ou la vie* is itself a book the author has spent his whole life writing; it is a book that overlaps a lifetime. When Semprun describes the episode that gave birth to it—it was born from another of Semprun's novels, *Netchaïev est de retour*, where the writing led Semprun once again to his Buchenwald experience—he says that it will still take years to be completed: "I'd seen it happen [. . .]:

---

39. Semprun's style has been compared in some respects to that of Proust, most importantly because of leaps in narrative time (See Brett Ashley Kaplan "'The Bitter Residue of Death': Jorge Semprun and the Aesthetics of Holocaust Memory," *Comparative Literature* 55/4 [2003]: 320–37). In his novel *Le grand voyage* (1963), Semprun relates how he passed his first night in the overcrowded boxcar to Buchenwald reconstructing in memory *Du côté de chez Swann* and thus reminding himself of his own childhood (Semprun, *The Long Voyage*, trans. Richard Seaver [New York: The Overlook Press, 2005], 72; *Le grand voyage* in *Le fer rouge de la mémoire*, 91–232 [Paris: Gallimard (Quarto), 2012], 130–1). In another section, a pastiche, Semprun mocks Proust's madeleine scene, describing how years after the war the taste of black bread brings up "with shocking suddenness" memories of eating bread in the camp (ibid., 126; 165). Kaplan shows how Semprun's evocation and dismissal of Proust's model of involuntary memory serves to show that the memory of the camp overrides any anterior blissful memory, and that after the camps, memory can no longer offer comfort. At any rate, the allusion to Proust here in *L'écriture ou la vie* is anything but naïve.

books taking years to ripen. Never reaching full maturity, either. I'd always felt that their publication, determined by external, objective circumstances, was somewhat premature" (231 En, 298 Fr). Books about the camps, specifically, are essentially interminable, and only external circumstances, such as the need to publish, not their inner structure, bring them to an end.

Both the unity of life and book, and the theme of writing as repetition emerge as central to *L'écriture ou la vie*. The next section will ground this unity and this theme in the very subjects of that book.

WRITING DEATH, AGAIN

The fantasy of one book, as I have described, is a fantasy of a book that is infinite, never-ending. As such, it is directly linked in Semprun's work to the central challenge he, like other witnesses, faces: that of expressing the unsayable. Difficult to say but not unsayable, says Semprun. Yes, everything can be said about Buchenwald:

> You can tell all about this experience. You have merely to think about it. And set to it. And have the time, of course, and the courage, for a boundless and probably never-ending account, illuminated (as well as enclosed, naturally) by that possibility of going on forever. Even if you wind up repeating yourself. [*Quitte à tomber dans la repetition et le ressassement.*] Even if you remain caught up in it, prolonging death, if necessary—reviving it endlessly in the nooks and crannies of the story. Even if you become no more than the language of this death, and live at its expense, fatally. (14 En, 26 Fr)

It is the story itself that demands boundlessness, to be "never-ending." The fantasy of an endless book is not, we see, merely a chance thought that comes to Semprun; it is not Fuentes's idea, nor an abstract meditation. It is, rather, intimately linked to Semprun's ability to write, and to what he has to say, for his story is in principle interminable.

In this citation Semprun links the infinite nature of his text, its fundamental openness, to the question of repetition, or of what he calls "*ressassement.*" Openness and repetition are indeed connected in his model of the never-ending book that is also actually a model of a book that rewrites itself over and over. The openness is then not only the book's length or the scope of life covered by it, but its internal repetition, the ongoing rewriting of the same experience.

Indeed, repetition is the hallmark of Semprun's writing. Again and again he describes the same episodes. The run in the tunnel at the entrance to Buchenwald, the killing of the German soldier who sings *La Paloma*, the fall from the train and the blackout that followed. In her pathbreaking chapter on Semprun in her *Crises of Memory*, Susan Suleiman demonstrates this process of continuous revision and reinterpretation that she sees as "Semprun's characteristic signature as a writer,"[40] and as the heart of the working through of trauma in his writing.[41] These repetitions—as opposed to the actual facts they repeat—are for her the clearest manifestation of literariness in Semprun. Even on the level of style, prior to the role repetition plays in recurrent variations of the same episode, repetition is Semprun's essential fingerprint. One step forward, half a step back, repeating, on and on. Everything is imbued with a sense of treading water or going around in circles.

Specifically in *L'écriture ou la vie*, recurring descriptions of episodes from other of Semprun's books are accompanied by admissions that earlier versions were not true, that Semprun has added details, distorted facts, changed names. The reader may understand that nothing prevents these practices from continuing to be implemented, preparing the ground for even further rewriting. So this return to the same episodes leaves the text open in much the same way as the dream of perpetual retranslation. These revisions also raise questions about an original and its truth. Which is the true version? Similarly, we saw in the dream of perpetual retranslation that the original disappears, fading into a multitude of variations.

Semprun repeats himself tirelessly, and does so because what he has to say is a mission that cannot be exhaustively accomplished. The blank pages of the book given to him by the Spanish publisher have an unavoidable resonance for Semprun. This blankness is the pure whiteness of the snow that descended upon his life—snow, the presence of death and a symbol of Buchenwald (240–41 En, 310–11 Fr):

> The snow had erased my book, at least in its Spanish version.
>
> The sign was easy to interpret, the lesson easy to draw: I had not yet accomplished anything. This book it had taken me almost twenty years to be able to write was vanishing once more, practically as soon

40. Suleiman, *Crises of Memory*, 141.
41. Ibid., 158.

as it had been finished. I would have to begin it again: an endless task, most likely, transcribing the experience of death.

Of all the copies of *Le grand voyage* that I've been given so far this evening, and that I will yet receive, the Spanish copy is the most beautiful. The most meaningful to me, because of its dazzling emptiness, the innocent and perverse blankness of all those pages to be rewritten. (273 En, 351 Fr)[42]

The snow fell on his book and erased it. His achievements vanished. Death haunts him again. Twenty years have passed, and he is back at square one.

Instead of totality and wholeness, Semprun describes a Sisyphean experience in which every time he reaches the summit he is forced to go back down to the foot of the mountain. The written book is not a closed object but a demand for a reopening: "This book [. . .] was vanishing once more, practically as soon as it had been finished. I would have to begin it again" (273 En, 351 Fr). Like the ever-renewing translation that does not allow the book's closure and leaves it as something alive and breathing, without an end, so it is with writing in general, the very attempt to represent on the white pages the death-that-was-experienced.

Openness in face of possible closure is essential to writing itself. It is neither a result of translation, nor a dream or a fantasy. Writing means rewriting, being sentenced to rewrite.[43]

And what needs to be written is death itself. Death here is the alpha and omega of writing, its beginning and its end: "an endless task, most likely, transcribing the experience of death" (273 En, 351 Fr).

Again and again Semprun comes back to the demand for endless writing: "It would take me several lifetimes to tell about all that death. Telling its story right through to the end would be an endless task" (35 En, 52 Fr). Death is then what asks to be written and what dictates the infinity of writing.

---

42. The incident of the banned Spanish book with its empty pages is also recounted earlier in another text by Semprun, *Autobiografía de Federico Sánchez* (1977), where it appears in Spanish, before being rewritten, in French, here in *Literature or Life*. Semprun, *The Autobiography of Federico Sanchez and the Communist Underground in Spain*, trans. Helen R. Lane (New York: Karz, 1979), 221.

43. For Tidd it is specifically testimony, rather than writing in general, that is structurally "condemned to a certain repetition." "The need to tell [. . .] can never be satisfied" (407).

But is the difficulty here that of putting the experience of death into words, or rather is it what Blanchot and others have pointed to, the problem of dying with the writing, the death that is part of writing itself?[44] Writing, says Blanchot, from whom Semprun took the epigraph for *Literature and Life*, is like an erasure, the disappearance of the writer.[45] Semprun elegantly gives expression to such thoughts. The pages of the book he was given are blank, erased. Ostensibly, a simple image: language is deadening, and once you enter the text you are lost in it. But Semprun, even when he is writing about "the murderous language of writing" (226 En, 292 Fr), is not dealing merely with textual death but with real death as well. This blank whiteness, this snow are for him direct expressions of the presence of death in his life (snow symbolizes for him the entire camp experience). Moreover, because of Semprun's life circumstances, death does not remain an abstract rumination: writing on Buchenwald sends him back to the experience of Buchenwald, to the experience of death. "[W]riting literally prohibits me from living" (163 En, 215 Fr).

And yet, was not death exactly what he wanted to write? Erasure is therefore actually a victory, the alchemic miracle of the wedding of content and form. Death has been successfully transcribed. Hence the delight: "Of all the copies [. . .] the Spanish copy is the most beautiful. The most meaningful to me, because of [. . .] the innocent and perverse blankness of all those pages to be rewritten" (273 En, 351 Fr). Semprun celebrates the blankness of the pages that demand to be rewritten. Writing is itself erasure. He writes, in white ink, death itself.

Semprun prolongs and complicates Blanchotian thought in yet another manner. Entering writing is perhaps a kind of death but, as he often emphasizes, Semprun experiences himself as someone who has already died, who has passed through death and who can at most re-experience it (89 En, 121 Fr). (Blanchot also thematizes this idea, especially in his *The Instant of My Death*). The theme of

44. As Tidd puts it, "Semprún's texts hover on an axis of writing to exorcise death and of writing as death" (410).

45. Blanchot, *The Space of Literature*, trans. Ann Smock (Lincoln and London: University of Nebraska Press, 1982), 23, 93; "Literature and the Right to Death," trans. Lydia Davis, in *The Work of Fire*, trans. Charlotte Mandell (301–44) (Stanford: Stanford University Press, 1995), 328.

having already died is actually common in Holocaust literature (see Deborah Lee Ames for a brief exposition[46]), and Semprun explores it in depth in *Le mort qu'il faut*. If he has already died, or in his own words, in *Literature and* Life, has "crossed through" [*traversé*] death (138 En, 183 Fr), if death is no longer merely a shadow of the future but also a reality of one's past, there is less need to survive one's autobiography.

Erasure and writing, then, even if they serve Semprun as channels of dialogue with one aspect of French thought regarding writing, never remain for him merely textual. Death is what erases and the erasure invites rewriting. Thus, at Buchenwald, when his camp companion Maurice Halbwachs dies, Semprun, who was working in the statistics department of the camp, takes Halbwachs's card from the card index and erases his name: "I erased that name: a living person would now be able to take the dead man's place. [. . .] [T]he rectangular card [. . .] had become blank and white once more, ready for another life to be written on it, and a new death" (43 En, 62 Fr).[47] Erasure and rewriting, real death and textual death: the perpetual movement of rewriting is based on death.[48]

In one section of *L'écriture ou la vie*, Semprun relates how he went back to visit Buchenwald in 1992. The text he was writing, *L'écriture ou la vie*, was finished and he wanted to verify "its coherence, its internal truth." There, in Buchenwald, on the assembly grounds, he discovers "that I would have to rewrite a large part of my story. That I would have to reimmerse myself once more in that long mourning process of memory. Endless, once again" (186 En, 243–44 Fr). Rewriting the story, and understanding that when it is sealed, the seal is only temporary and will have to be reopened and the text rewritten, that the story is never finished, turn out to be essential to Semprun's work and to the nature of the task he undertook, the interminable work of mourning.

46. Deborah Lee Ames, "Automortagraphy: Holocaust Survivors Remember Their Own Deaths," *a/b Auto/Biography Studies* 16/1 (2001): 24–38.
47. There is bitter irony here, for Halbwachs is a theoretician of memory.
48. The theme of erasure and rewriting is evident in other places in the book, and not necessarily in the context of the experience of the camps, though death still underlies the writing. Thus, for example, Semprun evokes Heidegger's erasure of the dedication of *Being and Time* to his teacher Husserl. Heidegger, Semprun says, "had deliberately erased it, as one erases a bad memory from one's mind. As one erases a name from a tombstone perhaps" (91 En, 124 Fr).

It was with Proust that we embarked on the theme of writing just one book throughout life. To end, let us return to the exact words of Proust's famous citation: "I realized," Proust writes, "that the essential, the only true book, though in the ordinary sense of the word it does not have to be 'invented' by a great writer—for it exists already in each of us—has to be translated by him. The function and the task of a writer are those of a translator."[49]

49. Proust, *Time Regained*, 926; *À la recherche du temps perdu* 4:469.

Contributors

EMMANUEL BOUJU, a former student of the École Normale Supérieure, is currently Professor of Comparative Literature at the Université de Rennes 2 and Visiting Professor at Harvard University. His publications include *Réinventer la littérature : démocratisation et modèles romanesques dans l'Espagne post-franquiste* (with a preface by Jorge Semprún, 2002), *La transcription de l'histoire. Essai sur le roman européen de la fin du vingtième siècle* (2006), and the volumes of the "Groupe phi," a research group dedicated to historical and comparative poetics: *Littératures sous contrat* (2002), *L'engagement littéraire* (2005), *Littérature et exemplarité* (2007), *L'autorité en littérature* (2010). He is also an editor for the Classiques Garnier collection "Littérature, Histoire, Politique" and for the Presses Universitaires de Rennes.

BRUNO CHAOUAT is Professor of French at the University of Minnesota. He has published on autobiography and death, as well as on French contemporary thought. He is completing his third book (forthcoming with Liverpool University Press) on the French literary and theoretical responses to the new anti-Semitism.

MARCUS COELEN is a psychoanalyst in Paris and Berlin as well as a researcher affiliated with the Department of Comparative Literature at the Ludwig-Maximilan-Universität in Munich and currently a visiting scholar at the Federal University Fluminense in Rio de Janeiro. He is the editor and translator of several books and compilations of texts by Maurice Blanchot into German, among which *Vergehen (Le pas au-delà)* (2012), and the author of *Die Tyrannei des Partikularen. Lektüren Prousts* (2006).

YFS 129, *Writing and Life, Literature and History: On Jorge Semprun*, ed. Razinsky, © 2016 by Yale University.

Colin Davis is Research Professor of French at Royal Holloway, University of London, UK. His interests lie principally in the fields of twentieth-century French literature, thought, and film. His most recent books are *Critical Excess: Overreading in Derrida, Deleuze, Levinas, Žižek and Cavell* (Stanford, 2010) and *Postwar Renoir: Film and the Memory of Violence* (Routledge, 2012).

Eran Dorfman is a senior lecturer in the Department of Literature, Tel Aviv University, specializing in contemporary French literature and theory, continental philosophy, phenomenology, and psychoanalysis. He is the author of *Foundations of the Everyday: Shock, Deferral, Repetition* (Rowman & Littlefield International, 2014), *Learning to See the World Anew: Merleau-Ponty Facing the Lacanian Mirror* (Phaenomenologica series, Springer, 2007, in French) and the co-editor of *Sexuality and Psychoanalysis: Philosophical Criticisms* (Leuven University Press, 2010).

Tsivia Frank-Wygoda is currently writing a PhD dissertation at the Hebrew University of Jerusalem, on the poetics of meaning and indeterminacy in Edmond Jabès's poetry. Other research interests include autobiographical writing in foreign language, literature of the Shoah, and French literature during the War and Occupation.

Richard J. Golsan is University Distinguished Professor and Distinguished Professor of French at Texas A&M University. He is the author of *Vichy's Afterlife* (Nebraska University Press, 2000) and *French Writers and the Politics of Complicity* (Johns Hopkins University Press, 2006), among other works. He is the Editor of *South Central Review*.

Sara Kippur is Assistant Professor of Language and Culture Studies at Trinity College in Hartford, Connecticut. She is the author of *Writing It Twice: Self-translation and the Making of a World Literature in French* (Northwestern University Press, 2015) and co-editor of *Being Contemporary: French Literature, Culture and Politics Today* (forthcoming from Liverpool University Press, 2015). Her articles have appeared in *L'esprit créateur*, *Michigan Quarterly Review*, *a/b Auto/biography Studies*, *Contemporary French and Francophone Studies*, and the *Journal of Romance Studies*.

Donald Nicholson-Smith's translations include Jean-Patrick Manchette's *Three to Kill*; Thierry Jonquet's *Mygale* (aka *Tarantula*); and (with Alyson Waters) Yasmina Khadra's *Cousin K*. He has also translated works by Paco Ignacio Taibo II, Henri Lefebvre, Raoul

Vaneigem, Antonin Artaud, Jean Laplanche, Guillaume Apolli-
naire, and Guy Debord. His translation of Manchette's *The Mad
and the Bad* won the 28th Annual Translation Prize of the French-
American Foundation and Florence Gould Foundation for fiction.
Born in Manchester, England, he is a longtime resident of New
York City.

LIRAN RAZINSKY is senior lecturer in the Program for Hermeneutics
and Cultural Studies at Bar Ilan University, Israel. He works mainly
in two fields: French and comparative literature, and psychoana-
lytic theory. His book, *Freud, Psychoanalysis and Death* was published in 2013 by Cambridge University Press. He has published
widely on Jonathan Littell's *The Kindly Ones (Les Bienveillantes)*,
co-editing a collection of essays on him, *Writing the Holocaust
Today: Critical Perspectives on* The Kindly Ones (Rodopi, 2012).
He has also published papers on Georges Bataille, Guy de Mau-
passant, and Elias Khoury. His current research project is called
"Fantasies of Self-Representation: From Classic Autobiography to
the Digital Age."

URSULA TIDD is Professor in twentieth century French literature and
thought at the University of Manchester, UK, with research interests in the literature and thought of Simone de Beauvoir, Jorge
Semprún, and in "memory work" of the post-World War II period
in France. She is the author of four monographs: *Simone de Beauvoir, Gender and Testimony* (Cambridge University Press, 1999);
Simone de Beauvoir (Routledge "Critical Thinkers" series, 2004);
Simone de Beauvoir (Reaktion Books, "Critical Lives" series,
2009) and *Jorge Semprún: Writing the European Other* (Legenda-
Maney, 2014) and two edited books, the most recent of which focuses on Beauvoirian existentialism and film (Berghahn Books,
2012). She is currently working on Semprún's collaboration with
Alain Resnais.

Yale French Studies is the oldest English-language journal in the United States devoted to French and Francophone literature and culture. Each volume is conceived and organized by a guest editor or editors around a particular theme or author. Interdisciplinary approaches are particularly welcome, as are contributions from scholars and writers from around the world. Recent volumes have been devoted to a wide variety of subjects, among them: Levinas; Perec; Paulhan; Haiti; Belgium; Crime Fiction; Surrealism; Material Culture in Medieval and Renaissance France; and French Education.

Yale French Studies is published twice yearly by Yale University Press (yalebooks.com) and may be accessed on JSTOR (jstor.org).

For information on how to submit a proposal for a volume of *Yale French Studies*, visit yale.edu/french and click "Yale French Studies."